WARRIOR
IN THE
MUD

CHILDHOOD TRAUMA, ADULT DRAMA,
AND RECLAIMING MY TOXIC LIFE

NICOLE MARTIN SALTER

Warrior in the Mud
Copyright © 2021 by Nicole Martin Salter

All rights reserved. No part of this publication may be reproduced, distributed, or transmitted in any form or by any means, including photocopying, recording, or other electronic or mechanical methods, without the prior written permission of the author, except in the case of brief quotations embodied in critical reviews and certain other non-commercial uses permitted by copyright law.

This book is a memoir. It reflects my present recollections of past experiences. I recognize that, because trauma biologically changes the developing brain, and because I subsequently killed countless additional brain cells, and also because nobody likes to read about how they were a baddie, others' memories of the events described in this book may differ from my own.

Most names of the living people described in these pages have been changed, either to protect the identity of those I like, or to protect me from the wrath of those I don't.

At the end of the day, I have led a rather eventful life, and have found no need to make anything up.

Tellwell Talent
www.tellwell.ca

ISBN
978-0-2288-6644-2 (Hardcover)
978-0-2288-6643-5 (Paperback)
978-0-2288-6645-9 (eBook)

For my mother and my father
Be easy, you earned it.

CONTENTS

Preface vii

Chapter 1   Happiness 1

Chapter 2   Jails, Marriage and Other Institutions 7

Chapter 3   Dream a Little Dream of Me 12

Chapter 4   Bye, Bye Miss American 19

Chapter 5   In Summer 26

Chapter 6   My Mother's House Has Many Rooms 32

Chapter 7   Love Me Tender 39

Chapter 8   Lockdown 47

Chapter 9   Lockup 58

Chapter 10 End of the Road 70

Chapter 11 Karmic Laws 77

Chapter 12 The Last Battle 86

Chapter 13 Call Me, Call Me Anytime 95

Chapter 14 The Revenge of the Gods 107

Chapter 15 The Golden Touch 112

Chapter 16 Jim's Not Here 120

Chapter 17 In and Out 139

Chapter 18 A Love Story 155

Chapter 19 And Then There Were Four 165

Chapter 20 The Pendulum.. 173

Chapter 21 Tidy Up, the Police Are Coming................................. 181

Chapter 22 On the Gaslight Express 190

Chapter 23 The Echo Chamber 205

Chapter 24 The Grandaddy of Narcissism..................................... 215

Chapter 25 Memos from the Border... 225

Chapter 26 Back to the Future 232

Chapter 27 It's Not Your Fault, Dear Ones 238

Chapter 28 Getting Out of the Mud 245

Acknowledgements.. 263

PREFACE

Like most people, I wore masks even before the COVID-19 pandemic. You might see me as a middle-aged woman, a mother, a Black lady, a drug addict, a successful business owner, a survivor, a wage slave or a volunteer, and you would not be wrong.

There are no letters after my name, and some of the titles I've held over the years have expired: Wife. Student. American. Only child. Criminal. Masseuse (not the good kind). Of course, not all these identities come into view all at once. You could have graded my papers, wondered why I cried so hard at the altar, or purchased soap from my company without ever imagining that any of these other parts existed.

All adjectives will depend on your perspective. Am I privileged or oppressed? Self-deprecating or narcissistic? Sincere or hypocritical? Redeemed or guilty? You will have to make up your own mind because there is no way to tell for sure. The idea of automating morality has already been tried, and it failed.

In 2019, one of the students at the college where I worked took an interesting approach to his final semester assignment. I was captioning lectures for the deaf in his beginners' web design course, and the assignment was to design a site that would achieve a single purpose, such as charity fundraising or recipe sharing. But this student had a more interesting idea: he wanted to build a program that would analyze user input to determine whether the user was the asshole in any given situation—it was like an AI version of "Dear Abby."

It made sense; who didn't want to be freed from the tedious business of figuring out right from wrong on a case-by-case basis? No one delights in collecting perspectives from biased friends and family members, sifting through the accumulated junk inside their own heads or swiping through podcasts about our morally relativist culture to try and make a decision. There are just too many trolls.

Of course, his website didn't work, even when his friends jumped onboard to help. None of us in the class could write code, and if the professor could, she didn't say. Instead, she tried to clarify expectations by praising a project from a previous year, which was a much more realistic example of what could be accomplished in four weeks with a rudimentary knowledge of WordPress. The home page featured a large, red "Danger: Hazardous Waste" sign mounted on two metal poles piercing a field of muddy brown soil that stretched to both ends of the screen. The student had created an environmental organization that collected donations toward cleaning up toxins that had been dumped on the land and then redeveloping the property.

So a discussion ensued on how, with habitable land dwindling across the globe, these contaminated sites that sat empty—called brownfields—could be rehabbed and whether anybody would live in a condo that sat on formerly polluted land. These were mature students with a lot of life experience, mostly from lower- and middle-income brackets, so there wasn't as much debate as there might have been in some of my other classes where I felt ancient in thought, word and deed. Most everyone agreed that if you gave them a free condo they'd live in it, even if the site had once been Chernobyl.

Both assignments got me thinking. I had tried all my life to figure out whether I was the asshole in every situation, see-sawing from the belief that my personality was basically flawed to the other side that most people took advantage of me. I had trouble with relationships; most lasted no more than a few years and ended poorly. I was pretty sure I had been abused as a child, though not in the conventional ways. But even if I had been, at what point was I supposed to get over it and move on? Was my past the real reason I often felt numb, unhappy, angry and with a gift for pushing people away? Or, if I really was just an asshole, was it possible to fully remove the most pernicious contaminants in my personality and rebuild on the brownfields of my life?

I was already working on a new book anyway. It was creative nonfiction, a kind of rags-to-riches memoir based on my childhood in the '80s as the unwanted daughter of an authoritarian Italian mother and a career-criminal Black father. It was supposed to show a woman rising out of shame and hatred, addiction and self-destruction to become a good, happy wife/mother/citizen with good, happy, resilient children. Never mind that my marriage was in tatters and addiction was creeping back into my life; my hope was the reader would find more meaning and hope in this ambitious project than I could communicate with the inconvenient facts.

Soon enough, my vision for that style of book collapsed under the weight of the complicated structure I realized I was using, in part, to protect my core self from the truth. But I didn't want to give up on telling the story and sharing what I had learned. Though the path was winding, I had indeed survived my childhood (and all the self-induced misery afterward) and, unlike many of my former friends and associates who had died as young men and women, I was still here. From a foundation so radioactive it practically glowed green, I had wrested all the things I wanted: a husband, varied and stimulating work, a clean house, a robust social life, several income streams and two beautiful children.

I decided to go full memoir and write about events as truthfully as I could recall them. Writing had always helped me make sense of things, and this time I would write with unflinching honesty, no gloss. I hoped that telling my personal story—the good, the bad and the ugly—would be more than cathartic; I wanted it to help me find the truth of what really mattered while finally measuring how far I had come. Then I could set about the transformation of all that guck into something nice; maybe a gleaming shopping mall, the kind that has onsite laser tag and everything.

Then my husband told me not to write the book because he didn't want to be implicated in my life story and have people know his business by association. Expecting at least the nominal support for this creative endeavour that he had offered for my paying jobs, I used his negative feedback as an excuse to stop writing. I told myself the book was structurally beyond rescue anyway, and that it was almost certainly so boring that no one would read it among the three million books published every year. I pushed the idea from my mind and focused on my grind.

When the COVID-19 pandemic locked the planet down in 2020, my husband abruptly separated from me—or more accurately, separated *me* from my already-uncertain sense of self. My carefully cultivated identity as a wife and mother was shattered as he executed a ferociously swift plan to erase my presence from his life, a process that was designed to strip me of my children, my assets, my home and my reputation—in short, everything. The assault was so sudden, so shocking and brutal, that I did not realize what I was dealing with until it was far too late. It even seemed he wanted to drive me insane so I would kill myself, which was a slightly grandiose assumption. I realize now that any physical harm that might have come to me was completely incidental to the main goal.

As far-fetched as it seemed even to the person living it, within six months I found myself in a crumbling high-rise apartment, seeing my children every other week and accumulating thick files of documents from police, Child Services, lawyers, judges and tax collectors. All these papers, photos and videos were tangible proof of a ruined life, but my mind could not accept what had happened.

After a decade of marriage, no husband. No house. No real job (partly due to the pandemic and partly to my battered mental state). No credibility. I had become a hysterical woman ranting about psychological abuse, lies and betrayal. Most of my social circle backed away slowly, and the casual friendships I'd had with neighbourhood families and mutual friends vanished in direct proportion to the number of police cars in our driveway and smear campaign emails in their inboxes. Some of our mutual friends, people I had spent many an evening entertaining in our home, judged me from the safety of their phones. Social media, which I had enjoyed, became tinged with the desolate colours of shame, fear and despair.

I felt completely alone, thoroughly isolated by some of the harshest and most prolonged lockdowns in the world at a time when I desperately needed human contact. There was so much to do, but nothing could distract me from the shock, anxiety and confusion that were my constant companions as I alternated between periods of frantic work and numbing dissociation. And seven years after the trickle of information and discussion about narcissism had become a deluge, I finally came to learn of this psychological phenomenon and apply it to the history of my life.

Slowly, as the months went by, a little light peeked through the solid wall of fog. Once again, I started processing what had happened by going back to the beginning. What sort of person was I to have participated in such a sad drama that had done incalculable harm to the only innocents involved: my children? How and when and by what means had I fashioned such a personality? And was I capable of changing it?

This is not a how-to book (though perhaps, it's a how *not* to book), or a book of psychology or philosophy. It's my personal story of, as they say in AA, what it was like, what happened and what it's like now. I had to write it quickly, before I slipped into the numbed state of passivity that had been my trademark long before the incomprehensible events of the pandemic, and before I forgot that I was even trying to do anything.

By the fall of 2020, there was only one title I was interested in adding to my name, one that had always eluded me: healthy. To heal, I had to find out if I was the asshole and find my way out of the mess. Then I could see if any good could come of all the pain and anguish, and whether solid structures could ever be built on that tainted ground.

Pre-Development

Pre-development lays the foundation [of the new building]. The developer conducts several analyses and determines any fatal flaws to decide whether the project should move forward. This is the riskiest phase for potential developers.

-The United States Environmental Protection Agency, Office of Brownfields and Land Revitalization, June 2019

CHAPTER 1

HAPPINESS

In addiction recovery, when you say you don't believe in a Higher Power, they ask: Would you rather be right or happy?

The two options are presented as if they are mutually exclusive, and the question is, of course, rhetorical. Obviously, anyone who finds themselves in front of a tepid coffee urn in a church basement waiting for a twelve-step meeting to begin can only answer it one way: you wouldn't have ended up there if you weren't already wrong about something. You aren't supposed to pause, let alone deliberate, when someone asks if you would rather be right than happy.

If the silence stretches a beat too long, it will visibly dawn on the person asking that, despite your relatively normal appearance, they might very well be speaking to someone without a shred of sanity left. They will remember that *Some are sicker than others*, and their expression will become one of earnest fervour if they wish to save you or detached sympathy if they feel you're past saving. Picture the face of a psychic healer who already has knowledge of your terminal diagnosis before you approach her pleading to know if the future is friendly.

Do not be surprised if, at this juncture, you are guided to a folding chair and advised to just keep coming back.

Unfortunately for me, I may be at a genetic disadvantage when it comes to the right vs. happy question. I come from a line of women who have somehow managed to eliminate the influence of doubt on their lives. No woman in my family moons around examining their schemas, auras or emotions; the pursuit of happiness is considered frivolous if you are a Martin. Grim satisfaction is usually as good as it gets. It may result as a by-product of being right, but don't count on it. Excess positive emotions—love, joy, elation—practically beg fate to reverse your fortunes quickly so someone else can enjoy grim satisfaction when your pride causes you to fall.

Steeped in this ideological stew, which is flavoured liberally with bad luck, divine punishments and the occasional gristly chunk of devastating failure, my bloodline puts as little stock in spiritual rewards as it does in material ones. The book of Job taught me that God is not a vending machine. You don't put in *right* and expect *happy* to just tumble down into your greedy, grabby hands.

It is pure luck that none of us ever came into direct contact with a cult leader. My mother would have been just the sort to unquestioningly devote herself to a charming doomsday fanatic, at least until some irritant—like not progressing quickly enough from the acolyte stage or someone putting too much sweetener in the fruit punch—resulted in contemptuous dismissal of the whole thing.

My family had essentially formed its own cult with a charter that emphasized superstition, self-reliance and silence. Despite the harsh penalties for speaking up or stepping out, I wasn't very old before I realized that most of the family rules clashed with the prevailing wisdom. Bruised cheeks, both above and below the waist, confirmed these suspicions more directly than any verbal explanation could have. Of course, no explanations were ever offered because I was a child; if the rules weren't good enough for me, I could always find another family. If I dared.

"I see what you're doing, Nicky, and if you think appearance is reality, you've got another think coming."

Mom could read my furtive glances at the dads who swung their daughters up into their arms and shouldered their backpacks after school. The children shrieked gleefully, and their sneakered feet bounced and skipped with mystifying excitement that didn't have to be contained. She knew what I was thinking when the moms crouched low with big smiles and open arms outside the school fence: that those families looked happy and I was jealous. She knew everything.

"That girl said she's adopted," I said, pointing to a Brown girl whose braids were pinched by colourful clips like all the other girls had.

"If anyone takes you in at that age—" she eyed my skinny six-year-old body, already nearly as tall as her curvaceous one, "it usually isn't pleasant."

Gripping my hand too tightly, she pulled me down the street, leaving to my imagination what it would be like to live with strange people who didn't really want me. Occasionally when we were licking the frosting off a Sara Lee cake or digging into a pint of Häagen Dazs Vanilla Swiss Almond, and she was in a good mood, I would ask her if foster kids got treats like that just to hear her laughingly say, "When they made you, they broke the mould."

Both my parents said this phrase with fondness, as if I were special. But if that were true, then why did "they" smash the mould so that nothing like me could ever be made again? I was an only child. I didn't want to be different, but at six I already understood that I was somehow both unique and awful. The corners of my mouth curved downward naturally, giving me an ungrateful, unhappy appearance that matched my ungrateful, argumentative, nasty personality. I could make anyone laugh but then boy could I turn on you!

It was not long before I concluded that happiness was something you wished for, like hot dogs instead of liver and onions, but it wasn't good for you. And besides, you didn't deserve it. Good things came from somewhere only to be taken away somewhere else. It was like this with school, the place that made me the happiest. The kids used to ask me why I even bothered to show up because I had no friends. What they didn't realize was that I didn't expect to have friends.

"Dickhole has a typewriter in her head," classmates jeered. "She's such a geek. Look, she thinks she's better than us."

"She thinks she's better than the teacher, never mind!"

"Don't you mean, *he*? Her hair's shorter than mine!"

"Go run home to your mommy, ya big nerd!"

They took their own advice, struggling into their coats the moment the bell rang, but I was never in a hurry. I was a hopeless loser four eyes teacher's pet; I genuinely loved school, if not the kids that came with it. I knew every square of speckled concrete floor, every locker that didn't close right, every detail of the view from the grimy windows. In winter especially, Canadian schools got dirty fast and stayed that way. If there was anything to be done about the greasy fingerprints, muddy shoeprints and out of service toilets, the permeating fug of sweaty boots and shit and discarded lunch bags slowly growing mould, nobody was doing it and it didn't matter. As a child, I relished my weekdays, especially when my mother declared me old enough to make the half-hour walk to school by myself.

There is a nerve-jangling exhilaration to simply being alive, anonymous and alone on a big-city street. Downtown Toronto has an incredible wealth of architecture and art, culture and commerce, but I paid little attention to the red-brick Victorians and shiny cars, the bustling Bloor Street falafel joints and Chinatown's seething outdoor stalls. My exuberance on these walks related to something more elemental. I gulped the sweet air and took in the rhythm of the seasons, the life that thrummed all around me. When I walked alone, I was happy.

Soon after the start of the school year, the sky was ceilinged by a canopy of maples whose huge, veiny leaves I collected if they were red and fresh or shuffled through as they browned in piles on the sidewalk. When fall rain speckled my glasses, I kept my eyes on my yellow rain boots and savoured the nutty aroma of wet earth. Walking home, I admired the mesh bags of knobby gourds and colourful ears of Indian corn filling the bins of vegetable stands before Thanksgiving, and I filled my pockets with the unblemished acorns near the roots of the massive oak trees. Squirrels raced in spirals around the deeply fissured bark, pausing to look over their shoulders as I stole their riches.

Next came months of snow. The hardpack of the school field was quickly churned into stiff, dirty meringue, but pristine clouds of white stuff lasted well into March if you knew where to look. The Annex's grand homes would be swaddled in flakes so lush and clean you could safely swipe the fenceposts a full week after a storm and pack pure white cold straight into your mouth. You could break an icicle off an eavestrough and lick it, hoping for something sweet.

In spring, the forsythia bushes exploded into golden glory. The individual flowers were frail and insignificant, but all together they smothered every branch in shades from buttercream to brightest yellow. The fruit markets displayed bunches of pussy willows nearly as tall as I was, their slender stalks bound together and jammed into white plastic pails of half-frozen water. Fingering their impossibly soft, furry buds was almost as satisfying as snatching drooping purple lilacs—the best-smelling flowers on earth—from branches overhanging the sidewalk to present as bouquets to my mother.

But when summer descended on the city in June, my steps really lightened. I seemed to float above the steaming pavement, giddy with feelings that were frighteningly intense yet maddeningly vague. School was coming to an end. Summer brought good things, but not always. I knew a thing or two about ricocheting from anxiety to expectation to disappointment and back, but I couldn't stop the process any more than I could stop the glorious sun from squeezing sweat from my forehead as it beat down on the tight coils of my hair.

It was easy to forget my manners in summer and find myself skipping down the street smiling idiotically, arms flung wide to catch the slightest breeze. Sometimes I'd see kids up ahead making a game of walking: *Step on a crack, break your mama's back! Step on a line, break your mama's spine!* It was ridiculous, of course, but for at least a couple of blocks the superstition would hold, and I would try to stay in the centre of the paving squares, dawdling to avoid the children. When it got too hot I would slip into the frigid air of a convenience store, maybe slide open the freezer case and poke around a bit as if I were going to buy something rather than just enjoying the chill. I was careful to keep my hands in plain sight at all times and to feign disappointment, as if they didn't have what I'd come for.

Nearing my mother's house, my pace slowed. I might run into someone I knew, a neighbour who would laugh at my foolish, awkward gait. On the narrow pathway that led to the stairs of our tall, skinny

Victorian on Howland Avenue, the concrete had hopelessly buckled; my large feet touched at least three cracks at once. I deliberately scuffed my shoe on an especially thick line, shivering with power and guilt. Climbing the stairs to the porch, I raised the knocker, a fierce-looking lion with bared teeth, rapped sharply three times and waited for it to open.

At some point in childhood, the solitary happiness of walking faded away, the simple satisfaction of being alive yielding to vivid fantasies of happiness that took place only in my mind. Gradually, unconsciously, the skipping and seeing and sidewalk-crack-avoiding became a smooth, no-frills stride. I started to march in lockstep with the person who taught me everything I knew: the woman I desperately loved, the woman who hollowed me out until there was very little left of me and then left the hole half-filled. She was impenetrable, but I never stopped hoping that if I pounded on the door long enough, she would eventually hear me and have no choice but to let me in.

CHAPTER 2

JAILS, MARRIAGE AND OTHER INSTITUTIONS

If a still, small voice within my mother's soul ever questioned her beliefs and actions—perhaps asking whether they resulted in happiness—she would have crushed its windpipe. When she first met my father in the visiting room of the Kingston Penitentiary, doubts that might have screamed at a less stubborn girl did not even dare to squeak. My mother had read about his moral and legal battles in *The Toronto Star* daily and began writing to him. Then the petite, slender young lady who had never been outside the city core began taking the Greyhound over 250 kilometres to Kingston to show her solidarity in person.

Though the circumstances were certainly less than ideal, it wasn't exactly a case of "delusional woman smitten by a three-named psychopath she believes only she can understand and save." Not quite. It was a different day; people were a lot more accessible back then. Even celebrities you bumped into at the airport would shake your hand, and not just to gain another social media follower. Incarcerated people were particularly approachable and always welcomed in-person chats. My mother preferred the underdog to Dudley Do-Right. She was the kind of person who could stare into the crazed eyes of a movie villain as he was about to kill again and be captivated; he was so much more *interesting* than the good guy. My mother was also very isolated. The kind of loneliness that produces instant kinship with an alleged criminal profiled in the paper might be alien to some, but not to her.

My mother was not so much sheltered from the outside world as she was confined. As a child she acted neither innocent nor childlike thanks to the things she had seen and been forced to do as the daughter of rural Italian immigrants who lived in grinding poverty, religious submission and ignorance of the modern world. Her parents, and especially her mother, kept her in permanent quarantine, the better to maintain her position as translator, housemaid and vessel for their disappointments.

Television didn't appear in their apartment until 1962, but when my then twelve-year-old mother finally tuned in to those three fuzzy channels, it was to watch firehoses being turned on Black protesters. The evening news showed clips of sit-ins, burning churches, Dr. King being led away in handcuffs, and wide-eyed little Black girls with pressed hair being heckled for attempting to enter schools that had been legally integrated for years. She heard about, and would later make me read about, important Black people like James Baldwin, Ralph Ellison, W.E.B. Du Bois, Alex Haley, Dick Gregory and Rosa Parks, as well as movements like SNCC, the NAACP and the Black Panthers.

Advertising also dominated the airwaves. It was an era of progress and prosperity that ushered in a wave of consumer goods ranging from shiny time-saving appliances to pre-packaged foods. To my grandparents, mentally and emotionally shackled by turn-of-the-century values, it was all a cesspool of sin. Far from sampling magical new products like Cool Whip and beltless stockings, my grandmother looked upon sliced bread with suspicion, leaving my mother to fantasize in front of the box alone.

Mom was teased mercilessly by her rich Forest Hill schoolmates for being too smart and having the audacity to look kind of Black while she was at it. It seemed the counterculture hadn't caught up to Toronto yet, and cruelty of all sorts was common: corporal punishment, violent bullying, homophobia and xenophobia were all in a day's work. Public school teachers cautioned their students to "Watch out for the nigger in the woodpile" when doing complex math problems.

JAILS, MARRIAGE AND OTHER INSTITUTIONS

Barely out of her teens and still scarred by the kind of *Lord of the Flies* upbringing we rarely think of boomers as enduring, she came across that article about a Southern Black man who had been accused of theft north of his border. He had been languishing in an Ontario detention centre for nine months awaiting his Charter-guaranteed jury trial which was constantly being delayed because Kingston judges didn't want to leave the cottage until the leaves began to turn. In hindsight it's not surprising that, inexperienced at romance, hypersensitive to injustice and seized by the prospect of escape, she was immediately filled with a righteous indignation that later turned to love.

My grandmother, Tecla, had been unmarried in her thirties and still lived on her family's spartan farm in a little mountain town near the Austrian border when Cossack invaders killed all her beloved livestock and raped every woman they could get their hands on. She supposedly escaped by pretending to be insane, but losing the animals, who she saw as precious friends, was bad enough. A vegetarian generations before it would come into vogue, my grandmother pulled herself through the rest of the war just as she had survived all the penury before: searching the fields for potatoes too small to harvest and surreptitiously eating them raw. Neither her revered uncle nor her eight brothers and sisters ever caught her doing this, which made her think the Blessed Virgin had drawn a cloak of invisibility around her.

Tecla's mother had died when she was only four, and she had been sent to live with an evil aunt who, among other tortures, made her do the family's laundry at a communal outdoor site where huge rats swam around in the icy water biting numb and reddened fingers. Her priest uncle was descended from the noble line of Petrarch, but that didn't save little Tecla from the hell in evidence right there on earth: a life of virtual serfdom marked by ceaseless toil and arbitrary punishment where, despite constant prayer, your sinful acts always outnumbered your saintly ones.

By the time my grandmother had resigned herself to spinsterhood, along came Angelo, a penniless charmer who drank too much. He accepted her even in her thirties, provided she would follow him to Canada and agree to obey him in all things, however strange or abusive they might be. Once across the water, he insisted she have all her teeth removed by a quack dentist and forbade her, on pain of death, from learning to speak English, which could have considerably improved their fortunes even if she had to gum the words sloppily. Silence and prayer were her only weapons against such a man, and it took a long time, if ever, for those arrows to find their mark.

Oh, that wacky Angelo! When Tecla got pregnant, she gained ninety pounds; he made her stand on the sidewalk outside the bar, waiting for him on hugely swollen legs, until he had finished drinking. Parenthood didn't make it better, starting with the fact that my blonde-haired, green-eyed grandmother didn't believe my swarthy, curly-haired mother could be her child. She had been anesthetized for the delivery, then separated from her baby while she recovered, as was the custom of the time. When finally presented with her freshly swaddled daughter for the first time nine days later, Tecla had screamed, convinced that someone had played a nasty trick in the nursery and switched the golden cherub she had laboured so hard for with a malevolent sprite.

Unlike some other Italian immigrants of his day, Angelo did not parlay his considerable skill as a master carpenter into a lucrative business, nor did he want to live in Little Italy. He isolated his wife, who could only effectively communicate with four people—her daughter, herself, God and him—and helped construct the city as a lowly contract bricklayer working sixteen-hour days. Later, he would become a superintendent in several of its finer buildings.

As a little girl, my mother lived in a succession of rent-free apartments, occasionally receiving gifts of crystal trinkets and castoff lace from the wealthy lady tenants who pitied the tiny, undernourished child with the unpronounceable name. She would follow her father into their luxury units like a puppy, translating their complaints about leaky pipes, loud noises and every other affront to Forest Hill sensibilities. How hard would it have been not to touch all the fine things? But punishment for bad behaviour was swift and severe, so she barely touched what they gave her outright.

She loved her father, who fed her nothing but candy until her mouth was full of silver fillings. She thrived on impressing the ladies with the kind of marvelous enunciation and common sense rarely seen in urchins. By the age of five, my mother was already booking her own immunizations because no one else understood how to do it. She was also sleeping in her father's bed without her mother, a phenomenon that would continue until she was eighteen, ostensibly because of the cramped space. Tecla said and did nothing about this arrangement, which my mother swore was completely innocent.

Acutely aware that her home life was medieval, my mother felt cornered. Italian girls were supposed to stay home and take care of their parents, and marriage was the only chance of getting off the hook. Vito Corleone famously said he couldn't refuse a favour on the day of his daughter's wedding, but he didn't have much to say about the relationship later on; once married, you belonged to the groom and his family, and what were the odds it would be worse over there? My mother was brilliant, graduating high school with top honours and getting her bachelor's in political science from the University of Toronto. She helped her parents buy their first and only home. But in her heart she was still the schoolgirl covering her ears, feigning deafness behind the bathroom door as my grandmother shouted through the keyhole that only whores went to dances. She had to get out.

"Did you have any friends who could help?" I asked her once.

"I had one in university," my mother said. "Cathy. That was back when I smoked for a while."

"You smoked?"

I couldn't picture my mother ever doing anything so dirty or so dangerous. But apparently, even nicotine couldn't best her; she gave it up as handily as she had started. Maybe it was the strongest rebellion she could muster, as her classmates danced around barefoot and smoked pot and dropped acid right on Bloor Street where the Mink Mile is today.

After a couple of brief and highly unsatisfying affairs that could, more or less, be considered date rape ended in shame and venereal disease, my mother opened the newspaper, got on a bus and met a very tall, very handsome, very smiley convict who promised to finally make everything okay.

CHAPTER 3

DREAM A LITTLE DREAM OF ME

Recall is sometimes a curse, but I wish I knew more about my father. Here is one fact: he was born on the 4th of July 1946, a Dog year, just like Bill Clinton, another lying, cheating, saxophone-playing Dog who was clever enough to conceal his intelligence when necessary. But Daddy, a Black boy who ran around barefoot in the red clay dirt of the Deep South till he was eight years old, would never claim his share of the boomer pie, let alone become an American president.

His name was Jeremiah, and he loved me as well as any man who had so many demons to wrestle that he gave up and embraced them instead. His Baptist parents apparently had a fondness for the apocalyptic when it came to naming their sons; his older brother, Ezekiel, ended up working for the Reagan Administration in a classified capacity and became a slumlord after his retirement. Zeke owned several run-down apartment buildings in which bedbugs and roaches proliferated like a biblical plague, while he himself lived in a sprawling home in suburban Maryland. He was known for this famous quote regarding his tenants' demands for fumigation: "What's a can of Raid between friends?"

Eventually, from what Aunt Kate said, he went insane and lost his fortune shortly after attending my wedding in Toronto (without bringing a wedding present). It should be mentioned that Aunt Kate is not really my aunt but an ancient matriarch who was somehow related to the family. She had always favoured my dad over Zeke because she said he was kind and generous. Or maybe, like my mom, Aunt Kate just rooted for the underdog.

Daddy also had a sister, quite un-biblically named Bobbie Jo, who became a nurse and developed a lifelong menthol cigarette habit that gave her a sexy, raspy voice and a lot of health problems. She lived in Birmingham, Alabama, which is not too far from the Dothan farm where they all were born.

Depending on who you talk to, my dad was a charmer, a black sheep, a criminal, a visionary, a compulsive liar and a good-hearted but naïve man. He was well over six feet tall, dashing and possessed of perfectly square white teeth despite a complete lack of dental care. He flashed them frequently, bestowing hundred-watt smiles on friend and foe alike as if he found the little things in life unusually exhilarating.

At first, he stole food to keep body and soul together after his parents died of alcoholism or cancer or domestic violence or whatever else kills the sons and daughters of sharecroppers in 1950s Alabama. While my mother's parents were ever so slowly on the way up in society, at least in terms of financial stability, my father's parents were already long gone, leaving young Jerry to lie his way into every job he would ever get.

"Can you pick cotton, boy?" a potential employer had once asked him, gesturing at the two-row combine that would one day become an instrumental piece of machinery in the second-biggest diaspora the South had ever seen.

"Yessir, why not?" my father replied, and confidently climbed aboard the mechanized picker.

He could learn anything by watching. Eventually, through observation and imitation, he would pretend to be an educated, sophisticated city man with skills he could not possibly have acquired but could make you believe he'd had forever. He loved to work and, by my mother's standards, was obsessed with it, although she allowed that Blacks did have to work twice as hard as everybody else just to get anywhere in life.

In his twenties, my dad moved north to the promised land of New York City only to find that the streets weren't exactly paved with gold. Nevertheless, the opportunities for a clever, hard-working man who didn't mind stretching the truth far exceeded anything available to him back home where he was still expected to step into the ditch to make way for the folks that mattered. In New York, he founded AAE, African American Enterprises, a chain of shoe stores that sold Hush Puppies and Pumas before they became iconic brands. He also worked for a publication called *The Monthly Review*, from which he embezzled money. I remember the word embezzled because, to my five-year-old ears, it was a funny word, like bamboozled.

All the time he was putting in the kind of long, productive hours that allowed him to park a snazzy maroon Lincoln Continental in front of our building, he still stole either because he couldn't stop or for the sheer hell of it. There was the night he ruined an expensive new suit by stealing a roast from the butcher shop; the meat juices dripped down his sleeve as he presented it to my mother, and I remember her panicked voice repeating that nothing in her vast arsenal of cleaning products would get bloodstains out of silk. Her Christian Dior kimono was another five-finger bargain, unfortunately cut for a much taller, slimmer woman. My law-abiding, God-fearing mother was mortified but resigned herself to the role of a sort of mob wife, accepting the stolen goods into our tiny bachelor apartment on Ocean Avenue without too much protest.

After their City Hall nuptials in 1974 (my mother wore a black-and-white checked dress and never gave a satisfactory answer as to why there was no real wedding), Mom tried to get an apartment in Bensonhurst, securing the lease with a deposit, but when the moving truck showed up along with her new Black husband, the unit was mysteriously unavailable. So my mother moved them to Midwood, and they lived choking on the thick smell of fried onions and cabbage that emanated from countless apartments full of the Russians her mother had hated so much.

Mom had one agonizingly painful, life-threatening ectopic pregnancy and one abortion before I was born in 1978, the Year of the Earth Horse. It's considered a bad year for girls to be born, as it makes us too wild and headstrong. The Horse is the most independent of the twelve Chinese zodiac signs, but the Earth element creates some frustration; Earth Horse girls are doomed to remain forever penned by life's insurmountable fences. And so we got off to a bad start: the birth was terrible, my mother screaming for pain relief (did she even have insurance?) while indifferent medical staff told her to just hold her horses.

I knew things would have been different, although perhaps in some ways worse, had I been born male as she had preferred. All the privileges denied me by my gender would have been granted a boy but with a very steep price in devotion. As it was, my mother was an only daughter, as I would remain for the longest time. The name on my birth certificate was Nicole Martin Salter, but my mom said she only chose the name so she could call me Nicky, as she would have called her son had she produced a Nicholas.

It was no secret that Mom hadn't wanted children in the first place. She delighted in surprising all who asked that she hoped it was neither a boy nor a girl but a goat growing in her stomach. This was all my father's fault for wanting to sow his oats; she had only ever wanted to be a housewife like Donna Reed minus the family, or like the '50s screen sirens who finally wound up with their dream man just before the credits rolled and who were never seen to ruin their bodies or their sex lives with babies. It would become the subject of many a low blow on my part.

"Why didn't you just keep your legs crossed if you didn't even want me?" I would scream in the middle of a battle over some freedom that had been withdrawn or never granted.

She considered it one of the worst possible insults since she had tried to be chaste and had sacrificed everything for me. Mom had a lot to say about mothers on welfare who ought to be sterilized, young mothers in short-shorts, White mothers with Black children who spoiled them rotten but didn't have a penny in the bank, and any other woman who visibly couldn't keep their legs crossed or make the necessary sacrifices later.

"Your *father* wanted kids," she would reply through gritted teeth. "Isn't that funny? I almost died the first time, but he wanted to keep trying. Now where is he? That's what you call *irony*, Nicky."

It was true. Not long after I entered the world, Daddy promptly left us to do his own thing. Well, two things, it turned out. One was to have sons by his secretary at African American Enterprises, Chandice, who once came to my elementary school to pick me up, impersonating my mother; the attempt failed, but barely. Judging by the odd Polaroid Chandice still sends me, she had definitely been in our apartment when I was a toddler, unbeknownst to my mother, and had even braided my hair once.

Dad's other business, which we knew about long before Chandice, was to shove loads of cocaine into his veins. At first, it allowed him to stay up and work more, but toward the end, anybody could see he wasn't doing much of anything else. My small finger would trace the track marks that ran the full length of his inner arms before I knew what they were: thick keloid scars that made him look like the victim of multiple suicide attempts.

He occasionally played his big, golden sax for me, and he taught me how to throw a punch by making me practice on his own huge hand till I could knock it backwards. I sat on Daddy's lap and did math problems and told jokes that made him chuckle with delight at my precociousness. He sometimes intervened with my mother, telling her not to hit me, but usually she was made happier and nicer just by his presence, which of course became less and less as his outside life encroached.

When he did come home, after my mother had raged against his absence and drug use, the tension would drop and we settled into the mundane routines of meals and nightly television. For some reason I could never understand, they both slept naked, even in winter, and indulged in unselfconscious nudity in broad daylight. Mom walked around topless in summer, rolling an ice-cold bottle of beer on her breasts while we watched the little black-and-white TV in the kitchen. Daddy patiently explained that I shouldn't poke his penis with my big toe when we napped together because it was wrong.

So many things were wrong, like singing and humming too much or saying I was bored or touching my mother's things because I had nothing else to do but read a book. Other things, like her washing my smelly privates once a week with her bare soapy hand, felt wrong but must be natural and right or my mother wouldn't be doing them.

Sometimes my mother rode Daddy like a horse in their queen-sized bed while I watched on the ground from my impossibly hard futon, trying to remain quiet. Sometimes without knowing it, I would be thumping on my futon in time to the rocking of their bed.

"She's awake!" my mother would yell, panicked.

"No, she isn't," Daddy would sigh.

"Yes, she is. She hasn't gone under."

My mother always called sleep "going under." She hated the new term "putting down," as in, "I just put her down for a nap" because putting down was something you did to animals when it was time for them to die. My body frozen, eyes squeezed tightly shut, I would sense her bending over me for what felt like long minutes. I could feel her breath on my face.

"Go to sleep! Why aren't you asleep yet?"

There would be a slight thread of hysteria, as if her voice were a fragile skein of embroidery floss that could snap at any moment. I have heard the same tone in my own voice when one of my children has been up sick or upset all night and I need so badly to sleep.

Eventually, of course, I learned to fool her. The secret is to relax your face completely, including your eyelids, and pretend your limbs were being pulled down into the bed. Breathe deeply and evenly. Don't lay still as a corpse when prodded, make little movements, sigh, turn over. Definitely don't lay in child's pose; even if your hands didn't stray to forbidden areas, it was an unnatural pose that no one could really be asleep in. And sometimes, when Daddy wasn't there and conditions were right and we had gone through our call-and-response ritual:

"Good night!"

"Sweet dreams!"

"Same to you!"

Which sometimes could be extended to include:

"Good night!"

"Sleep tight!"

"Don't let the bedbugs bite!"

… my eyes would close naturally and I would go under, sucked down like an exhausted swimmer finally surrendering to the depths. Even though I didn't know what bedbugs were—we had water bugs and roaches like everyone else in New York despite my mother's fervent ministrations with spray bottle and scouring pads, but nothing that could be called a bed-specific bug—it was comforting to know that the words would prevent them from biting. It was so good to sink into real, delicious sleep, comforted by the fantasy of my mother's sheltering love and not at all restricted, in dreamland, by her confining hands and peculiar ideas.

CHAPTER 4

BYE, BYE MISS AMERICAN

I did what I could to make Daddy stay. I wrote long letters to him on my little desk in the kitchen begging him to get drug treatment, but he couldn't or wouldn't. My mother, always tightly wound, graduated to a state that professionals might find multiple names for in the *Diagnostic and Statistical Manual of Mental Disorders*. Every night she pulled out the well-worn Yellow Pages to call the local hospitals and jails looking for any sign of him. It was a pattern I would repeat with my fiancé many years later, so I understand her fear and anxiety, though at the time I just thought she was rude. I hope I never sounded as obnoxious over the phone as she did.

"Yes, it's Salter. S-A-L-T-E-R. No." She sighed loudly, then took a deep, steadying breath like a Christian martyr being mortified by heathens. "S, as in Sam. A. L. T, as in Tom. E. R, as in—as in Robert. First name Jeremiah. Or Jerry. With a J. But he might have given you the name James Williams."

She always spoke too loudly, too slowly and too crisply on the phone, as if the person on the other end of the receiver was half-deaf, a foreigner, stupid or all of the above. I'm sure it did nothing for her cause. She was totally focused, stretching the curly cord and winding it around her fingers but refraining from pacing while on hold. Her right hand was always ready with a Bic pen poised over a scrap of paper or torn envelope, ready to take down the name of a manager who might have more information.

"I don't know why he uses the name James Williams. He doesn't always. No, his ID should say Jeremiah Salter."

There would be another wait, maybe an eye-roll, sometimes a hand covering the mouthpiece so she could whisper to me about the incompetent, illiterate fools they had answering the phones.

"I'm not sure. Just check it, please. I'm calling on behalf of my *husband*."

We began to take a car service—New York's answer, at the time, to having a personal Uber driver—to cruise around the ghetto looking for my dad in the middle of the night, visiting every known shooting gallery, bar and sketchy friend's house she could think of in the hopes of dragging him home by force. I was there because she couldn't leave me alone at night, and for the embarrassment factor, I think, although I got to stay in the car. When she couldn't convince the driver to go inside and ask for James Williams or Jeremiah Salter, she did it herself and always returned alone. It might have been then that the frown lines took up permanent residence between her eyes, even when she was smiling.

These night-time trips were terrifying and exhilarating. I was a big kid, and we were going to find my dad, and the car service gave free highball glasses to frequent riders! Not plain ones, but the good kind that were etched with all kinds of colourful words and pictures. Our glassware cupboard was full of them, and my favourite one for milk for the next ten years was the one with the playing card motif: a frowning King on one side, a stern Queen on the other, a sprinkling of colourful diamonds, clubs, hearts and spades.

Gradually, our lives shrank to a pinprick. We couldn't go out during the day lest we miss him, so there were no more trips to Coney Island to gather seashells on cloudy days (my mother disliked the sun as much as I thirsted for it). I had never visited the boardwalk, the rides and games and cotton candy that most people associate with Coney Island; I didn't really know what went on there, but the boardwalk was always full of people who would probably laugh at me or be mean. I looked different, and my mother would never let go of my hand no matter how hard I pulled. I missed the beach and the sight of the ocean.

"When I was little, Nicky, I got sunburned so badly my skin peeled off in sheets. That will never happen to you. The sun is bad for you; it makes you old and wrinkled!"

"Can we go when it's raining? Please …"

I wanted a hot dog from Nathan's. I do not remember if I openly asked for things like that in New York or if I had already stopped. I learned from constant proximity and lack of distractions to observe my mother very carefully. She once said she knew me better than anyone else alive ever would, but it was really the reverse: I knew her. She was the unchanging universe. If Mom hadn't proposed a thing or done a thing, that thing was never going to happen so there was no point in asking. She would buy Nathan's hotdogs to steam at home, but never from a stand. There was no more beach. Mom was always too tired, the train was too far, we couldn't waste money on fares.

Dance class—where my father had bitten my stockinged bum in a washroom stall when I was too scared to go dance with the other little girls—was not renewed once the initial sessions were over. Daddy had invented the bum-biting penalty when I started chewing the plastic arms of Mom's glasses as a toddler and had bitten her hand when she tried to take them away from me. She had enthusiastically adopted the punishment too—"Go on now, bite her back!" he advised, and she did—but he had bigger teeth and hands to hold a squirming little girl, so he was better at it.

There were no more outings to the brackish South Street Seaport to buy the kind of giant starfish and conch shells you simply can't find anymore no matter how much you're willing to spend. Nor did we visit Prospect Park again for faintly disastrous picnics like the one I wrote about in *Daddy's Chicken*, a short story that was published in a food anthology in my late twenties. Everything was winding down like Daddy's heirloom watch that had slowed until its golden hands froze in place for good.

I get my penchant for salty, fatty foods from my father's side of the family. My mother would tell you that my favourite dessert is key lime pie because they used to buy it for me at Just Desserts when I went to Toronto to visit my grandmother. We never actually sat in the café, as my mother wouldn't sit in dirty places even before the infamous shooting turned it from hot spot to not spot. But I don't really like sweets, not even the sour sweetness of key lime pie. It reminds me of fighting and tense silences and the blanketing humidity that can make candied lime slices curl limply against the glistening surface of a cheesecake and soften a graham cracker crust after just a few minutes out of the fridge. The heat could get a little merciless in July, even for my tastes.

The last pie Daddy would ever eat with me was in 1984, and I am sure I enjoyed every minute of it. The footing he provided was slippery at best, but I still saw him as a refuge from the endless days with my mother, a toehold of hope that only became more significant as weeks began to slip by between his appearances. He'd burst in suddenly, dressed in a tracksuit and visibly sweating his extra-stinky "coke sweat," as Mom called it, to rifle through the dresser looking for money. Most of the time, he left before I could even say hello.

These brief, frenzied visits followed by hours of debriefing with my mother left me feeling injured and wise. I drew pictures of a sea turtle and gave him undersea friends and adventures; we'd show it to Daddy next time so he could see what he was missing out on. The saxophone disappeared and so did the pieces of my glass music box, broken when Mom smashed it in an attempt to stop him tying off in our tiny bathroom. She was more than a foot shorter than him, so when breaking things didn't work, she scratched and bit, but incredibly, his Afro deflected every blow and there was nothing she could do to stop that needle from adding to the artwork in his arm.

Nobody at school knew this was happening because the kids would make fun of me even more if they knew my dad was a junkie. I was already a weirdo. Even my teachers disliked me and labelled me defiant. In my first days in kindergarten at PS 193, before the school was renamed in honour of Gil Hodges (that's right, who?), I had fallen flat on my face on the play roof and screamed so loudly that the teacher thought I had plunged to my death. I almost gave her a heart attack, she said; there was no need to scream like that, what was wrong with me? She didn't know it was my first fall. I had never run before, so I didn't have the sense to put my hands out to save my face. And anyway, falling on my face hard enough to loosen teeth actually felt a bit like I was plunging to my death.

School took time to become the refuge it later would. Cast as Orange in the kindie colour play, I spoiled the colour wheel by not wearing orange. I had been told to let the idiot teacher take it up with my mom, but I knew that would put me in the unthinkable position of being a tattle-tale on my own mother. In my mind, she and I were one and the same, equally liable for all our dark thoughts.

"I don't have anything orange," I said, truthfully.

"Well, you had a month to find something."

I am not sure if teachers are allowed to show their irritation quite so openly at five-year-olds today, but I certainly hope not. Mom wasn't about to go out and buy a new article of clothing in a ridiculous colour for a stupid hour-long kindergarten play nobody cared about. We had been to Broadway to see *Dreamgirls* and other shows, and this was definitely not it. And anyway, there was a little square of orange in the skirt. Not brown, burnt orange. Maybe more of a russet. But definitely in the orange family. Why couldn't the teacher see it?

Perhaps if academic brilliance had been at play, they would have forgiven me. But kindergarten has nothing to do with smarts and everything to do with human interaction. Everything terrified me; I'd shake and tremble, mumble and splutter when called upon. They brought in a tape recorder and every student had to say what they had learned or liked about dinosaurs. I blurted out that they had really long tails. Both the teacher (who probably still remembered the orange fiasco) and my mother, who had come early to pick me up, looked at me expectantly, but I didn't know what else to say.

"Do you mean tales, like stories?" asked the teacher. "Do you mean there's a lot of stories about the dinosaurs?"

I shook my head. "No, I mean their *tails*. Like, on their bodies."

"Okay!" the teacher said brightly. "They certainly do."

"Was that the best you could do? You embarrassed me!" my mother hissed after what had felt like a long, awkward silence.

She would never attend another class performance, concert or track meet again, coaching me from home instead.

My career as a public speaker ended the day of my Booker T. Washington presentation when I shook so hard the sweet potato and the peanut fell from my sweaty palms. I screwed up my walk-on in the production *How to Eat Like a Child*, despite knowing every word to every song; near-perfect pitch doesn't matter when you are too afraid to open your mouth. Mom could not help with this anxiety because she said that she herself had never experienced anxiety.

"You're probably just not interested because you know you're already smarter than that teacher, Nicky," she said.

The teacher wanted us to use a small "i" on purpose because she wanted the mural to look like it had been written by little kids, which we were. But she was not there to tell my mother that, who would not have consented to improper grammar anyway. We argued about it until I cried. I got in trouble for ruining my part of the mural.

My problems became more sophisticated in Grade 1 when I embellished Mom's statement that the teacher dressed like a hooker, telling everyone I had seen her smoke cigarettes in class and ending up in the principal's office unable to tell the visibly hurt teacher why I had said that.

"What is a hooky?" a classmate asked me.

Eventually I saw that it only made kids cry when I said they were dirty or that only crazy people walked on their tippy toes, or that herpes could form on both your lips and your private parts. The teacher said I did these things for attention, but I hated being hated and did not really know why I did it. One day I heard Mom say that words can cut like a knife. After that, I kept our home secrets at home and was nice to everyone, though I feared the damage had already been done. But fortunately, or perhaps unfortunately in terms of developing character, I was never held to account for my crimes at Gil Hodges. My mother had drawn a mental line in the sand and, although I wasn't privy to the particulars, was already planning to abandon her adopted country and move us back into the house in Toronto where I spent my summers.

It took Mom a long time to get us ready to leave, but when we did shut down our New York life, it was in secret; my father was informed after the fact, by letter. I left my second-grade class without a word to anyone. Given my reputation as a vicious know-it-all, I feared they might applaud the news, so the secrecy seemed reasonable. I sat through my last day of school wishing I could have frosted cupcakes like the other kids who had summer birthdays or were leaving PS 193. Instead, I ate the words that wanted to fly out of my mouth: *I will never see you again.*

After my seventh birthday, I would never again pledge allegiance to the flag of the United States of America (and to the Republic, for which it stands, one nation, under God, indivisible, with liberty and justice for all). No one in Toronto would know or care that from the Redwood Forest to the Gulf Stream waters, this land was made for you and me. No one would understand the significance of the rockets' red glare or the bombs bursting in air. My new home had also been born of war under the sign of Cancer. It, too, had a long history of exterminating its native peoples, presumably in some of the *plus brillants exploits* alluded to as we warbled *O Canada* in French every morning, our hands at our sides rather than pressed over our hearts.

CHAPTER 5

IN SUMMER

Brooklyn in the early '80s was a less than ideal place for a little girl, even one who loved every inch of the blistering hot, barf-stained blacktop on Ocean Avenue. New York hadn't been revitalized yet; it was still a cesspool of crime and corruption, with the mafia vying with crack-slinging dope boys over who could claim a higher body count on the evening news. I hadn't felt as though these things were close to us, but they might have been. What do kids know about the dangers of the world? New York was my home.

    I actually enjoyed the smell of cigar smoke wafting out of the laundromat even though it made my mother cough and stand outside while our clothes whirled hypnotically behind the round black orbs of the super loaders. The laundromat and dry-clean door was always propped open in the hopes of catching the faintest breeze, although even a hurricane could not have done much to cool the broiling room when all the dryers were going. How could elderly people stand to smoke cigars in that inferno? But for a little girl whose lungs were as yet undamaged, it was wonderful. The traffic noises drifting up through our open sixth-floor windows were reassuringly steady, like ocean waves, while at street level, cars rolled by with loud music and tanned arms broadcasting rebellion from open windows. There is nothing quite like a scorching, sweaty New York summer.

By contrast, Howland Avenue in Toronto's downtown west was too quiet. A car coming down the street was something to be listened out for in those days. This wasn't my first kick at the Toronto can. I had spent whole summers with Mamma, as we called my grandmother, since I was a toddler. The summers when Mom would fly me across the border and pick me up a couple of months later were strangely restorative. My grandmother didn't know what to do with me, so I watched *Mr. Dressup* every day on the grainy TV and did a whole lot of nothing, which was okay because I wasn't expected to do anything. There was no schedule, no routine. My grandmother couldn't even read properly, let alone do math, so I certainly didn't have to do homework.

Mealtimes, and food in general, were problematic when I was alone with Mamma. I liked eating meat, and though it wasn't served daily at home in New York, it was never served in Toronto at all. I never got enough to eat in either home if you asked me; snacks and sweets were all but forbidden, meals cobbled together with whatever raw, healthy ingredients were in the fridge. My mother was completely anti-sugar before its dangers were generally known, probably due to all the choco-cherries and candy cigarettes her father had fed her as a child instead of real, nourishing food. Once, Mamma tried to surprise me with some crocheted lace (*pizzo*, in our Friulan dialect) and I misunderstood, running through the house shouting "Pizza! Pizza!" even though I couldn't smell the pepperoni; my ingratitude caused her to go completely silent for a whole day.

Every summer, part of me missed New York, with its visible dirt and hidden dangers. How would I ever get used to living in Toronto? You didn't have to watch a Toronto sidewalk for pigeon-pecked chewing gum. The smell of urine never screamed out at you from doorways on Howland; there weren't any doorways, just hardscaped walkways leading to private homes. Besides, we never really went out. After the *pizzo* incident, Mom ordered her mother to cook me the occasional piece of protein, but Mamma didn't understand what I liked or my language or why I wasn't excited about crocheted dolls. They were masterfully done, with fully removable clothes and hats, but handmade toys didn't stand a chance against a rumbling stomach.

Mamma derided the games and dolls I saw on TV as plastic "jonk," a stance my mother adopted as well. If I pressed her to buy me something, she would raise her impossibly gnarled hand menacingly; I stared from her eyes to her crooked fingers and back, but she never made good on the threat. It was handmade dolls or nothing. I wasn't supposed to touch them, as they were precious, and I had nobody to play with anyway, but they were pretty to look at. She made a couple of them with chocolate brown yarn, presumably to help me relate.

The house was a huge, dark shrine to huge, dark antiques, and inside it I flung myself from room to room, watched over like a wild, dirty animal by immaculate statues of the Madonna and Baby Jesus. Mamma didn't wash my hair for two whole months one year because I lied and told her Mom had said not to bother. The washing would have hurt like hell because Mamma didn't even own shampoo, let alone conditioner. Anyway, it was next to impossible to painlessly scrub and comb my tight Afro at the best of times, even with the dog brush my despairing mother had purchased rather than consult a Black person.

Mamma phoned my mother about every problem, even when calling 911 would have been the more sensible course of action, but I knew their conversations about me would have more to do with behaviour than hygiene. I stayed happily stinky, except when we went to church and Mamma would scrub my armpits and face with a soapy rag. She'd squeeze me into clothes that had been a good fit the previous year, so I could stand and pray and sit and pray and kneel and pray at St. Peter's in a language nobody understood. Religion meant a lot to Mamma; she recited the rosary and spoke to God aloud constantly, even when brushing out her waist-length grey hair or shelling peas, but I learned nothing from those church services. To this day, I sometimes have to use the *Sister Act* scene to remember how to cross myself properly: *spectacles, testicles, wallet and watch.*

Mamma taught me to knit scarves, but her real passion was gardening that verged on farming, as most of it was practical rather than pretty. She gave me my own little space in the garden—*in tal ort*, in our dialect—so I could make my own things grow. I planted an acorn that, fifteen years later, became a twelve-foot tree that had to be cut down because it was casting too much shade. I grew corn and the sheaves got infested with earwigs. I grew squash and they were mostly eaten by squirrels. Finally I just watered the plants and helped Mamma till the soil, feeling the crumbly earth between my fingers and the sun on my face.

Though I wanted a pet very badly, my family only kept birds, so I contented myself with backyard wildlife. I could stand still long enough to observe bumblebees feasting on the cornflowers; I even touched their furry backs. The paper wasps were too scary to touch but very interesting as they chewed busily on the wooden fence boards. I pulled worms from the soil and drowned them in a bowl of water and then, disgusted with myself, buried them. I am easily bored, but at the time I remember only satisfaction from being outside from dawn to dusk, listening to the bugs at work and watching the light filter through all the leaves and branches above my face.

Mamma hated those towering trees and the neighbours who failed to prune them, leaving their yards a "jongle" and our own partially in shadow. She hated everyone on the street for reasons unknown—cats who shat in her carefully hand-turned soil? Stinky hibachis grilling dead animals on a daily basis? She hissed curses at the intrusive felines and stared at the neighbours as if daring them to start something. I assiduously avoided other humans, crouching behind the raspberry canes and running inside when I heard children coming out. The children would be less forgiving than their parents of my dishevelled hair and faded housedresses.

Mom wouldn't be caught dead in the garden when she was there. She said Mamma dressed like a peasant and it was mortifying to be seen with her. The uniform included men's work gloves, a broad, sweat-stained straw hat, long work trousers and a long-sleeved men's shirt over her undershirt, even in the hottest weather. She smeared various plant juices on her sweating face to repel insects and, after washing her hair every week with water she had used for cooking vegetables, she braided it and stuffed it under the hat so that she looked even more androgynous. Once girded for garden warfare, she would often spend a great deal of time doing nothing but standing out there, straight and still as though she herself had been planted deep in the ground. If you touched her during these moments, she would come back to herself as if she had been in a trance, smiling a frightening grin courtesy of the ill-fitting false teeth that had to go in before she went out. It was a jarring sight; she didn't wear them in the house, ever. She could chew nuts with her bare gums but insisted on wearing the painful dentures, which changed her speech and facial structure rather dramatically, just to greet a universe of bees and worms.

Mamma didn't just prefer working with her hands; she was decidedly anti-progress. She insisted on watering most of her crops by hand, trudging back and forth along a narrow, grassy path with two big watering cans filled with rainwater collected in big Rubbermaid trash bins instead of buying a longer hose. We had impressive yields of raspberries, strawberries, comfrey, potatoes, carrots, herbs, onions, tomatoes and even grapes; naturally, Mamma had built the framework for the grape arbour out of salvaged scrap wood and trained the vines herself. Though she won a City award for her manicured flower gardens and dwarf pines, Mamma's real triumph was the harvest.

We were living an enviably green lifestyle so many decades before it would become cool that I could not appreciate it properly. As I grew older, I cringed with embarrassment at the sight of Mamma and her bizarrely gleaming, perfectly even smile toting the heavy watering cans with her filthy slave hands, sweat soaking her back. A flowerpot was always nearby should she find a rusty nail or an offensive bit of paving stone in the dirt from which she wrung so much bounty.

When the day's work was done and our vegetable dinner eaten, Mamma crocheted at the kitchen table while I sat opposite forcing scrap yarn into tight, uneven stitches, telling lies. Once I made up a story about how the scars on my arm had got there. I said Daddy came home one night and cut me.

"Cots eh, cots eh, cots, eh," I said in pidgin.

She just nodded, occasionally glancing at my work and pointing out the holes forming where I had dropped yet another stitch. Who knows what she thought of my lies? Unlike me, the motormouth, Mamma was a woman of very few words.

Then summer would end and Mom would suddenly appear to scream at Mamma about my appearance and the state of the house, while I said nothing, watching to see who would have the final word. I would be whisked back to New York where we'd search under the bed for Daddy's used hypes and the discarded lipsticks and panties of his lady friends. That was, until the summer of 1985 when we didn't just visit. We stayed and, of course, three can be a crowd.

CHAPTER 6

MY MOTHER'S HOUSE HAS MANY ROOMS

If it seems crazy that my mother would move back in with a woman she hated, whom she thought of as illiterate, stubborn, dirty and crazy, please consider her predicament. Since before she could form the words, she had suffered years of brainwashing and was made to believe that the world was a terrible place and that loyalty to family was everything. The world had obligingly provided all the evidence necessary to prove the theory. Long before I would discover it for myself, she already knew there was nowhere to run and no rescue coming.

Mamma hadn't exactly provided her a secure attachment figure, but Mom didn't deal in the psychobabble of the past. She was much more infuriated by the daily indignities of living in close proximity to a woman who was too stupid to concede her daughter's superior intellect and common sense. Mamma routinely did idiotic things like stationing her bed in the living room after a botched burglary attempt so that next time she could be closer to the front door to detain the criminal. She also indulged in dull-witted cow behaviours like letting bills pile up unpaid and keeping jars of putrefying vegetables laying around for the bugs.

But Mom had made her own share of mistakes that made her vulnerable to critique. Her marriage had failed, and now she was stuck with a mixed-race kid. I was visibly Black, but as an Italian, she didn't need any more reminders.

"Don't call yourself Black, Nicky," she would say. "You're café au lait."

"Don't call yourself skinny, Nicky. You're statuesque."

"Don't call yourself ugly, Nicky. You're striking."

I hated these terms. Why couldn't my mother just talk normally like everyone else? Why did she have to show off?

Mamma turned my small brown hands over and examined the palms.

"If you look at this side, she's really almost White," she remarked in Friulan.

Speaking of failed marriages to convicted criminals from other races, we did wonder, of course, where my father had disappeared to so thoroughly. We had a partial answer within months of moving to Toronto: just after my seventh birthday, Mom was shocked to receive a letter with a bold red stamp on the flap warning that the New Jersey Sheriff's Office could not be held responsible for the contents of the envelope. Daddy had been locked up again for what was to be the last time. This time there would be no bail, no time served, no reprieve of any kind; he was accused of crossing state lines to commit a Federal offense, coked up out of his mind. They said he had robbed a bank in a small New Jersey town.

I found this out from my mother, whose conflicting sources were Daddy himself, who denied everything, and the New Jersey dailies available on microfiche at the Toronto Reference Library. According to the papers, Daddy or his partner had pointed an unlicensed weapon at the teller, who happened to be related to one of the town's lawmakers. They fled after an unsuccessful robbery and were captured hiding in a nearby marsh. Jeremiah Salter's ID—indisputable evidence of his real name—was at the bottom of the empty duffel bag. But after months of rotting in the system, my father, whose three strikes were already used up, went against the advice of his counsel and refused to take a plea agreement that would have freed him in five years.

Unwavering on the subject of his innocence and the State's frame-up, Daddy insisted on pleading his case to a jury even as his partner took the plea. Perhaps he imagined himself back in the relative luxury of a Canadian lockup, forgetting that Americans don't play when it comes to property crimes. Long before I would cheer for OJ, who had probably killed someone by the name of Nicole (but seriously, who even cared at that point?), Daddy was shown no mercy for wasting the court's time and resources in an expensive jury trial. He was sentenced to twenty-five to fifty years in Trenton State Prison without possibility of parole.

"We left just in time," my mother said. "He's really done it now."

Despite her formal education and off the-charts intelligence, Mom had only ever gotten a job in the secretarial pool in the hopes that office employment would yield a strong, sexy husband who liked fine dining and seersucker suits. She didn't want a career, she wanted to be taken care of. Thus she found herself, after years of unemployment, without viable job options and a withered will to work. She couldn't anyway, not with a child to care for. So we lived off the income from her savings and investments.

It was the era of 10 percent guaranteed returns; the money was not much, but it was regular, as was my grandmother's old-age pension, which was double what it should have been because the government had never caught on to Papa Angelo's death of a brain aneurism in 1983. That he had survived since his birth in 1900, through two world wars, decades of asbestos removal and breakfasts of half a dozen fried eggs every morning only to die from falling off a chair while changing a light bulb seemed yet more evidence of the hand of a cruel and random fate, but one that made it possible to keep the house. Mom gave her mother an allowance every week for knitting wool and porridge, and managed the household with what remained. Our lack of money was the subject of constant disputes. I knew my mother had some, so why didn't she spend it? Or get a job?

"Oh, so you want me to be like those mothers who spend all their money on designer clothes for their kids and don't have a pot to piss in? Or you want to be one of those latchkey kids raised by the TV?"

Well, yes, that sounded just fine to me. Looking back, we were in a better financial position than any but the wealthiest of my generation or those that followed could reasonably hope to expect; the enormous house had been paid off for years, we grew a fair amount of our own food and we didn't have the overhead of a car or even cable. This privilege seemed to flow from no discernible effort. We sat on a fortune's worth of antiques, but my mother would bend over to pick up a penny in three inches of snow.

Now that we all lived together, my grandmother complied with her daughter's wishes and rules in a stunning reversal of the old dynamic. She must have known, deep in her soul, how miserly she had been when it came to loving her changeling daughter and accepted this payback without much protest. They say the chickens always come home to roost, and Mamma was a great believer in the truth of such sayings, as well as home remedies, the evil eye and every cautionary tale, parable and fable she had ever heard. She knew one about a woman who ate only meat and starved to death (the doctors tried to save her but couldn't even find a vein). She told a true story about an immoral woman who had peed so much she drowned in her own urine.

Mamma never tired of warning me about the poetic justice that lay in store for thieves and liars and little girls who were just like their fathers. When I took a penny from the cashier's jar at the fruit market, my grandmother made me put it back immediately, her pale eyes blazing and her pale skin a terrifying shade of red. It would have been spurious to threaten me with Daddy's belt or teeth—we didn't know where he was—but the very real threat to tell my mother ensured it would be many years before I stole again. Alliances shifted: Mamma and Mom against me; me and Mom against Mamma. Although Mamma occasionally interceded for me, I never took up arms on her behalf.

Mom was all-powerful and all-knowing. She skillfully handled calls when the house's mausoleum quiet was shattered by the insistent ringing of telemarketers; she dispatched the bills and translated incomprehensible letters; she coordinated repairmen and directed sanitation, flying through the house shrieking about my grandmother's messiness, general stenches and innumerable other inadequacies. Mamma presented what, to my mother, was the feeblest of defenses:

"Vo-tu chi ti zuri?" ("Do you want me to swear?")

She would hold up one trembling hand, ready to place the other on the Bible if necessary to reinforce her declaration that she had acted in good faith or hadn't done the thing she wasn't supposed to do. Not surprisingly given the religious justifications for her abuse, my mother had a hate/fear relationship with anything that pertained to the Lord. Swearing on the Bible had nothing to do with virtue or innocence. It meant taking the Lord's name in vain, which was almost as bad as saying you didn't believe in Him or, God forbid, admitting you hated him; that was a surefire ticket to Hell in any language.

Impervious to the pleas that her belongings might be useful "someday," Mom shredded Mamma's cherished holey sweaters with her bare hands to demonstrate that they clearly needed to be THROWN OUT, NOT HOARDED. She discarded old yarn, broken crockery and yellowed newspapers with glee. Mamma would dig pathetically through the garbage trying to rescue these items, her once-powerful voice reduced to pitiful whimpers and futile prayers for divine intercession.

Eventually, Mamma moved into the unfinished basement and lived like a mushroom in the dark. Walking by the open doorway, we could hear her issuing reedy prayers to the Blessed Virgin, prompting conspiratorial eye-rolls upstairs. Sometimes there was an odd thumping noise as well. It wasn't the ancient furnace but Mamma pounding her legs with smooth stones to tame the pain of swollen varicose veins. Mamma cooked all her own meals, mostly concoctions of boiled grains and seeds and vegetables, and ate alone downstairs. She no longer made salads for herself even though it was one of her favourite foods. If she still had cravings for *pang e azet* (bread and vinegar), for reading the tabloid papers with a magnifying glass and giggling over alien abductions, for buying new lace patterns at Woolco, they were no longer indulged.

When she did come upstairs, Mamma lapsed into near-total silence, revived only by *Lawrence Welk* and *Murder, She Wrote* reruns that she watched in bed before falling asleep without saying goodnight. I felt guilty leaving the television on to watch my own shows in what was essentially her bedroom, but she never stirred or made a sound. Eventually, nobody said a word to her beyond the bare minimum. She developed sciatica, glaucoma and then broke her hip on the three concrete steps that led from the mudroom to the backyard. Even after weeks in a rehab hospital, she lay in bed for months, moaning for more medication when she had previously scoffed at weak people who took aspirin. She still sometimes had a big, toothless smile for me that only ignited my guilt and shame at the times I had been rude, dismissive, contemptuous. She *was* weak. She knew every bad thing about me, yet she continued to be nice even when I had so clearly chosen the other side.

Mamma yielded to the pain of not being able to navigate the stairs and wound up in a city-run nursing home eating steamed rice and microwaved vegetable niblets three times a day because they didn't have a real vegetarian meal plan. I knew she would never be back. The garden was an overgrown mess, and it would have killed her to see it that way. In my early twenties I'd go do her washing because laundry service cost extra. Sometimes I also washed her hair—a most unpleasant challenge in a shower chair, but better than subjecting her to the shame of a male personal support worker seeing her body. I made small talk in pidgin Italian, my Friulan vocabulary slashed down to pleasantries from lack of use.

As expected, Mamma did not come alive in the stimulating peer environment promised by the assisted-living brochures. Apart from occasional hallway fitness exercises, she didn't participate in any of the residents' groups, sing along at the piano or take part in excursions. She still didn't speak the language or understand the accents of the succession of strangers with whom she shared her room. Though I knew she enjoyed our visits and the flowers I brought, going every week became a dreaded chore as the years dragged on. I spoke English. What were we going to talk about? The sordid details of my life? Or hers?

"You're such a good granddaughter," one of the nurses said to me. "She doesn't get any visitors other than your mom. But she's always so polite and kind, just like you!"

Her family had never left Italy and hadn't seen her in over five decades, but we knew they prospered. She never stopped writing to them in the tiny, virtually indecipherable handwriting that had been necessary to conserve paper in childhood. Instead of describing how she had broken her hip, undergone lengthy physiotherapy and returned home to discover she could navigate neither the stairs nor her daughter's rages, Mamma spoke mostly of the distant past. She congratulated them on their grandchildren, offering lengthy prayers for their health and the happiness of their eternal souls.

In May of 2004, Mamma was baffled to receive a plaque from the government of Canada recognizing her ninetieth birthday. She hadn't felt old, or special. And by the standards of her healthy, robust family, ninety was no big achievement for a woman.

Three years later, she died suddenly of a hospital-contracted infection and was cremated—unthinkable sacrilege for a faithful Catholic—because neither my mother nor I were willing to pay for a funeral. I made many excuses to myself about why it wasn't my responsibility. I was broke, uneducated and stuck in dead-end jobs while my mother had that huge house she could sell, plus all her fine furniture and investments. She had lived off Mamma's pension for so many years and hadn't paid for school or given me a dime. I didn't know the first thing about making after-death arrangements. It couldn't really matter what happened to her body at this point, could it? Shouldn't I have done more to make her life better instead of feeling guilty now that it was too late?

It was good that the Friul family didn't come and visit her. The shame of them seeing her like that would have been worse than dying alone. I was often hungover and sometimes high out of my mind when I stood shoulder to shoulder with peach-clad orderlies in the elevator, scrabbling in my purse for gum that was useful for more than just masking my breath. I would do anything to take the focus away from the smells and sights of the seventh floor. It was the best floor in the place, the floor for residents who might think nothing of patting a visitor's ass but who hadn't yet completely lost their minds.

CHAPTER 7

LOVE ME TENDER

My middle school diaries either went to a recycling plant after one of my frequent moves or are buried somewhere in my storage locker behind holiday décor and small appliances. I have no desire to revisit these spiral notebooks of preadolescent rantings that gave me a permanent callous on the middle finger of my right hand from pressing so hard and writing so much. There is definitely enough dark energy in those ruled pages to fuel a small town for months, maybe years. Unlike Harriet the spy, who originally inspired all this journaling, most of the anger is directed at my mother. She was never meant to discover them, but she read them and retaliated with sabotage and silent treatment. Mom, I am sorry for all the mean, hateful, true things I said about you. Could you expect anything less from a Cancer?

Whatever didn't end up in my diary was shouted at the top of my lungs to my mother's face when I couldn't hold it in, which was often. Discussion having proven futile time and again, I lost the capacity for it; my temper escalated to nuclear in seconds, and I yelled myself hoarse calling her a bitch, a fucking bitch and many other variations on that unoriginal theme. Sometimes for variety, I threw in "I hate you, you ruined my life, no wonder Daddy left!" That was best said from the relative safety of the butler's stairs where I could escape through the house faster than she could run. I either gave myself up or she gave up the chase and punished me later.

Revenge could be taken, but only on my own body. I picked my skin raw, banged my shins and ravaged my fingernails knowing she'd hate people to think she was a bad mother for letting me go to school looking so ragged. She liked to restrain me with my arms behind my back and thrust my face in front of the mirror to show me how indisputably deranged I looked, my face greasy, my lips bitten bloody. How dare I damage myself like that? I told her that she looked even crazier with her teeth bared like a biting dog and the tendons standing out in her neck. I asked her why she clenched her teeth like that. I was daring her to physically hurt me, which would show, instead of just humiliating me, which wouldn't.

"I'm showing great restraint, Nicky," she spat through a grate of teeth that looked like they couldn't open even if she wanted them to.

She had been hospitalized for lockjaw as a young woman. Her anger terrified me; there was either something wrong with her that I could never fix or I was a rotten thing. Or both.

"When I was a little girl and I didn't get my way, do you know what I would do?" she said, as I stared at our grimacing reflections (the mirror had some black stains on it that seemed to come from inside the glass itself). "I used to hold my breath till I turned blue and fainted. Do you think I was born yesterday? I know all your tricks and they won't work either."

I once tried her breath-holding trick, too, but my burning lungs halted me well before unconsciousness.

Was this abuse? Abuse was when people touched you in inappropriate places. It was my bad luck that my mother was crazy and evil, but she was also funny, smart, principled, generous. The mirror I struggled in front of was the same one I posed for with my underwear flopping on my head, pouting, "Hey, sailor, want to catch fish in my net?" This made her throw back her head and howl with laughter at my sultry impressions. It was the same mirror she told me I was pretty in.

At ten I was easily my mother's height, but she loomed large, with the strength and will to spank me, twist my arms and slap me in the face. My dark skin was thick, yet another reason I wished she had married a White man who, at the very least, would have gifted me with normal hair and markable skin so people would know how miserable I was. I never considered hitting her back. She always said if I did I'd better make sure she stayed down, because if she got up she would kill me.

Restoring the peace usually required writing long apology letters in which I admitted my behaviour and promised to never do X, Y or Z again. If the letters weren't sufficiently remorseful and detailed, they were sent back to me for revisions—my first exposure to the joys of working with an editor. These apologies were never in the least heartfelt since I felt a psychopath's lack of remorse for everything I had said and done; I am sure she knew that, but the exercise persisted. No matter how often my mother expressed her preference for an average daughter who was kind and obedient over a fucking brat with a genius IQ, an admission of guilt written in my own hand justified punishment and exercised my mind. When the apology and request letters were finally up to standard, they were not acted upon but merely stored in the top drawer of her bureau in a neat stack of grovelling admissions, false promises and formal petitions. For all I know, those letters are still filed as evidence of my debauchery along with the legal pads full of pleadings to be allowed to go on school field trips, buy new clothes or visit someone's house after school.

With the exception of my grandmother, all living things—me, Mom, the budgies—spent most of our time in the kitchen. When I got a little older, maybe eleven or twelve, my mother disappeared more and more often to the upstairs level. She didn't say what she was doing up there, and I didn't ask. Only much, much later, when the real estate agent I worked for went in to appraise the house for sale, did I see the kitchen I lived in with an objective eye: bare plaster walls with giant cracks, ancient linoleum, vintage appliances, peeling window frames, salvaged furniture. I knew to describe it as "unspoiled" on the listing without my boss having to say a word.

In contrast to the faded quality of most of the house, the second floor sitting room was "a light-filled stunner," I wrote on the feature sheet. As a child, I called it the Fancy Room because it was brimming with crystal decanters and gold-embossed teacups that I was allowed to choose for tea on special occasions. "Boasting an impressive wall of windows, including coveted bay windows with lookout seats," I wrote, "the room is flooded with natural light, perfect for enjoying peaceful views and encouraging indoor plants to flourish year-round." Mom wasn't spending time up there in that room though. She wouldn't even sit on the rosewood settee she had rescued from the garbage, restored and reupholstered in gold brocade. She was probably just in bed.

Saturday mornings I'd be the first one up because she stayed in bed till at least noon. Before slipping out of bed, I would have lain awake for a while beside her trying not to squirm or cough for fear of waking her as I waited for the right moment to make my escape. I tiptoed down the hall, hugging the walls where the floors didn't creak so badly. Downstairs I'd watch *Pee-wee's Playhouse* (I had a crush on Cowboy Curtis) and *Saved by the Bell* (I had a crush on Zack). Every kid watches these shows and knows they are not representative of the real world, but I studied the characters as intently as an alien researching human behaviour. Everyone was so colourful and pretty, so different from real life.

Sometimes I lost track of time, and when my mother got up to make breakfast, I stared at her like an intruder. When the last *Road Runner* rerun had ended—a show I didn't even like because the bad guy, who was just trying to satisfy his totally natural urges, never, ever won—I felt a deep, unaccountable sadness. There was an eerie emptiness in the cheery jingles and dated credits, as if the voice actors, illustrators and every member of the orchestra, as well as many of the children these cartoons had originally delighted, already knew they would be long dead by the time these ancient programs aired in my living room.

Reality often merged into fantasy in the flickering blue light of my saviour, the television. I watched reruns of the original *Star Trek* on Saturday nights and pretended that William Shatner, who could wrestle alien life forms to the death in sync with the nerve-jangling soundtrack, had come to take me up onto the USS *Enterprise*. When Olympic skating was on, I swooned over the exuberant moves of Bowman the

Showman, pretending that I wasn't ugly and that he would one day marry me in a white wedding on the ice.

The armchair in front of the TV eventually became too small to share, and I started to resent my mother's too-soft body and the space it took up. It was as if she could read my private, lascivious thoughts, squeezing them out as surely as her round hips pressed my bony ones into the side of the chair. Even in bed, I found no peace from my resentments. If it had ever been cozy to sleep beside her naked body, as she said I used to beg her to do (quite possible, as I was afraid of the dark), I certainly had never been fond of her icy feet pressed against my skinny calves.

That I did not have my own room in such a large home was another bone of contention. Technically, I did have my own room, but it was the front parlour and had a glass-paned door that didn't lock and afforded absolutely no privacy. Just as the Fancy Room was a container for Wedgewood, the front parlour was a container for a lot of expensive stuffed animals perfectly arranged on the embroidered coverlet that was perfectly and perpetually spread on the single bed which was not mine to sleep in. On one shelf sat a vast assortment of tiny porcelain animal sculptures with rough, webbed bottoms that were somehow collected from ancient Tetley Tea boxes. They were also not mine.

"How dare you? Did you think I wouldn't notice they were missing?"

Staring at the sea of figurines, it must have been exactly what I was thinking when I had taken a couple of them to school. Who would count such tiny statues? I didn't yet understand that things that never moved out of their place were easy to notice once disturbed. I had carefully chosen a couple of animals that had duplicates, slipped them into my knapsack and rearranged the collection to cover my deception.

"Who did you give them to? And why did you give them away in the first place? These kids are not your friends."

I didn't know. To be liked? To be seen as owning something? To thank someone? To reciprocate a kind gesture or give a birthday present? I couldn't remember.

"I can't trust you with *anything*."

My mother redoubled her surveillance efforts and enforced the rules with renewed vigilance, resentful that I had given her the extra work of searching my bag for contraband and forcing her to make me strip naked if she found any. I would be locked in the bathroom so I could be cold while I thought about what I had done wrong. And she could hold her pee like a camel. I hated the shame of nudity, especially because I had nothing to be ashamed of, no burgeoning womanhood to hide.

"You're lucky you'll never need a bra, Nicky. And clothes will hang on you the way they were meant to. You're like Twiggy."

Maybe she really believed I was lucky, and maybe the contrast—not just my long, thin, brown body to her short, pale, curvy one, but my privileged life to her own sad, dispossessed childhood—made her jealous, the way I sometimes feel stabbed when my beautiful golden-haired daughter for whom a good life seems laid out in glowing neon says she is bored. I thought Mom held every conceivable card, but time has shown me another possibility: maybe I had all the potential. Given her boomer's terror of growing old, it's an explanation I can now glimpse through the abundance of floaters in my middle-aged eyes.

As stubbornly underdeveloped as my body remained, it was going through all the internal changes right on time. By the time I got my period at eleven, I was already boy-crazy and very ashamed of my feelings. Sometimes I'd fall asleep during *The National* with Knowlton Nash, wedged into the armchair beside her and wake to discover her gently licking the inside of my ear and my neck, which I didn't put a stop to because it felt good. Years later in therapy, I dutifully ransacked my memories hoping to discover more that was repressed: after all, sexual abuse by my own mother would admit me to a very special club whose members were excused from taking any responsibility for their actions.

Oh, you racked up your credit cards and declared bankruptcy? Dropped out of school? Cut yourself to ribbons just to see the blood? Tried to commit suicide? Drank pure grain alcohol till you went half-blind? Well, your mother touched you, so there's that.

Unlike the slow drip of daily occurrences I could not even begin to explain to an outsider out of context, let alone identify as abuse, being molested would have been both a conversation killer and a laminated hall pass. Every irrational thing I had done and more would be not only explained but entirely justified.

Except there was nothing sinister about her actions. I filled the companionship void left by my father, but I made a very poor substitute for the real man she wanted. The bedtime cuddling was, therefore, nothing but a reminder that since she had made me, I would always be hers.

Development

In weak markets, the desire for redevelopment, or a specific type of development, may precede an identified developer. As a result, the reuse vision may come before a developer is identified.

-The United States Environmental Protection Agency, Office of Brownfields and Land Revitalization, June 2019

CHAPTER 8

LOCKDOWN

A couple of weeks before Thanksgiving one year, Mom told me she had an unbelievable surprise to unveil. She refused to say what it was, no matter how often I pestered her for answers.

"Did you win the lottery?"

She laughed. "I don't play the lottery, Nicky. Don't you know the odds of winning are astronomical? You have a better chance of being hit by frozen poop falling out of an airplane. It's just a tax on the poor."

I pondered what it would be like to be hit with frozen turds: instant death before you knew what had hit you. I'd heard that if you dropped a penny off the Empire State Building it would go right through the sidewalk like butter. The only thing Mom had ever won was a local contest, when I was eight; the prize was some kind of giant marble table that either didn't really exist, wouldn't fit in the door or was not as specified. My mom made enough of a stink that the table was eventually replaced by the second prize: a stupid, boring Via Rail trip to a Northern Ontario resort called Minaki Lodge in the off-season. She hated every minute of it, so I did as well. I think I even wrote an essay about what a horror show it had been, though in pictures it looks incredibly beautiful—at least before it burned to the ground a couple decades later. The birchbark box with a porcupine-quill lid the gift shop yielded had sweetgrass stitching that was still fragrant years later. But we were done travelling.

"Did you get a job?" I asked hopefully.

It would solve so many of our problems. Almost every request of mine was rejected partly on the basis of finances; surely some drops of new-found income would trickle down to me—at least, so said my uncle's Reaganomics. More importantly, my mother was always home. I formed a mental picture of her alone upstairs, periodically leaking clouds of dark thoughts like a giant squid squirting ink. Once I was convinced she was stealing my life away from me, I felt her suffocating presence as the only obstacle to my freedom and could not forgive her for it. Sometimes I feel an avalanche of shame for interpreting every innocent question as an interrogation, every parental boundary as a personal attack and every loving gesture as a control mechanism, but at the time I only wanted to be left alone. It didn't matter anyway because she had never wanted to work. The surprise was not a job.

Had she met someone? Was a substitute Dad in the cards? Finally, she admitted that, yes, she had met a wonderful man who would be joining us for Thanksgiving dinner, but I had to act surprised because it was supposed to be a secret.

My heart pounded with the thrill of unleashed hopes. A new Daddy! We never went anywhere, so where had she met him? Who could it be? Surely not Stephen—never Steven, but Steph-*en*—the red-haired man who stocked vegetables at the grocery store. She had made many unnecessary trips to buy produce, returning each time in a flurry of excitement. He had flirted with her! He liked her! I thought it doubtful given his age, but she said younger men often liked older women because they knew what they were doing.

There was also a homeless man with a long, tangled black beard and piercing eyes who conversed with Mom at length, confident that she was unperturbed by his long rants and ill-shod wanderings along Bloor Street. The terror of the Ayatollah had passed and 9/11 was not even a glimmer on the horizon, so Reza was allowed to simply roam one of the city's busiest streets, calling out to people without their shrinking away from his robes and turban. Certainly the T-word could not be applied to Reza, who alternated calm, lucid pronouncements with animated political discourse; he was perhaps more like Osho, with a third-eye gaze that made my mother think him sexy, interesting and exotic. I thought he was filthy. But, like Steph-en, he was eventually swallowed up by the city, never to be seen again.

Meanwhile, I could think of nothing else besides this mysterious new man I had never met. I figured he was probably Jewish, of medium height with collar-length curly grey hair. A rescuer! Someone to show Mom how the outside world worked and occupy her attention completely, as was fitting—she had always maintained that the husband came first, children second. She had once taken me to a palm reader who insisted that, despite my still-developing hand, he could tell I would never give more than 60 percent of my attention to a husband. This had disturbed her as deeply as if he had said I would die before puberty. She couldn't think of anything worse than a wife not being 100 percent devoted to her mate. A husband meant she would forget all about me, so I could do whatever I wanted. If there was a downside, I certainly couldn't see it!

This magical thinking wrenched me out of bed early every morning, stomach roiling with excitement. What if New Dad had other kids? We might become friends. Even if they were much older and wanted nothing to do with an ugly weirdo like me, at least their father would know something about modern parenting that might rub off on Mom. I fantasized about darker scenarios too: if he was a child-molesting perv, well, hey, at least I'd get some positive attention for a change!

On Thanksgiving Day, I made sure I was clean and wearing something decent. The doorbell rang.

"Let me handle it, you stay here," Mom insisted, shooing me back into the kitchen.

When she returned a moment later, alone, it was with half a turkey with chestnut stuffing in a large box, fresh and hot from Holt Renfrew's dining room. My mother proudly said "Ta-da!" She did not smile often, but she was beaming as she set the various containers down on the kitchen table. I looked behind the boxes of food, searching for the man, but the delivery man had already left. I realized New Dad was probably running late, as dads tended to do; the food was obviously meant to impress and pamper him. But then she started opening the boxes.

"Shouldn't we keep everything warm till he gets here?"

My mother chuckled. "Oh, Nicky, there's no man. I was just teasing! *This* is the surprise. You didn't actually fall for it, did you?"

Whatever I said, she continued talking fast.

"I never expected you to actually believe it. I forgot how naïve you can be. I was just joking. Couldn't you tell I was just having a little fun with you?"

"Why would you do that? It's not funny."

I was too shocked to help as she set plates on the table. Her expression changed to one of annoyance.

"Look, I got us a real stuffed turkey. Aren't you excited? You're always asking why we don't do more for these holidays."

We didn't normally celebrate Thanksgiving so, as an often-frustrated carnivore for whom hot dogs were the ultimate treat, I should have been ecstatic at all that tender meat. But of course, I had believed her—she never lied! She didn't have to. Politicians lie to get your vote and criminals to get your money, but mothers don't bother; they do what they want. And Mom hated lies as much as I hated hypocrisy. Most of my punishments sprang from my deceitful sneaking around, so how could she have lied about something so important? It was like I was seeing the bits of my torn-up Get Out Of Jail Free card fluttering to the ground. How could I have been so stupid! I would never, ever be rescued.

Another Harriet the spy trick, this one to prevent crying: I stared at a single focal point on the perfectly roasted bird, which had thick, shiny, flawless bronze skin exactly like the Stove Top Stuffing turkey. It was just the two of us again. The drumstick blurred through a haze of tears that I wouldn't give her the satisfaction of allowing to drip onto my plate. She served us large helpings of food in silence, but I heard the familiar refrain as loudly as if it had been spelled out on the Jumbotron in Yankee Stadium:

Do you know what I have sacrificed for you? I could have had a man in the house—I wanted *one*—*but no one's interested in me now. I'm stuck with you, and you're not even grateful! Nothing is ever good enough for you. You're just like your father. You don't care about me at all, you only care about yourself. He gave me whiplash driving like a maniac in that car of his and I still can't move my neck and you never even ask about it. All you do is talk about yourself and that school of yours and those people you think are your friends. You never shut up, it's always "I want, I want, I want," whining and arguing and disrespecting me. It's never "THANK YOU FOR GIVING UP YOUR ENTIRE LIFE FOR ME." You want Daddy instead? News flash: he would have killed you by now. But instead he just left! He likes his druggie friends and his hookers more than he likes you! But who takes care of you and tries to knock some sense into you so you don't turn out just like him? Me. I could have snapped my fingers and given you up just like that, but I didn't. I stayed.*

"How's the turkey?" Mom asked.

"I don't like the stuffing."

"It's chestnut stuffing, you just haven't had it before."

"I don't want to eat the chestnuts, they taste weird. Do I have to?"

"Well, this stuff wasn't cheap you know."

She deliberated for a moment before sliding my chestnuts onto her plate.

In Grade 5, they sent me to HOBY, the Hugh O'Brien Youth Leadership Congress. I still don't know why; although I was arrogant about my academic achievements, it might simply have been affirmative action. Only two students from every school were selected, but my mother's no-holds-barred editing of my entrance essay practically guaranteed admission. In those days all I thought about was getting a boyfriend, earning money and impressing my teachers. Leadership wasn't high on the list, not when every day was a battle between the grandiosity that applied only to my intellect and the low self-esteem that defined every other aspect of my life.

While the other HOBY chosen seemed to form instant friendships, excitedly discussing the itinerary and how they would shower before bed and sleep in towels to save time in the morning for all the awesome activities, I panicked about how to even turn on the shower; I had never used one before. I lagged behind the group and tried to make myself invisible, then silently, bitterly judged them for not seeing me. I begged off doing the trust fall because of my fear of heights, which was real, but I also didn't want them to touch me and be disgusted. I was the youngest one there by a year, my social anxiety proving that the vice principal was right: I should never have skipped a grade.

Since my school didn't have an onsite gifted program, Mom had pushed hard for me to skip the fourth grade, a move the school administration tried to block. I wasn't emotionally mature enough, they said. Why that should hold me back academically was a mystery to my mother, so I was fast-tracked out of my grade. I didn't attend my third-grade year-end party because a kid who had called me a nigger counter-accused me of calling him a clumsy Korean. I didn't even know what a Korean was, but I didn't cry (Harriet having taught me to control those useless tears) and he did, so we were both banned from the party. It was fine because I could get cake at home the next time Mom bought one.

I had always preferred the company of adults to that of my peers, strange creatures who could tear me down in seconds when I lied about having seen the movie everyone was talking about or owning a video game I hadn't ever played. Adults practically had to be nice to you, even when they caught you in fantastical lies like pretending you had spent the weekend show jumping ponies instead of reading books (thank you, Merit, for calling me out on the fact that I had never been on any animal's back before).

Despite relating so much better to adults, I was never sure the teachers liked me. Maybe they wondered why a kid so clever and outspoken never returned a signed permission form, never packed a proper lunch, never wore a snowsuit. What, exactly, was wrong with me that I would rather sit in soaking wet clothes, hands too frozen to hold a pen after recess, than wear proper winter gloves? We lived in the Annex; there was no excuse. It wasn't like we had never heard of Gore-Tex. But my impermeable substance of choice was Teflon now, a miraculous new material from which I adopted a useful life strategy: pretend you don't care and everything slides right off you.

I made the mistake of telling Mom that I hadn't liked HOBY and that nobody there had liked me. She took this to mean that, for my own protection, existing social privileges ought to be clawed back and no new ones granted. She was already giving me the kind of home life she hadn't had growing up: stable housing, nutritious food, zero chores and active encouragement in all things academic. But it wasn't enough for me, living as we did in an affluent, progressive neighbourhood in the era of Kid Power where everybody else seemed to be given free rein.

Nobody intervened; I doubt if anyone even understood. What mother wouldn't give her child a washcloth for swimming lessons when it was a mandatory requirement for moving on to the next level? What non-Jehovah's Witness mother thought birthdays should not be celebrated and kept the house dark and shuttered on Halloween to avoid the evils of candy, begging and pranking? Of course, I must have forgotten to bring the facecloth, mention my birthday, wear my costume, and now I was lying about it. I was too tall, too nerdy, and had an uneven Afro. I wore my glasses on a cord like an old librarian because they kept falling off and breaking. I wouldn't have liked me either. Mom had an explanation for that too.

"You're different, Nicky. You're so far above them, it's not even funny," she would sniff as she went about her chores. "I knew that since the day you were born."

The worst thing would be for me to become a spoiled-rotten brat like everyone else; I was selfish enough as it was. Since the only practical route to success was via my brain, anything that didn't support that goal was an absolute waste of time. I tried to tell her about social skills and the importance of being well-rounded.

"That's like the *new math* they're teaching now. What's the point if you don't even know your times tables? Nicky, no one is going to care whether you can catch a ball or how many birthday parties you've been to once you have a law degree hanging on your wall."

Determined not to be what we called a social retard back then—the emotional equivalent of having your growth stunted by coffee consumption, which was definitely a myth—I pushed my curfew, hanging around in the field after school in search of friends and risking that the door wouldn't open when I came home. I openly scowled at her when using the phone after dinner, talking about boys and make-up right there in the kitchen doorway because there was nowhere else to go. She listened in, treating my requests for privacy with the same incredulity as if her left arm had demanded to be left alone. If her mood was bad, she raged at my audacity: it was her house! She interrupted, interjected, told me to either discuss school projects or hang up immediately. When I didn't, the receiver was torn out of my hand and smashed down onto its cradle. When a neighbour gave me a push button phone for my room for Christmas, she ripped it right out of the wall and destroyed the cheap Taiwan-made piece of shit altogether.

"Don't you already spend all day with these stupid people? Why would you want to talk to them even more after school?" She didn't add, "… when you could be having an intelligent conversation with me," but it was obvious.

A new mantra took hold, one that was perhaps intended to give me hope.

"When you grow up, you can do whatever you want. But until then, you will do as I say or you can go live with these wonderful friends of yours."

Before its demise, I had used my push-button phone to call American Express and apply for the golden card you weren't supposed to leave home without. I didn't meet the minimum annual income requirement of $30,000, but that was good information to know. I spent a lot of time daydreaming about the magical day when I could finally do whatever I wanted with the help of American Express, but the details were fuzzy. What, exactly, would I even do? Where would I do it? And with whom? I only earned twenty-five cents a week allowance, and I usually lost it anyway from being so bad.

When help came from an unlikely source, I didn't want to accept it. Like all nerds everywhere, I hadn't had the best luck with gym teachers—they didn't, generally speaking, seem to think much of me, nor I of them—but one track and field coach was sweet and kind. Track being the only thing I was even marginally good at, she offered to talk to my mother and explain how much running meant to me and how I could really be an asset to the team.

"If it's a safety issue," she said when I explained I wasn't allowed to stay past 4:30 or exercise on weekends, "I'll tell her we don't practice alone, we have group runs that I personally supervise. This is the nineties. Safety is our top priority."

Mom's rules were about safety. The perverts always preyed on cross-country girls like poor Alison Parrott anyway, not sprinters who, if anything, were well-equipped to dash to safety. I was almost six feet tall, not the frail, blonde type who was forever getting herself snatched while jogging alone in the woods. No, it wasn't about safety.

A conversation with my mother would kill Mrs. Panagiota because she was a normal person and would not understand that my mother would make her cry just for the fun of it. The prettiest teacher at school, she nevertheless had a loud, scratchy voice and a thickly-muscled neck. She wore shiny track suits instead of skirts. Mom would either tear her to shreds just because she could or she'd say she was only following my wishes, that *I* was the one who didn't want to run track but was too scared to admit it.

"I mean, it's no secret that Nicky has a bit of a problem with lying," she would say. "I'm glad she's finally awakened to the fact that extreme physical exertion is better suited to the opposite sex, but she can't stand to disappoint you."

I knew how to protect Mrs. Panagiota, who always encouraged me. I told her not to worry about it, that I had joined the science club and track would cut into my lab time. She looked bewildered and a little angry, her hands on her hips with the thumbs at the front and her fingers cupping her backside, her feet planted on the track's shimmering black surface with the toes of her sneakers turned out: a strong pose that Mom would have said was the stance of a duck. I wouldn't have made it very far in track anyway. I had taken up smoking, I ate penny candy for lunch every day and I lacked muscle mass. People who thought I was The Great Black Hope were already disappointed in my mediocre performance on the relay and the 100-metre dash.

Those who doubted I was really half Italian quizzed me on what my mother put in her lasagna, but I never tasted lasagna until Victor made it for the class in home ec (overly salty, but delicious AF). Naturally, my peers were skeptical of my claim that Northern Italians ate gnocchi and polenta instead of lasagna—what the hell was that? And whatever it was, why didn't I eat more of it? I was built knife-straight, with no discernible waist, hips or butt. Even the whole sticks of butter I crammed in my mouth didn't help my body grow the shapes that had been forming on other girls for some time. I remained so skinny that even the flat-chested girls made fun of me.

"Someone drop a bag of rice on this starving Ethiopian!"

"Where's the brainer? Oh, she must have fallen down the sewer grate."

"I haven't seen her. She stepped sideways and just disappeared."

"Look at those legs! She's walking on needles!"

Nobody dared say this kind of stuff at HOBY, but they were probably thinking it.

Don't they say that children are resilient? It's either that or they have no choice but to adapt, just like political prisoners in the Amnesty International newsletter learn to eat roaches for protein in between regular torture sessions. The indignities I was subjected to by my peers can in no way be compared to actual torture—they were quite common: pebbles and sand thrown in my hair, exclusion from games that led to self-excluding, purposeful dodgeball hits to the face. My mother had two pieces of advice on the subject of teasing—or perhaps it was just one piece: stop snivelling about it and stand up for yourself. Depending on the circumstances, I should yell back, hit back, make them respect and fear me or feign indifference and coolly walk away, tossing a devastating comeback over my shoulder. Anything but shake with fear and panic. But ultimately, of course, it wouldn't matter when the law degree was hanging on my wall.

"Sticks and stones may break my bones, but names will never hurt me," Mom insisted.

She had been called a brown-noser and worse, but it was all out of jealousy and didn't stop her from getting ahead. Someone had even put a bar of soap in her locker once with a crude note telling her to use it because she hadn't been taught basic hygiene and the bathtub was always full of laundry when she was growing up. I simply didn't appreciate how lucky I was because I lived in a clean house where I could take a bath every single week. I was tall and graceful; I should stand fully erect with my shoulders and head thrown back like she did, instead of slouching to fit in with these Asian pipsqueaks. Why reduce myself when I would never be like them?

She reminded me that Daddy always said I would have to beat the boys off with a stick when I grew up, and he should know. I was a swan, even if the backs of my arms had that unfortunate little pocket of fat and I would probably inherit the flab on the insides of my thighs that plagued the Petracco women. She constantly reminded me about the story of *The Ugly Duckling*, who had emerged from the crucible of chicken judgment to spread his wings in his true element: a bigger pond populated by beasts just like him.

It all sounded like a death sentence to me.

CHAPTER 9

LOCKUP

Books were the main refuge from the confusing world of my peers. I had always been given plenty of reading material (Dickens and Orwell and Steinbeck, but also *People* magazine and *Newsweek*), but the game changer was finding the stash of trashy sci-fi novels in the upstairs laundry room that Mom had saved to ship to my father. It was quite a procedure: First she would acquire the paperbacks at yard sales, then wipe down the covers with soap and water lest they contaminate our home. Once they had dried, she tore the clean covers off and discarded them. Finally, she would flip through the thin, yellowy pages to ensure no scrap of loose paper or bookmark remained, as per the exacting standards for penitentiaries in the state of New Jersey.

While all incoming mail was rigorously inspected, hence the mandate to remove the covers before shipping (which, unfortunately, took place before I could get all the way through *Var the Stick*, but not before the alien sex scenes), outgoing mail was apparently not; all the letters from Prisoner #209866, of which there were suddenly several per week, seemed to get through. They were filled with updates on new hearings, new trials, new appeals, new lawyers, new transfers, new evidence. All I wanted to know, of course, was when he was coming home.

His weekly missives were long on confidence and short on hard details. He railed against the White Establishment's lies but always assured us that justice would prevail … in due time. Blissfully unaware of the gravity of the situation, I responded faithfully to these letters at first. I made elaborate cards out of colourful construction paper (never blue; the colour was forbidden, lest an inmate somehow extract the pigment to fabricate a guard's uniform). I told him how I was doing in school and, of course, how much I missed him. I didn't speak of my struggles at home.

As the years passed, the tone of Daddy's letters gradually changed. Instead of reminding me how he used to throw me high in the air and catch me as a baby (seemingly unaware that the game left me rigid with terror), he wrote now in painstaking detail of appeals and new legal strategies that had failed, enclosing a copy of each motion he had filed or planned to file. He described the crushing frustration of trying to get parts for his worn-out, obsolete typewriter in a place where no system worked like it was supposed to. Guards tossed his cell and stole his special diabetic food. They seized or destroyed his possessions just for kicks on a regular basis. A simple hole in his clothing led to an accusation of inappropriate conduct with his female lawyer and a restriction on their future legal consultations.

I didn't entirely disbelieve him. Everyone knew the American justice system was a cruel joke, racist and corrupt and infuriatingly arbitrary. I knew this from my mother, but also from the news, the papers, the culture itself. A couple of years later, the Rodney King beating and the incendiary police acquittals achieved by moving the trial to a rich, White neighbourhood and proving that the police had been following actual LAPD policy, would burn this into my rageful consciousness like the dirty flames of the riots at Florence and Normandie.

But Daddy was actually guilty as sin! Wasn't he? My mother certainly thought so. He had been in jail many times before this. He was a con artist, a manipulative liar. He should be contrite and penitent, that's why they called it a penitentiary. Sometimes his letters were so full of bravado, they made me cringe. He wanted to act *pro se* because all lawyers were crooked anyhow; he was proud to have been thrown in solitary for antagonizing a guard; and despite seemingly doing his damnedest to ensure he would never come home to us, he always said he was going to be released … soon.

"He should stop denying the truth," my mother said.

Mom was terrified of the law and thought it should be respected at all times. Even jaywalking could get you into trouble.

"When exactly are you getting out?" I became bold enough to ask over the phone one day.

"Soon," he promised. "Are you treating your mother right?"

"He's never getting out," Mom said as soon as I hung up.

To be fair, Daddy was in the same maximum-security prison that had let Rubin "Hurricane" Carter, who would later visit my school as a motivational speaker, rot for eighteen years for a crime he obviously did not commit and that someone else had confessed to. One of the oldest jails in the United States, Trenton was not a place you wanted to be. The New Jersey DOC did not like to admit mistakes or spend money on inmates. Supposedly, if you had AIDS in there, they gave you an aspirin and left you in a wheelchair until you died.

Daddy's letters began to commence with the words "In the Name of Allah, the most Beneficent and Merciful." I couldn't be sure whether he had converted for the relatively better food and freedom of movement or that he had legitimately found, as Nation of Islam Prophet Elijah Muhammad had called it, "The natural religion of the Black man." Either way, who could blame him? For anything?

Gradually, the letters came less frequently but with the same intense content, sometimes concluding with what he wanted to do when we were reunited. These plans were long on fresh tomatoes from Mamma's garden (now defunct, but he didn't know that) with a pinch of salt and lashings of olive oil and short on anything relevant to me. In his mind, I was forever frozen as a little kid, free of the pubescent challenges of hair crimping and how to get my hands on a Walkman.

For a class assignment I pounded out an essay on my electric typewriter on the four goals of sentencing and how only two of them were being met by the American justice system since actual rehabilitation was low and recidivism disturbingly high. It examined the troubling phenomenon of *institutionalization* in the context of how someone like Daddy would adapt to modern life one day, without, of course, admitting that my insight sprang from personal experience. The research reinforced my decision to become a trial lawyer instead of a ballerina. My life's work would be to get my father out before he lost any more time in the real world.

Spoiler alert: I did not become a trial lawyer, or a corporate lawyer (my backup plan) or any kind of lawyer. I did not become a ballerina either. But the habit of reading cheap paperbacks never left me. While reading Daddy's letters became increasingly painful and irritating, reading the cheesy fantasies and post-apocalyptic sagas that helped him escape reality never did. I read every fantastical story I could get my hands on and developed a strong affinity for Robert A. Heinlein, with whom I shared a birthday. But any writer in any genre who could plunge me into another world would do, and I came to love Ernest Hemingway best of all, with his flawed but heroic characters who drank and hunted and sailed their way to dark nirvanas.

I read somewhere that Hemingway killed himself when he could no longer write the perfect sentence, a standard I admired because I could see little more important in life than the words on a page. Fiction did more than stave off loneliness; it provided an important education. Even the most absurd and far-fetched stories with two-dimensional heroes and villains unlocked a door to how people should live. Villainous assholes often remained that way and worlds could be impossibly harsh, but there were always people who made the right and difficult choices, who valued sacrifice over shortcuts.

It was there, alone in the quiet house where nothing exciting ever happened, that I developed the damsel in distress fantasy that would characterize my future romantic relationships, both real and imagined. I wanted to be rescued, which happened often in the fantasy genre, but I was no delicate flower waiting to be plucked; yes, I would surrender and melt, but then I would make a vital contribution that would bind the hero to me forever, whether that was shooting down the deadly monster he didn't see coming or discovering life-saving plants on an otherwise inhospitable planet.

The person I saw in the mirror didn't look at all like the irresistible heroine I longed to be. I wasn't buxom and bold or perky, accessible or pale and helpless. Unlike Mamma, who judged your worth by how many flats of peat moss you could shoulder, my mother thought personal appearance was very important, and I tried to look more like her. She was, after all, a woman who could make carrying overstuffed plastic grocery bags look elegant. She carried herself like a queen, her posture impossibly erect, her enviably muscled arms toting a week's worth of provisions well away from her long swing skirts while my bags bumped my legs and left deep welts in my palms.

Mom's underwire and waistbands were on a par with armour, her bra cups cut with darts for that pointy 1950s look. Her dainty feet—a source of pride despite the bunions that had developed from wearing unsuitable shoes as a child—were always beautifully manicured. She taught me how to walk, sit and speak like a lady should, even though my calves would never touch and my elbows were always on the table (apparently a very serious problem for a girl who would soon be going out into the world and having to meet its exacting standards).

I was more concerned with my coarse features and many flaws. I spent so much time in the bathroom, either voluntarily scrutinizing defects in the mirror or locked in as punishment, that I taught myself French from the backs of product labels and perfected my singing voice until I was told to shut up. It never occurred to me to do something worthwhile like write a symphony, start an NGO or even teach myself toilet paper origami, but then again, I wasn't supposed to be having fun in there. What I could have done with a smartphone in there! Maybe less. Or maybe I'd have achieved fame on TikTok by recording when the cosmetic improvements I tried made me more hideous, not less, like the time I put toothpaste on my eyelashes and pretended it was mascara.

My sixth-grade homeroom teacher was Mr. Brown, a British man with the exact same dent in his chin as mine, except his was black with hairs that a razor couldn't reach. My mother said the dent was a sure sign of a sex addict. Mr. Brown bore a striking resemblance to Prince Charles—indeed, his first name was actually Charles—and he had the accent to match. He was not a particularly emotive man, but he highly praised the work I handed in. He had gotten in the habit of giving me extra assignments as a hedge against boredom and to hone my academic skills. He fed my desperate need to be noticed, to feel that I mattered, to garner approval and praise.

In those days, in that school, single-parent families and even single-child families were a rarity. I sometimes hung out with another unpopular only daughter with no dad named Mahrishi (Mahrishi: Suddenly, the Obvious) and a sweet girl that was teased for absolutely no reason (Jeannette: The Worst a Man Can Get). From afar, I worshipped the girl everyone said was a slut but who seemed to have the most power in the room (she didn't give me the time of day). There were so few other misfits that they stand out in my mind: A bully named Jason who decided to pierce his own ear with a pin and shove one of his mother's huge, skull-shaped earrings inside the bleeding hole, necessitating a trip to the nurse (years later, volunteering at the Don Jail, I would see him in it). A boy named Billy who slapped me across the face on the jungle gym, said I needed putting in my place and called me a nigger (I never saw him again). A boy named Eli, who smelled bad and was even lower in social standing than me, who cried when someone fed him a Slurpee laced with something unpleasant (years later, working in a massage parlour, I would see him in it).

I know more about how this relentless, automatic comparison and ranking is part of every child's life, but at the time, this was the whole world, one that had to be endured to get to the other side. The future was all that mattered. After Grade 6 I would be graduating from Huron and moving on to Lord Lansdowne, a transition I viewed with anticipation and dread. Would I finally be set free? I told my friend Lauma (dubbed Glaucoma by my mother) that I wished my mom would just beat me in the face with a hairbrush instead of the mental abuse (a term that didn't exist in my vocabulary). Lauma thought that was completely insane.

"You mean you actually want to get hit?" she asked incredulously, her light-coloured eyes making big round Os behind thick lenses. Lucky Lauma was farsighted, so her glasses made her eyes look bigger, instead of shrinking them like mine.

"But at least then people would know."

I thought it was so obvious, but my failure to adequately explain my situation even to myself made as little sense as trading physical abuse for whatever it was I was suffering. I'm sure I loomed over Lauma to convince her of my point as we strolled around the schoolyard. Everyone was always so much shorter than me.

"What do you mean? Know *what*?"

"What she's doing to me."

"But what is she doing to you? I know she's strict, but if she's not hitting you …"

It was not a winnable argument. Nobody talked about verbal abuse or neglect back then, much less psychological, emotional or narcissistic abuse; even physical and sexual abuse were not part of the conversation unless it was severe and preferably happening to you from outside the family. All the lesson plans in class and the gossip circles in the field centred around randoms leaping out of the bushes and showing you their privates, or trench-coat-wearing men with bushy beards taking pictures of you playing innocently in the park. The worst kind would lure you into their vehicles, which always had tinted windows, with promises of puppies and candy that might or might not actually materialize before they molested you, perhaps chopping you into tiny pieces for good measure. The sight of a white, unmarked van parked on a quiet street signals danger in my mind to this day.

As kids we didn't know that the odds of anything like that happening were pretty long compared to your average, run-of-the-mill child abuse. All threats were perceived as external and extreme, courtesy of the American news Mom had been steeped in for years and that everyone seemed influenced by—the milk cartons with pictures of missing kids, the newscasters who chided, "It's ten o'clock, do you know where your children are?" Though I was never out past five, all this must have only validated my mother's fears and her desire to control my every movement. If anyone suspected my home life was a bit off, they kept it to themselves or, if it was being discussed, nothing ever came of it. At least I wasn't in danger of being snatched.

Lauma was unique in that her dad, a rare single father, invited us over for dinner once—maybe to see for himself. So did Kok Yan's dad, whose wife I believe had died, and whose unfortunately named daughter taught me how to shave my legs dry without any water or shaving cream to avoid parental notice. What would these men have seen? A well-behaved girl, cautious and polite to the point of timidity, asking permission to sit down or visit the washroom. Not someone who was being hurt, but who was shy, mannerly and enviably well-raised. They probably could not have guessed that their homes, kitchenware and culinary skills would be subject to my mother's scorching mockery the moment we escaped. There were no second invitations.

Things I never told Lauma:

Some things do not leave a mark. No one was there but my mother when I knelt in front of a toilet full of my own shit and used my teeth to take out the empty cardboard toilet roll I had carelessly tossed in there. In Mom's mind, it was the best way to remember that my thoughtless actions could cost her hundreds of dollars in plumbing repairs.

When I shivered in the empty tub with my bucket and my bar of soap and she shook the grit and hair from the bathmat on top of my naked body, nobody saw it except the two of us.

When she made me kneel so she could kick me more effectively when she thought I, and not her beloved budgies, had shredded paper all over the birdcage floor, Mamma, the ghost in the basement, had nothing to say about it, as she only spoke to God. No one in the holy trinity appeared to be listening.

Toward the spring of my Grade 6 year, it was announced that I had been chosen, by some mysterious non-popularity contest, as valedictorian of my graduating class. I was only eleven, and I felt sick with anxiety on the day of the ceremony. I stared up at the underside of the kitchen table, with its cobwebbed supports, clutching at my stomach. The kitchen rug, whose lint always got trapped in my hair, was also very familiar; I had stared at them often in between gasps of pain from the anxiety-ridden stomach-aches that had torn through me since I was little. I knew the cramps wouldn't pass until my intestines relaxed their grip, and that wouldn't happen until I was no longer nervous—which wouldn't happen until the graduation ceremony was over. The pain was made worse because I constantly held my stomach in so I wouldn't look fat.

As I remember it, graduation fell on a beautiful, hot, cloudless day, the kind that are so precious in Toronto that you want to wake up early and get outside right away. I sat stiffly erect all afternoon in my room, looking out at the empty street through a hedge of flowers that nodded indifference to my plight, practicing diaphragmatic breathing so I wouldn't get a truly incapacitating stomach-ache. I had already put on my graduation dress, a super short, super tight number Mom had picked out from a boutique on Bloor Street. It was probably more suited to Naomi Campbell than to a sixth grader, but I thought it looked really good on me. I was all right from the neck down. I had the body of one of those mannequins at The Bay who didn't even need heads.

I was supposed to give a choir solo before my speech, and since I always choked, I cursed myself for having agreed to do it. It was one thing singing "Four Strong Winds" or "The Logical Song" in the music room, quite another to step up alone in front of the assembled crowd and do my best impression of Dorothy wondering why she couldn't fly beyond the rainbow. I was terrified that everyone would see my underwear if I sat wrong or notice I hadn't shaved my legs because I had, for once, obeyed my mother. I didn't know how to walk in the heels, and practicing hurt my flat feet, which completely rejected the notion of bending at any angle.

At some point that graduation day, with the precious heat and sun flooding through the picture window, I fought with my mother over something—I don't remember what—and she threatened once again to call the Children's Aid Society and have them take me away then and there. With characteristic defiance, I called her bluff.

"I'll save you the trouble," I raged. "I'll call them myself."

Since I no longer had a phone in my room, I pushed past her to the kitchen hall like a chopstick shoving aside a dumpling, straight lines and hard angles and all-consuming fury. I threatened not to go to my own graduation, hoping the embarrassment alone would strike her dead. I picked up the receiver and tried to call the operator, but Mom reached the phone, pressed the white button over and over, pulled it away from me and said I was going whether I wanted to or not. I don't think she said she was sorry. But I can't help but wonder now: What if she hadn't tried to stop me? Would the white van of my imagination have come and bundled me away, high heels and all?

As the hours crawled by in a stalemate and I hadn't shown up for choir rehearsal, the vice principal called my mother to negotiate. Somehow I got to the school. Unbelievably, I don't remember whether Mom came with me or if I forbade her to and took the cab alone. I will never know exactly what happened that night, as if a tide of negative emotion has scrubbed the fragile sand of reality clean. The solo happened. I do not know if my mother was there to see me mount the stage, although I must have done so, because I have the valedictorian plaque to prove it. Relatively few people had signed my yearbook, but I discovered later that the slut girl wrote: "Don't forget me K?" which made absolutely no sense since we weren't friends. Maybe she wrote that same message to everyone. Despite forgetting most of graduation day, I have never forgotten her twelve-year-old face.

The other kids and their parents attended the grad dinner afterwards without me. It used to be common to see dressed-up sixth or eighth graders all on their own at big family restaurants, obviously celebrating the end of school, but in those days we had parent chaperones. They would have congregated merrily at Mr. Greenjeans or The Old Spaghetti Factory, popular downtown spots for teens then. I hadn't been invited, nor was I expecting to go, nor would I have been able to face the soul-melting shame of having someone else cover my bill. I went home and nothing happened.

How do you continue on with your parents after such unequivocal evidence? This sentence originally read *evidence of lack of love*, but that is not quite right, not to an eleven-year-old. Of course they love you … right? The nuances we can sometimes see as adults—that our parents were acting out of their own trauma or flaws or immaturity or preoccupations or addictions—aren't available to children. It's a zero-sum game: you either love me or you don't.

The problem was that if I concluded they loved me, which I basically had to in order to keep the charade going, the dissonance would make life impossible unless I further concluded that there was something terribly wrong with me. If I reached the life-threatening conclusion that they didn't love me, I wouldn't see that as something wrong with them either; I once again would have thought it was me. I gathered this from talking to childhood sexual abuse survivors, but the same applies to any type of boundary-breaking abuse: it always has to be internalized so the child can continue existing with the magnitude of knowing they are helpless to stop betraying themselves over and over again for meals and a place to sleep. This is a foundational principle of how narcissists are made.

It was summer, school was officially over, and I would never be going back to Huron. I spent very little time in the garden and lost touch with the smell of my own hot skin, falling in love with the ballads of *Classic Queen* and Elvis Presley instead. Freddie Mercury, who believed above all else that the show must go on, and Elvis, whose biography revealed him to be essentially a grown child, made the perfect music for rising to the occasion. It was a kind of magic all right. That summer I saw *The Godfather Part III* when it came out in theatres and fell hard for Al Pacino, an emotionally unavailable man ruthlessly doing what had to be done for the good of *la famiglia*. I played the soundtrack endlessly on the tape player in my room, giving equal due to the frantic pieces like *Cavelleria Rusticana* and the bittersweet crooning of Harry Connick Jr. until the tape was ruined from flipping it over so many times.

I was so impressed with Sofia Coppola's French manicure that I quit chewing my nails cold turkey that summer. I had always had long, elegant fingers and good nail beds, and hand care was something that even the unattractive could and should prioritize. I cast a critical eye on my beautiful neighbour Maia's broken, dirty nails. She may have lived in a far nicer house than mine and possessed far greater assets—lush lips and a prematurely ripe body that made the kids call her Maia Rent-a-Pussy—but her nails were just awful. I grew mine out and painted them perfectly in glossy, neutral colours. My mother not only allowed this but helped me write to Paramount Pictures to request head shots of my hero, Michael Corleone, which they graciously sent. I spent two months lying on the Persian rug in an agony of raging emotions and acetone, escaping into full-fledged fantasies of rescue and love that always ended in tragedy because I couldn't conceive of anything else.

Of all the music I heard those two months, my favourite by far was the work of Milli Vanilli, a singing duo with exciting hair and snazzy suits who would later be discredited and hilariously spoofed for lip synching, something all acts did. Mom found one of their tapes at a yard sale and brought it home; once it had been sanitized, I snatched it up like the find of the century. Their pop message was simple, upbeat, full of cheap sugary bubbles of empowerment and hope: "Take it as it comes, girl. You'll make it through, no doubt. It'll all come around."

CHAPTER 10

END OF THE ROAD

In Grade 7 I speed-walked a half hour each morning to Lord Lansdowne, the octagonal building off Spadina Crescent with the outlandish red panelling where John Travolta would film parts of *Hairspray* on location in 2007. The challenge of attending a large middle school that was known for its high academic standards, dedicated faculty and wealthy student body meant I was a small fish in a big pond.

It's funny how perceptions can change. While riding the Spadina streetcar to Kensington Paulet as an adult, I noticed that The Scott Mission, the Centre for Addiction and Mental Health, and a large rundown strip club (all three surrounded by faintly desperate crowds) flanked the school. They had always been there, but it took awhile for Lord Lansdowne to fall victim to the same entropy I later would. It became the beneficiary of a Chapters Indigo fundraiser to buy books for inner-city, at-risk schools, and its 200-metre track grew cracked and potholed; but I like to remember it as it was in 1989, when it had a great reputation.

Because most of my peers hadn't come from Huron, I could reinvent myself. I think it was in seventh grade that I started shoplifting—stealing gum and chocolate bars from the 7-11 near the school—but it could have been a bit earlier or a bit later. Remembering specific calendar years is difficult for me; it's all there, but the lack of organization could be the result of inadvertently killing those brain cells responsible for maintaining the filing cabinets of my mind. I do know the Gulf War broke out when I was in the seventh grade and, like a virulent rash, so did my unpopularity; that it could get any worse was shock-and-awe-worthy, but it did. My homeroom did a penny drive for the soldiers, and instead of bringing in rolls of coins, I parroted Mom's then unpopular, now widely-accepted theory that the war was unjust and had nothing to do with liberating the Kuwaitis and everything to do with controlling the price and availability of oil.

Fortunately, neither I nor the war were important enough to talk about for long. The teacher shut me up fairly quickly, and we all moved on to the scientific method and how to dissect a crayfish. I studied Cantonese as an elective but never learned much more than how to count to ten despite my hopes of listening in on the conversations around me in my predominantly Asian school. It was the one class where I could relax because the expectations were very low. The teacher was used to Chinese kids who mostly spoke English but had at least grown up hearing the language spoken around them. She was thin and unsmiling and did not even know what to call me. We decided on Nei-goh.

"Nei-goh? That doesn't mean anything," scoffed my Chinese friends.

They weren't friends in the usual sense—we didn't go to each other's houses for play dates or talk on the phone, but they respected me enough to leave me alone. I hid behind their voices while we chanted mysterious words every session.

"Lam yoc wui. Teen hon meen."

But I was good at making paper lanterns. I tried harder and did worse in this class than in any other, and that was probably good for me.

At lunch and recess we played Sho Tai Ti, a card game we all took very seriously. Whoever won was nicknamed dai lo (gang leader/bawse) and while I never got the title, the other players did let me run and buy their lunches from local fast-food joints for tips so they could have more time to play. The dimes, nickels and quarters from their change bought plenty of sour keys, fuzzy peach slices and malted balls from the jars at the corner store cash register, and that's where I first noticed kids palming packs of Bazooka and Junior Mints. For me it was Oh Henry bars (so much more filling—anything with nuts, really), but I would never steal from the elderly couple who ran the tuck shop and sold single cigarettes for a quarter to supplement my all-sugar diet. They were nice and didn't deserve it like the 7-11 staff, who followed me with their eyes the moment I walked in the store.

Decades later, my therapist would say it was unusual for a child whose mother knew better to have to eat candy for lunch.

"How did it feel to know you were buying your friends' lunches for dimes just so you could have something to eat while they played without you?"

My mouth opened and closed like the fish at the Dragon City aquarium those same friends had once taken me to see. I'd never thought of it in those terms. How do you feel left out when you are already an outsider? Whatever I answered, I'm pretty sure it wasn't satisfactory; she was only ever happy when I cried, and I wasn't about to sob that it hurt like hell when it was actually the most acceptance I had experienced to date. By the time I came to sit in her office, I knew something of real bondage, and it didn't look like racing through the slush with other people's steaming brown bag lunches.

My own lunches had been discontinued long before because I complained about them too much and didn't eat them. Mom froze yogurt cups to make them last longer, pre-peeled oranges and wrapped them in soggy waxed paper, and spread bone-dry organic almond butter on thick black pumpernickel. Most of this food tasted awful compared to the fries-and-gravy lunches my peers ate, but it also took longer to eat, so I'd end up outside trying to play while eating half-frozen, watery yogurt, great smears of which ended up on the front of my coat.

Toronto winters are very cold, though warmish compared to the rest of Canada. Some people wear a full parka for eight months out of every year. When I first had children, I enjoyed winter because the parks were empty and the snow endlessly fascinating for them. Besides, my body still ran far too hot from hormones and milk to necessitate buttoning my coat. Now I see the Canadian winter as more of a menace than a guarantee of outdoor fun. It's the kind of cold that makes you scurry for the closest subway entrance even if it means navigating a much longer path to the train. It's the kind of cold that brings on asthma attacks, cuts cigarette breaks short and chills your morning coffee before you can get it from the bus to the office. The icy wind puts men down like dogs when they sleep in the streets. You cannot eat frozen yogurt outdoors without serious consequences.

There was no breakfast either because every morning, despite knowing that there were starving children who would cut off their own limbs for a chance at such food, I pushed my oatmeal down the kitchen sink drain. It was easy to do because I ate alone; my mother would have gone back to bed, leaving me to choke down a huge bowl of extra-thick porridge that had been cooked one or two nights before and left out on the stove to be reheated. It was served without any milk or sugar, a brown sludge with the occasional sharp husk just to keep me on my toes. I could have invented a new way to eat, like the tanned, leotarded proponents of diet shakes on TV: nothing for breakfast, penny candy for lunch and then a sensible dinner.

One of the budgies shit in the open pot of porridge once, unfortunately on a weekend when I had to eat with Mom. I showed her the little greenish black coil and said I didn't want the oatmeal.

"That is absolutely not bird shit," she scoffed, wiping the counters with a sponge (she was always wiping something). "Eat your oatmeal, Nicky."

To prove what a monster she was and make her writhe with guilt, I didn't scoop out the shit but deliberately ate it all. It all tasted like shit anyway, and taking poison and waiting for the other person to die was already a deeply ingrained habit.

Nothing changed the menus, and my bony frame didn't fill out at all. A particularly bright mind at Lord Lansdowne who was tired of flinging skinny jokes coined the name "Dickhole" for me. Despite the complete lack of supporting evidence, it stuck. Four years ahead of me and just an hour west, my ex-husband already weighed three hundred pounds, and the joke was "Don't piss him off or he'll sit on you."

"Yeah, I will!" he'd reply, and it was good-natured backslaps all around.

I glared silently, shot back ineffectual insults and remained Dickhole.

Those were the best years of my life, and the last level of education I would ever complete on schedule. Eventually, I lived up to a little of my so-called promise. My mother had no objection to me sitting on the yearbook committee with a future Toronto politician who famously defended the poor exposure of the black-and-white yearbook pictures by saying, "We just don't know how to shoot Black people." He was later caught up in a Clinton-type scandal that ended his political career, which was astonishing because he was absolutely the last person I could envision getting jiggy on his office couch with anyone. It was tall, nerdy Adam, not Mr. Brown, who was the sex addict after all.

"End of the Road" by Boys II Men was our grad song at Lord Lansdowne and probably everywhere else as well. I was not asked to be valedictorian in Grade 8.

At some point that summer I went to visit Daddy: the ultimate fantasy finally fulfilled. Only not really, as fantasies so rarely are. If you think a two-hour visit to a maximum-security penitentiary can satisfy the father-longing of a hypersensitive twelve-year-old girl who hasn't seen him in person for half her life, you would, as my mother would say, have another think coming. The story, as I repeated the interesting part, went something like this:

"Have you ever seen the movie with Tom Hanks called *Big*? You know, the one where the ad has a giant piano on the floor with this kid walking on it?"

The answer was inevitably "Yes," to which I'd excitedly reply, "Yeah, so that kid who played the kid in *Big*, his dad is a friend of my dad."

That was as far as I got in telling the story to my peers. If I ever knew, I no longer remember the exact nature of this friendship or how it came to be; I just know the actor's father was a Jewish lawyer with a big fro who looked like he'd stepped out of the seventies, and my mother had arranged for me to stay with him and his accomplished family so he could drive me to the jail in Trenton for a visit. My mother said I was beholden to these people and should obey them in everything they said.

My first night back in the States was spent with Steve and Bram, my mother's gay friends whom she had randomly met at LaGuardia and instantly clicked with. Bram was severely pockmarked, but no wonder—he was from Guam! Who had ever heard of Guam? I later found out they had both cautioned her that if she continued to keep me on such a tight leash, I would one day rebel and it wouldn't be pretty. Of course, she disregarded their advice; they were gay, not parents. All I remembered of them from New York was their exotic kindness and their ancient, vicious white cat, Bink, who did break-dancing moves when they petted his stomach. He attacked me when I tried to pet him, and I pretended it was completely unprovoked because I wasn't supposed go near him. Also, I did not like the Rice-A-Roni they made at dinner, and Steve laughed, saying, "She doesn't like the rice," while my mother kicked me under the table and told me through clenched teeth to eat every single weirdly over-seasoned grain on my plate.

Six years later, I was stinking up the close confines of their car on the way to their apartment, having nervously held gas in for hours in the airport and on the plane. Again, they laughed and simply rolled down the windows, but I vehemently denied that the stink was mine. Not for the first time, I hoped to be struck dead from the shame of a relatively minor incident. If I were dead, there would be no more nerves, no more embarrassment, no more dread. Of course, death is too much to ask for at twelve; even *numb* is elusive. I couldn't figure out how to operate their shower in the morning, so I just ran water from the faucet and washed squatting in the tub before they dropped me off at the *Big* boy's house.

The only song in my head was "Happy Together"—call me a very late adopter—and the lyrics ran through my head constantly when I wasn't singing it outright. I loved the simplicity and romantic idealism of the songs I had heard on car service radios back in New York: "Raindrops keep falling on my head..." This time, the lyrics couldn't soothe me; I didn't feel free and a lot was bothering me. I had an irrational terror of staying in the lawyer's comfortable home. There were no words for this then and nothing to do but try to imitate what was expected of me.

I don't even remember what the son, the actual kid from *Big*, even looked like, only that there seemed to be a lot of teenagers there who were perfectly at ease doing alien things like sitting on the floor eating snacks and watching movies. I finally drifted off in my big bed in the luxurious spare room and got my period during the night, bleeding a round rusty circle right through the sheets to the mattress. Horrified, I got up before dawn to try and scrub away the evidence in the bathroom sink, exhausted but too keyed-up to fall back asleep.

The Polaroid I have of that prison visit tells me I wore a beautiful plaid tunic top, but I don't need a photo to remember that my skinny arms were covered in goose bumps as I shivered in the freezing air conditioning of the lawyer's car all the way from god knows where in New York to someplace in rural New Jersey. It never occurred to me to tell him I was too cold or to request that he open the window more than a crack when he smoked. I simply hugged myself and endured it, insisting that everything was fine when he asked. He was already doing me a huge favour.

In the Polaroid, taken in front of the prison mural that had considerately been erected for the benefit of the children, I am smiling my usual close-mouthed, serious smile, the one that hides my pre-braces buck teeth. Seeing the picture now, I think I look young, awkward and beautiful, but at the time, I had a sense of the wrongness of the visit. It was too long but impossibly short. There was nothing to talk about and nothing that needed to be said. My eyes are very wide and I'm clutching Daddy's hand, which I didn't want to ever let go of; the one time my mother went to visit him, they are posed in almost exactly the same way.

CHAPTER 11

KARMIC LAWS

As the youngest student enrolled in my high school in 1991, I was called upon to present an award to the oldest living graduate of the school in front of the entire student body. At just one calendar year younger than everyone else, I was no Doogie Howser, but it was still a big deal to me and proof to my mother that her plan to accelerate my education was paying off.

The walls of Harbord Collegiate Institute were lined with pictures of the young men, mostly Jewish, who had died serving in both world wars. By the time I got there, at least 60 percent of the student body was Asian, mostly Hong Kong kids whose parents enrolled them in extracurricular activities and pre-university programs at places like University of Toronto and the Royal Conservatory of Music. They also bought them the standard issue uniform: Vuarnet shirts and tight-waisted, tailored pants with forty-inch cuffs that completely concealed cherry Doc Martens.

My summer job, working for the Toronto District School Board in the office at a summer sports camp held at Lord Lansdowne, had paid for a new wardrobe for me, too, replacing the boys' collared shirts and ill-fitting thrift shop finds I had always had to wear. As an eighth grader, my home ec teacher had gained confidence in me when I pierced my right thumb through with an industrial sewing needle while trying to make a pair of shorts. Instead of yelping or panicking, I had politely raised my good hand to let her know my other one was pinned to the machine, and she marvelled at what she thought was my cool headedness but was really just pride.

"How would you like to work for us this summer? We need someone who can remain calm under fire, so to speak," she quipped.

I was twelve years old and loved her. I would have said yes to anything, but the job paid serious money for a kid, though not so much as my husband-to-be was making playing weddings and socials all through the year in his uncle's band. I would like to believe I made better use of the salary than he did amassing an enormous collection of porno magazines, but eventually I would prove just as wasteful.

The well-paying sports camp job came, like all things, with a price. I was so un-athletic that I couldn't really support the counsellors, which was part of the job description. When it rained, I proved to be no good at organizing crafts or corralling rambunctious kids in the gym; their ball skills were usually superior to mine anyway. I began to diet, eating only a small bag of chips each day to maintain my concave stomach, since it was clear that my boobs were never going to grow and I had to make them look bigger by contrast. My mother helpfully told me about a scam company that ran a newspaper ad promising to send you a miracle way to increase breast size if you mailed a cheque to the address provided.

"What is it? Some kind of pill or something?" I asked hopefully.

"All they send you back is a pair of paper hands," she said knowingly.

"What is that supposed to mean? If I rub them or stretch them enough?"

"No, Nicky," she laughed. "It means tough titty. Nothing can make your boobs grow bigger if you're not built that way, but it won't matter when you meet the right guy. He won't care."

I took that to mean the only way to feel good about my body was to have someone else grope it, or at least want to grope it. I wanted that to happen more than anything but had no takers from the young men on staff. The required camp apparel was a hideous bright red polo shirt made out of some synthetic material that felt like a cross between polyester and an IKEA bag. I had to wash it daily because I couldn't wear deodorant because of a mysterious bleeding rash I'd developed in my armpits. An ancient doctor, while examining my raw armpits, touched my small, hard breasts a lot more than I thought necessary, and kissed me wetly on the lips when the examination was over. I felt none of the expected exhilaration at being groped, and my boobs didn't get any bigger, but at least I hadn't lost money sending away for a pair of paper hands.

My co-workers showed contempt for my ineptitude and probably wondered whose ass I could have possibly kissed to get such a cushy job; one of the counsellors was the school principal's son, and the school board, like many public sectors, ran on nepotism and favouritism and every other kind of ism. On field trips they told me I needed to use better judgment, which was true because even the littlest kids could easily manipulate me into allowing them freedoms they certainly should not have had. They weren't the only ones.

One handsome counsellor who loudly regaled us with his sexcapades on subway field trips asked me to type out an essay for him. Of course, I agreed. The primitive office typewriter was at my disposal, but he had no idea how slow I was on it and that it would take a whole bottle of white-out and several days to deliver. I had not only promised to do it immediately, despite the fact that my workload left little time for extracurricular typing, but had assured him of editing skills I didn't possess. He demanded to know why I hadn't just been honest, to which I spluttered that I would find a better machine and do it over. My answer was always yes, a bad habit it has taken three decades to reduce, whereas he probably enjoys a successful career in management now. The following summer I fell hard for a good-natured stoner counsellor named Stan, nicknamed Stan the Man. He treated me well, which I translated to mean true love, another unfortunate habit I still haven't entirely grown out of.

Joe Carter, the famous Blue Jay, sent his daughter to day camp one year and let me take a picture with him long before selfies were a thing. In the picture his arm is slung around my shoulder, indisputable proof that I had met a famous athlete besides Pinball Clemons, who must have toured every single school in the country three times over giving speeches to inspire students to greatness no matter what their financial, racial or physical stature.

The home ec teacher put in another word that year, and I was promoted to registrations for Saturday morning classes at Castle Frank Public School, a job I could do all year round. The Board of Ed paid monthly; the joke was, "I'm bored of education. Just pay me already." I would put almost my entire paycheque into locked-in GICs, so I was always broke, and I began to steal a little of the registration cash to pay for bus fare and incidentals. Eventually I got caught by a young woman who worked at the school. She literally walked in on me counting small bills into my wallet. She didn't say anything, and despite my feverish imaginings, there were no meetings, no confrontations or penalties. I simply didn't get called back to work by the school board or hear from any of my mentors there ever again. It was the Canadian way.

In all five years of high school—we still had that extra year of OACs, Ontario Academic Credits, and only maniacs tried to cram all six of them into their already-full four years—my only B grade besides gym was in eleventh grade clavigraphie: keyboarding, in French. All my mother's clenched-toothed drills on how to correctly pronounce "Pierre," a character in one of my children's books, plus all that time reading product labels in the bathroom, had paid off in the sense that I was nearly fluent in Canada's other official language and took many of my courses in French. My peers made lots of jokes about *fromage* but still often struggled with what was, for them, a third language, whereas I could analyze Moliere or toothpaste ingredients with ease. The STEM posters telling girls not to drop math and science lest they turn their pretty behinds on more than eighty different jobs didn't move me; math and science required far too much work and lowered my grade point average. Getting a B in a French course, any French course, was unthinkable.

When I challenged the teacher—a B? What kind of blot was that on my transcript, not to mention the certainty of being denied a beer at the next restaurant outing with my mother?—he was maddeningly calm behind his handlebar moustache.

"It doesn't matter," he said. "The only thing they look at for university is Grade 13."

"Still, it lowers my average. I did better than this on the tests."

He turned to me from chalking the board and said, "Mademoiselle, you spoke in English throughout the course. It is called clavigraphie, not typing."

What could I say to that? It was true. My voice was loud, my words perfectly enunciated. You couldn't *not* hear it. It was a radio voice, said Russ Holden, the one-time Eye in the Sky above Toronto at a work training many years later. The man who would be my husband, who worked with voices for a living, concurred. Some might have called it piercing, and it would soon help me hold philosophical discussions above the din of noisy bars and clubs. Angry at being heard for all the wrong reasons, I stalked away with my transcript, not knowing that that single junior class had taught me the skill set on which I would make most of my living as a transcriptionist and content writer for many years. The universe is funny like that.

Oh, the longing in high school—it only got worse! The longing for romance, to be accepted, to triumph! Harbord Collegiate was known as an academically-focused school, despite the sporty and competitive leanings of its school song:

Onward, Harbord, onward, Harbord, on to victory!
The orange and black are on the track; we pledge our loyalty, rah rah rah
With a virtus et doctrina, we will reach our goal!
And yours will be eternally the spirit we uphold.
[Followed by the spoken chant:]
Virtus et doctrina, is our battle cry
We shout and fight for the orange and black and the honour of HCI
Sha-boom hey, sha-boom hey, sha-boom boom bah
Hey, Harbord, hey Harbord, hey, rah rah rah
Heeeeeeyyyy, Harbord! Fight, fight, fight! Grrrreat!

I'm still convinced the last word came from the Frosted Flakes commercial. We were, after all, the Harbord Tigers, and the song was meant to bring out the Tiger in you—a tall order when we had to travel to the jock school up the street, Central Tech, just to practice on a proper 400-metre track

I spent my free time in high school puffing cigarettes at the edge of our little 200-metre track or outside the arcade where I could play *Streetfighter* and eat French fries. I had to work at smoking very, very hard, but fortunately you could buy cigarettes for less than eighteen dollars a pack back then and I eventually came to like it. Smoking kept my hands busy for well over fifteen years the first time around. Most of my peers were willing to welcome another puffer to their mostly counter-culture ranks; oddly enough, it was the smartest, nerdiest, weirdest loners who smoked, not the cool kids, who could choose to be cool by healthier means.

Apart from smoking and having a bad attitude toward authority figures, I did my best to uphold the honour of HCI by bringing back awards for the school like library grants and shiny plaques for essays my mother had heavily edited or entirely written but that I successfully passed off as mine.

Then I started up a little crime racket.

For what I thought would be an easy grade, I took Italian, squeaking into the OAC level without the prerequisites. From my years working at a college, I can easily spot profs who have simply given up; at the time, I thought Signora Colombo was just a little simple, but now I know she was deliberately looking the other way when, one by one, the Southern Italian boys began to approach me, furtively holding out their assignments.

"Can you help me with this? You're the brainiac, right?"

At first I tried to talk them through the work, hoping to earn their admiration as I did so. But they were too busy getting driver's licenses, dousing themselves with cologne and grooming non-existent facial hair to do any work. So I did it for them, for money. Signora Manuele would just pop a tape in the VCR and leave us alone in the room to watch bad Italian movies, a true feat because there is no shortage of good Italian movies. The boys spoke mostly Calabrese dialects at home that sounded more like standard Italian than my Friulan, but they couldn't conjugate a verb to save their lives. I told my mother how stupid they were and she nodded approvingly.

"You know what Mamma always says about those Southerners, right?"

I snuck a surreptitious glance at the gaping maw of the basement doorway. Technically, we could just ask her ourselves.

"She says they're so ignorant that when people were making donations to them in the war, they couldn't tell a bar of soap from a piece of cheese. They literally didn't know what soap was. Can you believe it?"

But dumb and hungry as they may have been, these Calabrese and Sicilians had money, and I was motivated by even tiny amounts of it. Eventually they got caught because the homework didn't look enough like theirs, but true to *omerta*, they didn't turn me in when they got zeros.

I made only one serious enemy in all those years, a mysteriously vicious Italian girl who threatened to hit me behind the bleachers for looking at her the wrong way. She did slap me, but only with an open hand; I am still not sure of my crime. She used to get in my face and say, "What, you think you're better than me? You fucking think you're better than me?" If someone said that to me now, I'd respond with an ironic laugh, but at the time I found her anger both scary and confusing. She had big, beautiful hair; big, beautiful boobs; and a big, beautiful butt. How could I possibly think I was better than her?

At some point, a boy named Duy died in an accident at school. His neck was crushed by a European handball net that fell on him during gym class, and everybody talked about it without seeming to know any details except that he did not survive and that there would be no more European handball played at the school, ever. He had not been exceptionally smart, nice, or brave—at least not that I remembered—but at the assembly, he was called all of those things and much more. A school photo of him was blown up and elaborately decorated with white flowers; wreaths and candles covered the podium and the stage where staff and students gave tearful eulogies that made me cry, too, for a boy I had barely known.

The incident proved what I had already learned from TV news and commercials: serious personal injury or illness granted you special privileges. Death was a little extreme because you wouldn't even be around to see how sorry everyone was, but the wheels started turning in my head. If something bad happened to me, the reaction would be even better than love. Along with finally receiving the love I coveted, I would be showered in sympathy and praise for my fortitude while my faults would be either excused or overlooked by my devoted caretakers. I had held this belief since reading *Pollyanna* as a young girl, completely missing the actual takeaway and earning a slap for wishing ill health on myself aloud. Rubbing my sore face, I tried to defend my thinking.

"But Mom, wouldn't it be nice to get attention and have people say nice things about you and do everything for you?"

"That's the stupidest thing I've ever heard you say, Nicky. Don't ever wish you were sick. All you have is your health. Your health is the only thing that matters," my mother repeated over and over.

She seemed very agitated by the way my mind worked. Or perhaps by the possibility that I was inviting the wrath of God down upon myself.

"Do you want to be like those people who live in a bubble? In my day they had the iron lung, but now it's a bubble. You wouldn't even be able to move!"

That was the first time I heard about the flipper babies, whose name I would invoke a scant few years later when I had my first abortion.

"I didn't want a flipper baby," I would say, ashing my cigarette, scanning the listener's face for any trace of understanding or forgiveness. "By the time I found out, I had already poisoned the shit out of it."

Health was all a person had, and flippers instead of arms did not constitute good health. I could not forget my mother crossing herself as she spoke about soundness of mind and body—invoking the Lord was something she normally only did before a challenge that required divine luck to pull off, like a new recipe or the Bills winning the Super Bowl.

I knew she was right. Even if I took drastic measures I wouldn't be like poor Duy, elevated in death to a status he had never enjoyed in life. Nothing would ever earn me the affection and attention I craved. With my luck, I'd end up a vegetable, connected to machines, unable to communicate, helplessly soiling myself during visiting hours.

The kid who had so long ago accused me of calling him a clumsy Korean now suffered his own unspeakable tragedy when a drunk driver drove through the plate glass window of his parents' convenience store, killing them both. I contemplated how adults would talk about this in hushed tones and cross themselves, at least mentally, but the kids wouldn't have much to say because if it hadn't happened to us, it hadn't happened. There was no big picture, just the immediacy of trivial or downright ridiculous matters like, Did he get to run the store himself now?

Kids: no empathy and a weird way of seeing the world. I fit right in. I thought about this as I walked to and from high school, ripping out people's flowers that were hanging over public property to make bouquets for Mom that she would reprimand me for stealing, even as she trimmed the stems and put them in a fresh vase.

CHAPTER 12

THE LAST BATTLE

They say there is no longer any sort of reliable test of adulthood. My son already called himself a man at the age of eight, but even if he had been eighteen, few rituals in modern society exist as proof of the milestone; he didn't kill an animal and drag it home, go on a vision quest or even learn to drive. Growing up in the age of the dinosaurs like I did meant that no matter how much Judy Blume I devoured at the school library, the gateway to womanhood wasn't guarded by periods, first kisses or best friends. I didn't finally become a woman when I threw out the thin white cotton T-shirts that showed everything and bought my first forbidden bra even though I still had nothing there. No, I crossed the line into womanhood when I straightened my hair.

There had been many a pitched battle over my desire for straight hair, which could only be achieved through chemical means. My mother insisted that Black girls, with their elaborate weaves, braids and/or liberal use of hair care products, were sluts who had rejected their race in favour of enslavement to an unrealistic beauty ideal that wasn't worth attaining. I relentlessly argued that the White girls used hairspray and mousse in the bathroom all the time. And if we were all meant to remain exactly the way we were born, no one would paint their toenails, pierce their ears or even wear clothes. But every line of reasoning fell flat: I had to embrace "Black is beautiful," a message that was represented exclusively on the cards Daddy sent me from prison. My profile just wasn't meant to resemble the Roman cameos carved on conch shells from the South Street Seaport; nature had struck me on the head and pronounced me Queen Nefertiti, who proudly wore a tall, perfectly-trimmed cylindrical Afro I could not dream of duplicating if I wanted to.

To Daddy's credit, he must have given some thought to something other than garden-fresh tomatoes to send me cards like that, but I'm not sure how much he could fathom the life of a Black girl living in a White neighbourhood with a mother who thought of her as a badly-behaved appendage. Did he, like Chris Rock, grasp the overwhelming significance of our hair? Perhaps he tried to. He certainly put precious greenbacks into someone's canteen to produce those meticulously detailed pictures of Nubian queens to try and convince me of my natural beauty. Maybe my mother had told him I was insecure about my natural hair, that I wanted to look White; he called collect every week like clockwork, trying to bolster my self-esteem with meaningless phrases.

We increasingly had little to talk about. Perhaps he sensed my growing hostility. I was turning into a savage who cared less and less about the feelings of others, and I didn't feel the need to be nice or make small talk to put people at ease. Mom and I had always had a tacit agreement not to say anything that would upset Daddy when he called. She may have had other motives to pretend life was just hunky-dory, but for me it was a protective instinct; wasn't he suffering enough? He was captive, we were free. My throat constricted whenever I imagined the tiny steel cage that enclosed my strong, vigorous father who, like me, sought the comfort of fictional planets to deny the reality of the bars around him.

Daddy would never again feel the caress of open water in any country. He would never feel soft snowflakes settle on his hair and slog through drifts of it, looking back at his muffled footprints. He lived in an overcrowded hell of inescapable sounds, awful odours and two kinds of lethal movement—time and frustrated male humanity—one or both of which would eventually kill him. Was this justice? Or, guilty or not, was he the victim of one of humankind's most colossal mistakes, one that would make aliens who observed us shake their bulbous heads in perplexity and sorrow? It was not my place to determine justice. But the privilege of freedom made me the adult responsible for safeguarding his emotions instead of the other way around.

My mother broke our unspoken contract only once that I knew of, telling him about my terrible behaviour and back-talk.

"Agata told me you been calling her names," he said when she handed me the phone. (She was always Agata, even to me, except one time when he had written to his mistress Chandice and sent us her letter by mistake. He pretended to be referring to my mother as a sacred chalice, only with typos.)

I don't remember whether I said nothing or whined a plaintive, indignant denial.

"If I ever hear you been giving lip again, you know what I'm gonna do?" he said in the sweet, slow, seductive Alabama drawl he'd never been able to shake. "Imma strip you down and tie you to a tree, upside down. Then I'm gonna cover you with molasses, and you know what'll happen?"

It took a moment for his words to penetrate because I could not make sense of what I was hearing. For once, I was struck dumb, picturing the horrific shame of my body exposed for all to see, dripping syrup onto my glasses until the lenses were gummy with it and they slid right off my upside-down head.

"The ants will come running. They can smell it. They gonna cover you all over, and pretty soon, they gonna start stinging you. Until you die. It takes days."

When the words finally unfurled themselves across my consciousness, I pulled a reverse Grinch: my heart shrunk three sizes that day. I didn't know that parents talk a lot of shit and aren't to be taken literally. I didn't know him as a person either, so I held him to his word. His eviscerating, betraying, unjust word.

My letters continued, of course, though they became soulless. Mom insisted, claiming that she was no longer his wife so I was the only one who could improve his bleak reality. As long as someone else was picking up the slack, she didn't have to feel guilty about not writing to her husband, the man who had ruined her life.

I had always seen Mom as an adversary, but the knowledge that Daddy had joined her opened up a howling hole in my chest that I quickly plugged with an invented advantage. He didn't know me, nor could he reach through the receiver and actually do anything to me; his was the desperate threat of the powerless, and it had been made to an image in his mind, not to the real me. Our time on the phone together was very limited and we never dealt in truth, especially with my mother sitting right in front of me waiting to say a final, cheery goodbye before the operator cut us off. Therefore, it wouldn't be hard to never let him hurt me again.

It makes sense, then, that my father would never learn of my struggles with my hair, how anxious I was to look *normal* and how every glance in the mirror was shameful confirmation of my ugliness, even though my mother said I was beautiful just as I was. It made me want to punch her in the face. She often told the story of how she had been approached by a baby modelling agent back in New York who took one look at me in the stroller and said, "I want that face. I must have that face!" My mother hadn't even considered calling the agent because my father forbade it, even though we could have had money. How dumb could a person actually be? Let alone two people? They deserved each other.

Despite my protestations, Mom said that anyone who couldn't tell that I was a girl was just plain stupid, "plain" being the worst thing a person could be.

"You don't have to change your natural appearance to please these people who are just plain stupid," she'd fume, never considering that I might have wanted to please myself.

"What about all your creams and potions and lipsticks? How is that not changing your appearance?" I screamed.

It had taken her years to begin wearing lipstick, and when she did, it was without acknowledgment of her lifelong insistence that make-up was for sluts. I once repeated this phrase to the delicate passenger sitting next to me on a delayed flight back when we were still making frequent trips to Toronto from New York. The lady, who I only remember as very pretty and a little bewildered, explained with great kindness and patience that a little lipstick does not a slut make.

Reluctantly, Mom took me to upscale White hair salons whose staff recommended expensive, plant-based anti-frizz products that did just about nothing. In *The Autobiography of Malcom X*, I read that his friends had introduced him to the hot comb back when he was still Malcolm Little, so I heated a butter knife on the gas stove and used it to crisp at least some of my hair straight, trying for a version of his famous red conk. But at the slightest hint of humidity, my hair reverted back to an impenetrable thicket of frizz. So much for fried, dyed and laid to the side; I burned off an alarming amount of hair without ever achieving the straight, glossy results I was hoping for. Plant extracts and knives weren't going to cut it.

Mom tried next to encourage other ways of asserting femininity, such as dangling earrings. Although I shoved enormous hoops into my lobes on a daily basis ("Hey Dickhole, where's the canary?"), I was somehow exempt when she lectured that Black girls wore too much fake gold. At least I didn't laugh too loud or put an ounce of grease in my hair every day.

She also tried to relate to me.

"I know how you feel, Nicky. I used to straighten my hair with an actual iron, the kind you iron clothes with. I used to stick my head on the ironing board and everything!"

She made a swooshing motion, demonstrating what it was like to straighten her waist-length hair when the limp, bone-straight Joni Mitchell style was popular. It was the ultimate rebellion against her own mother, who had always forced her to pile her hair high on her head with the help of a whole sleeve of bobby pins. One day when she was in her 20s, she said she just couldn't be bothered anymore and had chosen feminist freedom by wearing her very curly hair cropped to a two-inch length.

Next on the list of acceptable solutions, Mom took me to one of the Jamaican men's barbershops on Bathurst where I endured buzz cuts and the curious, pitying stares of neighbourhood men who sat waiting for fades. It was unendurable. I started cutting my own hair, unevenly, over the bathroom sink with craft scissors until, without permission or blessing, I went to Shoppers Drug Mart to buy a chemical hair straightening kit. The quarter-aisle that housed these exotic and mysterious products was already familiar because we had made fun of the men on the boxes, who all looked like Lionel Ritchie, and the women who gazed vacuously off into space between massive clouds of spiral curls. Even the brand names: Dark and Lovely? What's the opposite of that, Light and Ugly? My mother had told me that the so-called "fading creams" sold in that aisle were really skin bleaching products marketed to ignorant Black people. It wasn't their fault, she said; they didn't know they were puppets, subscribing to an artificially-imposed beauty standard that was enforced by Western culture to trick them out of their money and make them hate themselves.

"This is exactly what destroyed Michael Jackson," she said sorrowfully. "All that plastic surgery and he ended up looking like a freak."

The problem with everything my mother said was that there was always at least some truth to it, which made it difficult to reject the harshly judgmental, absolutist nature of her comments out of hand. At least our scornful condemnation of the products on those shelves had shown me exactly where to look.

My only chance was when Mom left the house on Saturday mornings to run her errands. I estimated how much time it would take her to line up at the bank, fill out a withdrawal slip and walk around the corner to buy her vegetables versus how long it would take to apply the contents of the forbidden box I had hidden away. I should have read the instructions in advance, but even if I'd thought that far ahead, I might have gotten caught reading them. All I knew for sure was that, once done, a chemical reaction could not be undone. I would deal with the punishment later while tossing my suddenly-flowing mane of gorgeous locks instead of just pretending with a towel.

I had worked most of the smelly cream through my Afro as best I could when I heard the key in the lock. The TD line-up must have been shorter than I thought. There was rage, which I had expected, but also destruction, which I hadn't. The crucial de-activating shampoo was poured down the sink and the instruction sheet, with its advice on timing and aftercare, torn to shreds.

For the uninitiated, which I was, the thing about a "no lye" relaxer kit—comprised of cream, activator and neutralizing shampoo, plus a pair of ill-fitting plastic gloves—is that you can't actually straighten hair without lye, just as you can't make soap without it. The chemical reaction of lye is necessary to relax the bonds that curl the hair. The so-called no-lye formula, which was really lye in the way that "seasoning" is really MSG, applied inexpertly by a young teenager, burned my scalp as thoroughly as lye would have. I couldn't neutralize it without the special shampoo. The smell of the cream frying my hair and skin, and the resulting chemical burns whose interesting scabs I was still combing out weeks later, did not at all deter me. I had a lot of hair, and most of it, though weak and brittle, had not fallen out. We did the kit-hiding, kit-destroying dance once or twice more before my mother accepted that I was going to relax my hair whether she liked it or not.

This was a defining moment in my struggle to finally be my own person (at least on the outside). Once upon a time I had naïvely assumed that Mom needed a boyfriend to distract her into leaving me alone. Now I began to realize that all I had to do was stop entertaining her, stop agreeing with her, stop being just like her, and she would no longer have the energy to mock or block all the new and disagreeable thoughts, preferences and behaviours. It was Grey Rock with a twist: showing defiance worthy of a psychopath, I became so stubborn that she could not get me to agree the sky was blue or water was wet. There was no one left worth smothering.

It was a laughably simple solution. She lost interest in me practically overnight, which led to the dismantling of another naïve assumption on my part: being left alone was equal to life, liberty and the pursuit of happiness. Not so. The emotional emancipation only led to anxiety and fear. Who was I now that the one person who knew me best wanted nothing to do with me? I was more alone than I had ever been, with fewer resources at my disposal than ever. Still, pride would not allow me to reject the terrifyingly infinite choices in front of me and crawl back to her side where it was safe. I had my own demands before that could happen: she must become more co-operative, wise and generous. Our relationship would be like a friendship among equals.

    I am sure you are already laughing.

Re-Development

Brownfields often are in struggling neighborhoods and areas with blight, deteriorated infrastructure, or other challenges. These properties often are eyesores as well as potential health and safety concerns.

-The United States Environmental Protection Agency, Office of Brownfields and Land Revitalization, June 2019

CHAPTER 13

CALL ME, CALL ME ANYTIME

Every week, my mother clipped articles out of the paper for my information and edification, but my favourite were *The Sunday Star* clippings about little children with special needs who were up for adoption. Some mean part of me wants to believe those were to show me how good my life was compared to the siblings who were doomed to be parted or crack babies with holes in their hearts. But I know she felt for those children, who would be so grateful if adopted that they would love her forever and never want to leave her.

Studying the grainy, heart-wrenching photographs, I begged her to adopt me a brother or sister, especially a little one who came with severe emotional and behavioural issues that my love would quickly iron out. We did have some experience with adoption, in feline form.

"No, Taco Maco! Bad cat!" my mother would exclaim, pushing his lithe body off the kitchen table over and over.

"You can't teach a cat like that, Mom," I said, rolling my eyes at her stupidity. "Cats aren't like dogs."

I had argued for a cat in terms that I knew would appeal to her—their cleanliness and independence, the relatively inexpensive cost of maintenance—but really, I liked cats because they weren't dogs. They didn't just automatically fawn over whoever owned them; you had to earn a cat's love and respect its wishes. If it eventually did what you wanted, it was only because it had been their idea all along.

Unfortunately, Taco Maco (named by my grandmother, as it was something she could pronounce) proved totally incompatible with my mother's beloved budgie, Ringo (named after the Beatle who shared my birthday). Taco Maco tried to kill Ringo for the ninety-six hours he lived with us before going back to the shelter. If hunting with a view to kill doesn't constitute irreconcilable differences, I don't know what does. Maybe our increasingly toxic environment wasn't the best place for a troubled sib after all.

Never-ending silent treatment initiated by one or both of us meant that we had to orbit around each other as though the other person did not exist. The moment we'd start talking, we would fight. I was convinced that my mother was the only barrier to whatever slight enjoyment I could ask of life. It's called "splitting" in psychology: I had converted her into an all-bad object, a process that had been in the works since before I could remember it. I often wished for telekinetic abilities so I could burn her to ashes where she stood re-washing the dishes I had already washed, her round butt wiggling hatefully as she wiped down the countertops as though it was the most important thing in the world. She acted as if her mere presence wasn't ruining every waking minute of my life.

The one thing she had never interfered with was work, and a means of escape began to form in my mind. Not a single math class appeared in my high school course load, but Money = Power + Freedom was a simple enough equation. It had always been assumed that I would parlay my intellect into scholarships, go to the best schools and eventually settle into a lucrative career. But this conventional way of doing things had a serious drawback: it would take years. I couldn't endure years of this hell with a woman I literally wanted to kill with my bare hands when I wasn't too busy feeling ashamed of myself or pretending to be someone else. I had always been told that when I grew up, I could do whatever I wanted. Well, I had never felt like a child, so why continue to delay? I knew the boundaries of "whatever I wanted" would be defined by what was in my bank account; freedom required cash. I was sixteen and ready to launch.

The mixed-race heritage that had caused me to feel like I never really fit in anywhere finally began to work in my favour when I joined the workforce. Who wouldn't want to employ a smart girl with a sharp Toronto accent who would work for minimum wage? If she was Black, so much the better. Through school contacts and neighbours, I easily secured various tutoring and babysitting gigs. I was a terribly impatient teacher ("Here, just let me do it for you") and didn't like babies ("Seriously, not sure why she keeps crying like this"). All the money went into guaranteed income certificates for a future I couldn't picture in the slightest.

There was no need to try my hand at the traditional student mainstays of retail and food service; to this day I cannot fold a sweater properly because in Grade 12, with only a year left till graduation, I found an evening job at a telemarketing company. It was owned and managed by a real live matriarch who employed a couple hundred workers on a whole floor of a midtown office building in a firm we dubbed Doesn't Make Sense, due to its ever-changing policies and rules. I glimpsed the lady herself a couple of times at motivational staff assemblies. She was short like my mother, with short, curly hair like my mother's, but it was fashionably dyed and styled, and she wore enough make-up and nail polish—not to mention pantyhose and high heels—to earn Mom's official slut stamp for sure.

Almost any job would have been easier for a nervous, sheltered shut-in like me than rushing home from school to spend four hours calling total strangers and asking them to sign up for, accept or purchase new products and services as if my life depended on it. We competed against each other for unrealistic sales quotas; if your name didn't have enough sales beneath it or hadn't even made it to the whiteboard, there was a process in place that involved you parting from what we also called the Land of Oz. Heedless of my own preferences and quick as always to sell myself cheap for immediate gratification, I took the position because it was available. I made the 8 in 1978 look like a 6 on my application form, and no one questioned it. I certainly didn't look or act sixteen.

The call centre required you to work a minimum of three nights a week and two Saturdays per month, which I very optimistically calculated would be enough to keep body and soul together if I got a roommate and moved into a tiny bachelor apartment; after all, there were performance bonuses that could take me all the way to thirteen dollars an hour! Considering that a quarter-century later, minimum wage in Toronto is only a dollar more than that while rents have at least tripled, it might have worked. In our gig economy, educated people need a side hustle, and delivering food is considered a perfectly respectable way to pay for your transit pass and your data overages. But back then, life was more stable. Many of the people I met at work were getting promoted or eventually going on, like my fellow Harbordites, to post-secondary education in pursuit of real careers. I had no such ambitions, certain that everything would unfold properly once I had escaped. This job wasn't going to be permanent; it was just a vehicle to carry me to the lofty heights of freedom.

Student welfare would have been the easy alternative to killing myself in pursuit of a buck. You could also be emancipated from your parents by legal decree if they were crazy enough to make you sleep on the floor or in the same bed with them—child actors did it all the time—but the last thing I wanted was government involvement in exchange for a subsistence cheque. I feared and disliked the law, personified in my imagination by bearded White men in white vans. I wanted real independence. I wanted the thirteen dollars so I could prove to everyone, including myself, that I didn't need my evil cunt of a mother, and she could never throw it in my face that her tax dollars paid for my living just as surely as if I were under her roof.

At work, I would broaden my horizons in a way that most high school students, cocooned in their insular world of intramurals and "What's your average?", never would. Since it was forbidden among my peers to say you hated your mother, I didn't tell my friends I was moving out; it required too much explanation with words I didn't have.

When she discovered the details of the escape plan in my diary, I tried to convince her it was in both our best interests.

"What do you expect? My help?" Her brows crept up then dropped abruptly as she frowned, causing the familiar deep line to appear between them. "I suppose I can't stop you, but that doesn't mean I have to make it easy for you."

Fortunately, I was my mother's daughter and was used to proceeding in the face of opposition. Since all I could take with me were my clothes and the rock-hard futon, I convinced myself that her blessing was irrelevant; opposition only strengthened my resolve. She used to say I would catch more flies with honey than vinegar, but challenge, adversity, fear and hatred drove me like kindness never could. Dishonesty entered the soup when the TD Bank accidentally handed over $12,000 to me. I had been prepared to live like a monk if I had to, but when I went to our local branch at Bloor and Bathurst to withdraw the $3000 I had saved over the years to start my new life, the teller turned her computer monitor toward me with a quizzical expression.

"You wanted to take the entire amount today?" she said, pointing to a figure close to fifteen thousand. "Our policy is that withdrawals over $10,000 require a manager's approval."

I nodded, playing dumb while my brain churned. I didn't know how the money had gotten there, but I wanted it. Maybe they were only ushering me to the back office because I was a minor and could not be expected to make wise financial decisions without counsel. Maybe the manager would try a win-back approach, like the ones we were taught at the call centre, to try to keep my business. (Well, it was too late: my work friends had told me that a rival bank gave out credit cards like candy and charged lower fees.) Or maybe it was a test and, instead of a manager, the police would be called into the office where I sat waiting on a padded green chair.

But the manager asked no questions as to how I had obtained such a substantial sum at my age. Before Y2K, computers didn't lie. He prepared a bank draft which I immediately deposited into my new Canada Trust account (ironically, TD would merge with Canada Trust shortly afterward). The records indicated that they thought I was the *other* Ms. Salter, my mother, who had a hell of a lot more than twelve thousand saved but who happened to have a GIC in that exact amount which had inexplicably been duplicated and listed under my assets as well as hers.

With nearly $15,000 I was easily able to put down my share of first and last on a bachelor at Yonge and Davisville, and even furnish it. I paid a roughneck from school, a guy named Ali who was at least twenty and still trying to get his OACs, a hundred bucks to drive my stuff over in his little beater. The futon didn't fit and wouldn't bend, so we drove the whole way from The Annex to Midtown with the trunk half-open.

"Holy fuck," he said, reeking of weed as he wrestled garbage bags into the mirrored service elevator. "These walls are a trip."

The glass walls had been broken up into a mosaic, so our reflections leered back at us from a hundred different angles. I leaned against the wall and closed my eyes. I was so keyed-up about spending the night alone in my very own home. Except I wasn't really alone. The apartment on the seventeenth floor was one block from work, one block from the subway, one block from no less than four different pubs and a steal when shared with a co-worker I'd just met. I no longer needed a roommate for financial reasons, but being underage, I couldn't sign a lease on my own, so I paid and Connie co-signed. I did need her; she knew how to use a coin laundry machine and schooled me on what supplies might be required to live independently. She would later throw a two-dollar bill at me when, after only a few months of adulting, I couldn't afford coffee one morning before work.

If they ever invent time machines, I want to go back and not spend all that free money on bar tabs for myself and my new work friends. I'm not greedy; I don't expect to go back in time to invest in Big Tech or buy the Coke URL. I just want to be a little bit wiser, stay in school, pay my bills. But I had already discovered the magic of liquor, a friend that, when poured down my throat as often as possible, turned me from a wallflower to the life of the party. Liquor made me stupider, which was the whole point. I could talk to anyone about any topic. I could sparkle, even flirt, before the window of opportunity slammed shut and I started slurring, stumbling and puking.

I wasn't able to buy booze at the liquor store because I didn't possess ID, let alone a fake one; but servers thought I was legal, especially when I went into The Ploughman in the company of my much older work friends. The same went for the clubs where I regularly thrashed around on the concrete dance floor to industrial music, dressed head to toe in black, my hair bone-straight and white-blonde. I couldn't decide whether to be a Goth or a Gina like Connie.

Connie thought I was weird, but she showed me the basic ropes of how to be a person in the world. They were expensive lessons. In exchange for stopping me from folding the dirty clothes before they went in the hamper and informing me that a clothes dryer—which I had never even seen before, as there wasn't one at home—had to be turned on by means of a button, I paid the bills and kept the party going. We went on a whirlwind trip to Montreal with the last of the bank proceeds. I mostly remember dancing the night away at clubs, drunk enough to finally be un-self-conscious in the same little black dress Connie had bought. It was Connie who taught me to dance, whirling around me, swinging her massive curly mane and stomping her pointy-booted feet, aiming her long, elegant index fingers at me as we spun around and around. At home, we fought about my bringing the boss's son upstairs in the middle of the night; she slept on the pull-out couch and had to witness a lot more than she'd wanted to. I couldn't remember how I had even identified a Millman, much less invited him upstairs for a grope-fest, but we lived so close to work that our apartment was everybody's crash pad.

When the money was gone and so was Connie, taking the rented Bell phone with her but considerately leaving me all the essentials and a few overflowing ashtrays, a creditor named Mr. Wilson came looking for me. He knew exactly where to look because my mother had quickly sniffed out the fraud and reported it to the bank, who said they could do nothing until their semi-annual audit.

"I'm sorry, Nicky. I told them to stop you before these *friends of yours* take everything, but they just wouldn't listen to me. If you confess, they'll probably let you do a payment plan."

I hadn't talked to her in some time, and now I laughed harshly, lighting another cigarette. I did what I wanted, when I wanted to, in my home. Just like she'd always said I could.

"Do you really think a used couch, a synthetic rug and a TV would equal twelve grand plus interest? The money's gone."

"Every little bit helps, Nicky. You wanted to be independent so badly. Well, this is what it means: being responsible for your actions."

I hung up the phone, furious at her for ratting me out and then presuming to tell me how to live. It was friends who helped me pick up the pieces. Two sisters from Newfoundland lived upstairs and also worked with me. They and their boyfriends were sweet and, though we shared the bad habits of drinking together constantly and watching *The Tick* on Saturday mornings while trying to hold down greasy hangover breakfasts, the younger sister, Colleen, was kind and conscientious. She asked me if I really thought I was doing the right thing by partying so hard. She hadn't liked Connie and wanted me to do better next time.

I couldn't bear the concern, though I certainly didn't doubt the sincerity. The sisters and their boyfriends took me to the hospital when I half-assed a suicide attempt by systematically taking everything in the medicine cabinet and washing it down with liquor because my crush had come right out and said that he didn't like me back. After I got off the phone with him and went to bed, I had no recollection of events until I found myself in a wheelchair and, hours later, projectile vomiting charcoal onto the wall from my hospital bed.

"Why did you do this to yourself? Can you tell me why?" a faceless doctor asked me.

I really had no idea. Who does that over a crush? Later, the older sister's boyfriend, Peter, told me what had happened that night. He was a funny guy, unafraid to speak his mind. He had inducted me into the adult world of shining floors and clean corners through teasing. I didn't know how to clean anything but dishes, so after a few months he informed me that I had mould growing on the bathroom floor while pretending to unfurl yet another cotton throw rug to cover the mess. Peter said nobody knew I was eating pills, they thought I had just passed out from drinking.

"The next thing we knew you sat up all of a sudden and said, 'What would happen if someone had a tracheotomy and you tied a scarf around their neck? You could kill them just like that, with a scarf!' Then we tried to talk to you, and you couldn't talk at all."

The next day, Martin, Colleen's exotic Malaysian boyfriend, came over with three wilted pink roses and a tangle of baby's breath. From the sofa, I watched him wrestle with the rubber bands and tape until he finally just sliced the wrapping off with a bread knife and left the litter of leaves, stems and bits of plastic all over the kitchen counter. I was tired and drugged, but despite my protests he heated a can of soup, which he brought to me in a shallow bowl with a plate underneath it. Even the spoon wore a little paper napkin coat. I was Pollyanna for a day.

We all went to Newfoundland for Christmas one year—two locals, one Malay, one White west coaster with a curly red Afro and one tall Black girl. The family loved me because I drank Newfie screech and could sing all the carols so nicely, but I woke up on New Year's Day in a pool of my own vomit on the mother's immaculate pillows. They were so nice about it, I couldn't stand it. They introduced me to fries, dressing and gravy at Mary Brown's and glossed over my excesses, saying I was one of them because east coasters drink, that's just what they do. Spirit of the West's famous jig with the line, "I'm so sick from the drink …" had us linking arms and dancing our way through the holidays. They told me that joke about the Newf who'd been asked by his doctor why he didn't just stop drinking if he knew he was going blind from the screech.

"Well, bye," said the old man, "I guess I likes what I drinks more than I likes what I sees."

The worst was finding my faded underwear, which I had bled through in a drunken stupor without realizing it, perfectly bleached and folded for me. There were eight siblings, and the mother still washed their clothes and those of the guests. I couldn't stand it. They were too nice, too good for me; they'd eventually figure it out, and concern over problems like the collection agent would turn to judgment over my irresponsible behaviour. I began to distance myself. I thought I knew what I was doing.

It was months before Mr. Wilson got organized enough to try and get blood from a stone. He called and sent letter after harshly-worded letter, his indignant tone suggesting he took my fraud personally. Apparently he didn't believe that my only remaining assets were canned goods and a suite of hideous dinnerware Connie chose; the rest had gone down my throat by the glass. Undeterred by the lack of response, Mr. Wilson would stalk me for the next ten years, long past the point where the bank must have written off the bad debt. He left voice messages warning that my credit rating would be ruined forever if I didn't make reparations (I didn't and it wasn't). One day, his attentions ceased so abruptly that I wondered if he had simply walked into the sea.

The landlord was more efficacious. When the property management company taped eviction notices on my door—I was working full-time, but my daily drinking habit exceeded my daily salary and left nothing for accommodations—I moved back in with my mother for three months. Once again, the futon was dragged back to one of the peak-roofed attic rooms. My mother couldn't stand it. I'd come home drunk, throw up in her fancy wicker wastebasket till the acid ate through the unfinished wood floors and argue for bath privileges instead of using the spider-filled basement shower stall Mamma forced me to squeegee after each use.

I had already dropped out of high school for the second year in a row; Harbord was a termed school, not a semestered one, but with only a couple months left to go each year, I got spring fever and couldn't see it through. My grades had dropped 10 percent from my erstwhile high 90s, and I felt defeated, coming to class in yesterday's make-up and thinking obsessively about what I saw as my real life. No one else I knew lived on their own and partied with people who treated them like an equal. That was the thing worth hanging onto.

In my last attempt to graduate, I took the creative writing OAC in the certainty that, like the other liberal arts courses, I would ace it. I already knew the teacher from an earlier writing course in which I had memorized *In Flanders Fields* for my poetry recitation. It seemed to disappoint him, but whether that was due to my shaky, stage-fright delivery or because he expected some kind of deep analysis of *The Telltale Heart*, I never found out. Still, I was sure he would spot my talent for fiction from a mile away, and the class would boost my GPA to former levels so I could finally graduate with pride and maybe get some kind of a bursary for university. Instead, my work came back with Bs written in red ink. I wasn't living up to my potential, he said. I had finally been exposed for the fraud I had always known myself to be.

Before my eighteenth birthday, I had dropped out of school altogether and, on another break from the call centre, found what I hoped would be stable employment at the front desk at a large insurance company at Yonge & Eglinton, replacing an ancient receptionist who was finally retiring to enjoy her Belmonts on a full-time basis. Underqualified and immature, I could not seem to get the hang of the enormous old-fashioned switchboard or when it was imperative to let calls through to the executives or how long was too long to leave someone on hold. I took too-frequent smoke breaks and even stretched out on the waiting room couch when I was tired after lunch. I hated being so exposed every minute, but reception and phone work were the only jobs that would overlook a lack of higher learning, so what else was I going to do?

I didn't realize I was being watched. Most of my attention was directed all the way to the very, very back of the office, where the firm's only other person of colour, a ridiculously handsome fellow with a penchant for close-fitting pastel business shirts, sorted mail for the adjusters and examiners. But before I could get to know him, I was called before a very angry lady with high, sculpted hair who was apparently my boss to listen as she compared her career-fast-track life to my pitiful performance. She was a power suit, I was faded pajamas. By age seventeen *she* had already been a single mother but had bootstrapped in a largely male industry, and if she could do that, she certainly expected more from me. My behaviour was unprofessional and insubordinate, she said, and I would never succeed in life unless I humbled myself enough to seize my own bootstraps and pull very hard indeed.

"You're fired," she concluded, as my throat closed and embarrassing tears leaked from my eyes.

It still didn't make sense to me; anyone with half a brain should be able to pull off such easy monkey work. Most of the people I saw on the rush-hour subway—dead-eyed, half-asleep, holding on for dear life—could accept that work was a painful necessity, so what was wrong with me? Why couldn't I just put in my time, unlock my potential, find my why or even show up long enough to collect a paycheque? Why did all my talk of maturity, independence and hard work evaporate in the face of the real thing? It was a puzzle I would try to solve for decades.

Somehow I managed to trick a succession of HR reps into hiring me by projecting fake assertive confidence just like my naïve but magnetic dad who, when asked by a New York City bartender if he wanted his drink on the rocks, confidently replied, "No thanks, I'd like it on ice." This faux pas earned Daddy a drink on the house in exchange for a night of yokel jokes with a strongly racist bent. He had beamed strongly throughout the roasting.

After that I ricocheted from one casual, on-call temp assignment to the next, mostly reception relief and admin jobs that didn't require any special skills or even reading an instruction manual. I was earning money a day at a time, and more went out than came in. Working the front desk at offices and hotels required money for coffee, bus fare, cigarettes, food, high heels and tailored business clothes, except for when I ended up in the cavernous mailroom of a much bigger insurance company. There was not a pastel-shirted heartthrob in sight.

CHAPTER 14

THE REVENGE OF THE GODS

There was no man in my life. A guy had circled around the insurance company on my smoke breaks and asked me to go for a drive with him, taking me instead to an underground parking lot where he unzipped his fly, guided my head and then gave up when I proved to have an overactive gag reflex; that didn't count. Nor did my fellow telemarketer on the drunk driving fundraising campaign where, on a dare, I deliberately botched the sales script so that potential donors would think I was the mother of a drunk driver pleading for his release. He took me to his apartment and performed elaborate tricks with the ceremonial nunchucks he pulled down from the wall above his bed, pinning me to it with moves that would have been scary had I not already learned to go somewhere else in my mind. Men brought out the worst in me and made me desperately thirsty and immoral. It wasn't a personality disorder, love addiction or limerance back then, of course; PD stood for professional development. I just thought I was slap crazy.

I lost my virginity to a much older supervisor who hung out with the one I really wanted—the one I puked charcoal in front of and whom I would later date and discover I only liked because he reminded me of my mother.

"Love the one you're with," Daddy would say.

When not discussing birth stories, women sometimes discuss these things, but fortunately the question of "What was your first time like?" is not as common, because I couldn't really say. I floated above my body as he grinded on me in his hotel room, complete with onlookers, for what seemed like hours after our booze-soaked company Christmas party. We continued to socialize in our group of friends even though I wasn't good at doing the things he wanted to do, like smoking weed all night (it made me too paranoid) or having sex in the morning (I had to shower first).

When I sensed him losing interest, I made up a story about a traumatic abortion courtesy of a boy at school who'd dumped me. What did I think an outrageous emotional manipulation like that would accomplish other than screw up my karma forever? I laid the lies on thick, simulating a slow and painful recovery process, and the story seemed to pay dividends in sympathy and attention at first. He even gifted me a night in a nice hotel, a gesture that was presumably meant to show me that all men weren't assholes and I deserved better than a boy who got me pregnant and then threw beer caps at me for sport (I may have been foolish, but I was nothing if not inventive). But close to Valentine's Day, he told me he was dating other people. Such honesty may be commendable in today's world of non-exclusivity, but in the nineties when you told someone you couldn't commit, you were basically telling them to take a long walk off a short pier. It didn't work.

"You mean like lots of other people? Or just one in particular?" I asked.

We were at Tim's late at night drinking coffee because I had run out of cash from using the ATM to withdraw drinking money in twenty-dollar increments—twenty was all I ever intended to spend—and paying a three-dollar service charge each time. He was vague on answers, which I found encouraging. Surely there was enough of him to go around for all of us! I pity him now. How gravely he had miscalculated the extent of my loneliness and the energy I could pour into my fantasies! He left a shirt at my house and I kept it, immersing myself in the scent of Blue

Jeans until it faded. Eventually, I took to calling him with a blocked number so he'd answer and I could ask him why he wasn't calling me.

One night I walked into The Ploughman alone. The main floor was almost empty, and I went to climb the stairs to the quiet level where I could station myself near the jukebox. The supervisor sat at a table at the top of the stairs, and on his lap sat my best friend from school, Christy.

I froze. They froze. I wouldn't leave my bar for them. Did he walk over, buy me a consoling drink? I don't remember. I drank a lot that night, like I did every night. Then I went home and that was it, on the outside. On the inside it felt as though my already-shrivelled heart required a microscope to find. I had no idea he even knew Christy, a friend I'd casually introduced him to once at the same company Christmas party. She was the plus-one I'd abandoned in favour of spending most of the night in his room. I had confided every detail of our "relationship" since then, constantly asking her opinion and advice on how to make him like me. The idea that they were laughing at me behind my back all that time almost turned me inside out.

Christy wrote me a rambling letter explaining that she had never intended to hook up with the supervisor, but it didn't even approximate the kind of apology I expected. In fairness, nothing would have sufficed; once wronged, I never forgot. She was sophisticated and two years older with well-off parents who fostered troubled teens, so she knew what to do when someone tried to stick his dick into you when you weren't paying attention (if that was even what happened, it was a hell of an accident considering they stayed together for five years, an eternity at our age). There was no excuse. Her letter accused me of telling the supervisor about her life—the ultimate betrayal, Christy wrote. She added that I didn't understand her. Inside the envelope was a copper disk she had made for me on the arcade machine that would stamp your chosen message out for a dollar. It said: LOVE YOURSELF AND YOU WILL BE HAPPY. I'd given it back to her because it wasn't that easy. I countered this message with a prophetic hand-lettered sign which I posted on my wall shortly after: I WILL NEVER HAVE SEX AGAIN FOR FREE.

There was never time to process anything that happened, let alone heal from it. I was back at work the next day, reporting to the same supervisor. Life seemed to proceed at a frantic pace, and when it didn't, I was immobilized by apathy and loneliness. Transferring my devotion to a new and, I hoped, better person by plunging into yet another doomed liaison too brief to ever be called a partnership was as close to therapy as I ever got. I wish I could say I learned something. I suppose, in a way, I did. I learned I could not even stick to the principle on my bedroom sign no matter how many casual disasters followed. This weakness and stupidity only reinforced the idea that I would never find happiness on my own because I obviously could not be trusted to even preserve my own basic welfare.

Everything about my life became wretched, and it was a lucky day doing *whatever I wanted* that yielded any sort of relief. The city was in an unprecedented stage of growth that has continued ever since; I dodged cranes and open construction pits every day to get to my Wellesley Street apartment where I was surrounded by brackish fluids and unpleasant odours of many varieties. The toilet in the unit above me leaked, so it was impossible to use the bathroom without getting wet. The super, annoyed that I wouldn't sleep with him again, taped a black plastic garbage bag over the hole in the ceiling and poured something caustic down the drain as a perfunctory fix. The shower drain smelled of rotten eggs and clogged easily. The laundry room dryers left clothes reeking of curry. I was terrified of being alone and spent weekends trying to stave off the anxiety by listening to 102.1 The Edge, making tomato sauce, drinking and sewing little frilly curtains for my bedroom windows.

As I sank deeper into debt, I could no longer afford the laughably inexpensive unit on my own. Along with a thirty-three percent interest consolidation loan, I acquired a roommate, Ian, a burly bear of a night shift supervisor who positively overflowed with witticisms from his native Thunder Bay such as, "It's black as a nigger's ass on a moonlit night." The call centre had moved into a much nicer building downtown, and we could once again walk to work. I kept the bedroom and he, rather unfairly for a man in his fifties, had to sleep on a mattress in what I thought of as *my* living room. The inevitable roommate conflicts occurred. He was a slob, but I'd come home at two in the morning, stumbling around looking for something edible. Tension simmered like the beef stew he always had on the stove. As a peace offering, I got him a kitten, but she got sick from swallowing the used dental floss he would casually drop on the carpet. This caused another fight, after which he left for good, taking Min with him.

The situation became untenable. The dance wasn't working: drink today, eat tomorrow. Buy a couch today, pay it off for three years. Pay rent late, pay the phone bill every other month. I had come up against the hard realities of Toronto life, and I was barely eighteen.

Then it began to dawn on me that I could do something about this. If for every person I slept with there were two more who seemed interested, I might have something to offer the world after all. Of course, my paltry assets weren't enough—would never be enough—for true love to find me; nobody I really liked had ever really liked me back. But I was no longer the girl who only got high school kiss-o-grams on my hand, and only then from my girlfriends. Now it seemed like I was not only damaged goods but fresh meat to be sniffed out by a whole kennel's worth of dogs. In an otherwise forgettable series of drunken, uncomfortable encounters, I had lost keys, phones, wallets, substantial amounts of money, even my floor-length faux-fur coat from The Shopping Channel in the middle of winter. It was time to reinvent myself into something other than a loser. For that, I would need a wrecking ball.

CHAPTER 15

THE GOLDEN TOUCH

Even if my mother had allowed it, I was never going home again. I moved farther south to a small brownstone on Carlton Street right across from the city park with a substantial homeless population, never realizing the huge glass dome at one end contained a breathtaking greenhouse. There was beauty all around me, but I didn't see it. I kept my eyes, like my head, down; one foot in front of the other. This was a place that didn't require a co-signer, and rent was less than $600 a month, so they even took welfare applicants.

The building was rather ambitiously called Coral Gables, but my unit was more reminiscent of a cell than a beachside villa. The kitchen was in the living room, and the bedroom was actually a walk-in closet; with my double bed wedged inside, I couldn't close the doors, but at least it provided a modicum of privacy. The floors were painted black, which showed every speck of dust and grain of cat litter. The bathroom walls were caked top to bottom with thick teardrops of brown residue that no amount of scrubbing would remove. I don't think we had magic erasers back then. Those miraculous electrostatically charged dry dusting cloths would only be invented four or five years later, when I was just about ready to leave.

The call centre had switched me from outbound—cold-calling people to make sales—to inbound, which was much more bearable and secure but offered no bonuses. I was considered a senior employee in the call centre world, trained on dozens of programs so that whether people thought they were calling the bank to ask about their student loan status or the insurance company to apply for travel coverage or the long distance carrier to discuss international savings and freedom, they were actually routed to my headset in a cubicle amid hundreds of others in the Atrium on Bay.

I didn't speak sufficient French to command the bilingual wage, and though I tried working overnight for the extra hourly dollar, I didn't last long. I wasn't built for walking home down a trash-strewn Yonge Street as the sun rose, trying not to outpace my Eritrean and Djiboutian friends who strolled slowly, gossiping and telling jokes as if we were at the coffee shop on a morning break rather than having just pulled an all-nighter. I envied them. My mouth was dry and bitter from too many cigarettes, my head muzzy and my face greasy, but they didn't seem to have a care in the world.

The whole walk, I would have my admiring eyes on Fatemah. She was Eritrean as well, a Black Sephardic Jew from Montreal who was six years older than me—an eternity back then—and the model of what I thought a woman should be. Fatemah was beautiful, elegant, petite and curvaceous. Her demeanour was always kind, confident, wise and composed. She was afraid of nothing ever since her estranged boyfriend had slashed her with a straight razor when she was my age and left her for dead. It had taken hours to wash the blood out of her waist-length hair, she said, and her face still bore the scars. She was my sister, friend and mother at a time when I needed all three and didn't know how to respond properly to any of them. I wanted to be the only one who loved her, but there were so many other admirers. And one of them, it turned out, had the solution to my financial problems.

This friend of Fatemah was a girl she had known forever who was now working, of course, in telemarketing. She told me she stripped on the side, and if I wanted to make real money and get out of debt, I should too. What else would give me the kind of coin I needed to pay for the wonderful consumer goods I drooled over in the catalogues I studied between calls?

While I didn't really like Tasha and her haughty bilingual-ness, I was a chameleon who would have a laugh with Hitler, I joked, as long as he bought me enough beer. Tasha didn't buy me anything. She already had another pet project, an immigrant girl who she was going to bring to work with her, but that girl couldn't afford the proper clothes to get started. I helpfully agreed to spend almost $200 on sexy lingerie to get her ready. It was less of a loan and more of an entry fee into a business I would never have explored unaided. Tasha got me into a massage parlour when I proved too chickenshit to get on the main stage and shake what God had not given me.

"What do I even do in a massage parlour?" I asked.

"Oh my God, it's super easy and totally private," she said, flicking her long, black ponytail which was in need of conditioning. There was a time lag before the new call on the screen would connect in your ear, but she both muted her phone and curled a hand around the mouthpiece of her headset. "You just massage him. You know how to give a rubdown, don't you?"

I thought about it. There were massages, and then there were *massages*. I didn't want to look stupid by asking too many questions, a trait which had been my downfall more than once.

"You have to dress sexy, obviously, but not slutty. You're not going in there looking like a stripper," she continued, then raised a finger and switched abruptly into the French greeting for the phone company.

Our conversation was going to take a lot longer than it should have, especially since we kept getting interrupted by supervisors who were patrolling for the upsell, the cross-sell, and all the other types of sells deemed necessary.

"So, they're like, in their underwear, or what? I don't get it. Like, how can you make so much money just … massaging?"

She gave me a withering micro-look before her face smoothed into a smile for the French caller ("Smile while you dial!" they used to exhort us). Who did this bitch think she was? I could tell she wasn't eager to divulge any details with so many ears around, even though no one was really listening. The cavernous room was as loud as a stock market trading floor on a movie set. All morning she had been ignoring me and massaging hand cream into the patches of eczema that lined her fingers. Her nails were shit, and she wore big, ugly plastic glasses. She was utterly inconspicuous, a disguise I didn't yet realize allowed her to compartmentalize so thoroughly that she didn't need substances to get her through the day, not even nicotine.

When the call ended, she said, "Most of them are naked, Nicole. You cover the guy with a towel if he didn't already do it, and you rub him down while he jerks himself off. If he wants you to do a sexy dance or take your top off so he can get off faster, he has to pay to play. But there's no touching. You don't let him touch you."

I tried to process this information while she re-crossed her long, shapely legs, the one thing she didn't bother hiding.

"You'll totally figure it out. Oh, and obviously don't use your real name."

I don't know why she lied to me. Maybe she didn't want anyone knowing what she really did behind closed doors, or maybe she was being rewarded for recruiting unwitting girls who, once they had crossed the first line, would keep on crossing all the rest like a kid playing hopscotch. I highly doubt she managed to convince any of her clients that the only thing they could get from her was a provocative dance, not if she hoped to make any money.

Perhaps I am being too hard on her. Hers, and then ours, was a world where everyone lied, not just on a micro level (pretending things were going well to save face, complimenting someone's appearance to be nice) but on a big, bludgeoning level (spreading malicious rumours, claiming to make stacks of cash for doing practically nothing, stealing each other's regulars). Everyone pretended to be saints then pointed accusing fingers at other girls for allegedly doing "dirty" things like full service, Greek, bareback, blow jobs or—heaven forbid—kissing, things that gave everybody in the business a bad name. From time to time a used condom would be found under a massage table and brought forth like a sad, shrivelled snakeskin nestled in a mound of tissues. It was surefire proof against the room's previous occupant, who would have to loudly insist that the room hadn't been cleaned properly since the last girl, and so on down the line. *By the time you were working in a massage parlour*, I wondered, *did it really matter what, precisely, you were doing?*

I didn't even know what I myself was doing. I was one step up from the stereotypical runaway teen who, fleeing her hellish homescape, winds up huddled up in a bus station only to be discovered by the friendly neighbourhood pimp. I thought I was making my own decisions, not realizing it is very difficult to make any decision, let alone a good one, when you have no real sense of identity. Obviously, I was rejecting my strict upbringing which had failed to provide me with much of a moral compass, but even when my own results were dismal I did not know how to reverse the process.

Adding to the confusion was the fact that not only did I lack experience, I wasn't even 100 percent sure how much Tasha was dissembling. There was no way to prove anything. Maybe she had found a way to manipulate the custies with softly spoken lies, exotic fragrances, suggestive movements. She let her waterfall of black hair down and the glasses came off, transforming her into someone altogether different. I, too, had put together a uniform: printed sarongs a friend had brought back from Mexico and skintight spaghetti-strap bra tops. Compared to many of the other girls, I was positively swaddled in clothing, but I thought it showed my body to best advantage.

The only thing I remember about my first client at Golden Touch was that the room stank of feet. So as not to intimidate the custies with my height, I had to take my shoes off (even the highest massage table was too low for me), so my feet immediately became black with dirt from the baby-oil-soaked carpets. What I didn't know about seduction could have filled a book. I stayed dead drunk most of the time, hiding in the basement whenever a group came in because I knew they would put their heads round the kitchen door to pick the girl they wanted. If they didn't look like the right sort of man—White and old—my smiles were slight. The Asian girls usually didn't smile at anyone, nor did the prettiest girls; they didn't have to.

I didn't like that these men could just invade our privacy, wake us up, interrupt our meals, TV shows and conversations to choose who they wanted like they were plucking a banded lobster out of a tank.

My heart pounded. I was terrified of being picked and mortified by the rejection when I wasn't. Technically, we were supposed to work on a turns system based on who had clocked in first, and the managers did maintain this unless the man wanted to pick. I took my turns, kept the lights low and often let the men do more than they had paid for. I was so practiced at sending my mind away already, it was nothing to run through my to-do list or rehearse all the things I should have said and done in a long-passed situation; massage required little focus. There was nothing that could not be ravaged for a price, a bit of affectionate approval or just for a quick exit. To feed the beast of independent living, I learned to make my body an unfeeling husk.

The happy ending was standard—hence the baby oil we went through by the litre—but I kept prices low, taking my tips at the end like a waitress and failing to mention extra services unless the customers asked for them outright.

"But if you don't tell them what's on the menu, how are they supposed to order?" asked one baffled girl when I admitted I didn't offer topless, nude and bodyslide right up front. "Like, don't you think they would take more if you asked?"

Her expression of disapproval suggested I was more suited for working fast food than taking up space on the sagging couch. But I half-wanted them not to ask for anything more because it was sometimes preferable to being probed or mauled for the entire session and always preferable to rejection. I wasn't going to beg. I had put myself in a double bind: determining advance intent also ensured getting tipped upfront, whereas when someone asked for more halfway through, I was so painfully tied to having everything go well that I felt it ruined the hard-won mood to force him to get up during the massage, covered in oil, and pick money out of his wallet. Some clients claimed they only had credit cards, which would mysteriously decline during processing or drew too much management scrutiny if the amount put through exceeded the amount of the massage by three or four times.

One particularly rough evening, a custy said he had to go to his car to get his wallet after the first hour. I watched, naked and with a mounting sense of dread, through the dusty, parted blinds of the upstairs window as he climbed in the car, backed out of the space, and drove away. I felt frozen to the spot, staring after him. An ancient TV jingle chose that moment to run through my head: "Lift one of our blinds and what do you find? You find, our trustworthy NAME!" I tearfully confessed to the girls that he had run without paying because I wasn't collecting right away.

"But they could run without paying," someone said, as if this hadn't just happened. "Aren't you here to make money?"

Yes, I was. Stupid, stupid! It wasn't like I trusted them—I didn't. I was just too stubborn to change my ways. It would be like admitting what I already knew: I had failed at this, just like I failed at everything. I had to feed the beast, but it seemed I was feeding other strays too. I appeared to have a bottomless unconscious need for the punishments the custies were only too happy to dole out. I did not then, nor do I now, like to be pinched, slapped, bitten, hair-pulled, brutally finger-banged or humiliated on the rare occasions when my body responded positively against my will. But these things were familiar and endurable. Every night was a new episode of *Survivor*: I had agreed to participate in a never-ending contest of outwit, outlast, outplay, where I collected insults along with paper money to be held up later as sticky trophies that proved I was in the right place.

"These are too small. You should get them done."

"No way you're eighteen. Everybody says that, but you look at least twenty-five."

"If we could just cut off your legs right here [side of hand to my knee] you'd be perfect."

"Come on, just put your mouth on it for a minute."

"So-and-so fucks me with her titties until I come."

"Just let me put it in. I'll wear a condom."

"Oh, come on. I'll come really quick, I promise."

"Could you help me get a green card? I'll make it worth your while."

"Why are you doing this? You a single mother or something?"

"You are a highly sexual being, I can tell."

"Ooh, you like that, don't you? You should be paying *me*, not the other way around."

"Do you have a five-year plan? Just picture in your mind where you see yourself in five years."

"You know what, Serena? I bet you could work in an office if you went back to school."

"Crawl around on the floor. No, not like that, like a dog. That's better. Show me your bark."

"Do it or I'll tell them you're terrible and I want my money back."

"Guess what? I have AIDS. And now you have it too."

I would venture to say that none of us, despite these experiences and innumerable others, ever came to hate men as a group. Contempt would have been closer, but I reserved that for individuals, not the whole gender who buttered our bread. It helped that a good man would walk through the doors every so often, someone lonely and misunderstood—perhaps someone with a minor physical defect, crippling shyness or some other affect not conducive to attracting the opposite sex. The knowledge that I was being paid to soothe and comfort these men made me feel desirable and powerful. I stood still for whatever they wanted, thanking them, providing hot towels and sweet caresses to speed their journey through this land of thick fluids and fetid smells. I pretended I was a love robot and they were Martians with strange bodily protrusions that needed to be stimulated. I pretended I was a nurse and they were patients who would surely die without my lifesaving ministrations. I pretended they were soldiers about to die and, with oily hands, I saluted them.

CHAPTER 16

JIM'S NOT HERE

Judy, who was elevated from masseuse to Golden Touch manager when her pregnancy advanced too far, told me in broken English that we were making life better for the men we serviced, and she was grateful for the work. At least that's what I heard, swaying against the wall, drunk and resentful at how she wielded her new-found power over me. Before the promotion, ugly Judy, with her terrible dye job and lumpy body, used to beg me to trade massage rooms with her so she could have the one with the working dimmer switch—as if any amount of darkness would have concealed a six months' pregnancy. Now, the baby delivered and safely cared for by relatives, she bossed me around. I was always trying to leave early, a trait I haven't really grown out of.

"Serena! Room Two!"

"But it's two o'clock, we're almost closing," I'd whine, "and he never tips."

"Tips for good service! You go now!"

Management didn't want to hear about tips. She ordered me not to drink so much, as if it was any of her business.

I imagined the reactions if I'd told my day job acquaintances what I was really doing for a living. Certainly, they'd be full of assumptive questions:

"They're all lonely and pathetic, right?"

"They're all ugly and fat, right?"

"They can't get a woman any other way, right?"

"Are any of them really young, like virgins or something?"

"Do the married ones take off their wedding rings?"

Fatemah knew, of course, but not the dirty details. Like a serial killer who wants to be caught, I flashed my money around. It wasn't hard, we didn't come from money; it was a rare customer service rep who could afford smokes the day before payday, but despite my newfound prosperity, no one ever asked.

Fatemah and a couple of her friends thoughtfully laid out a business plan to start our own massage parlour. All we'd need was an apartment, a bed, a phone, a blonde and an Asian. But they weren't really in it; they were too normal. No one was willing to take the risk.

I, too, tried to inject some normalcy into my life by visiting my father in prison again. Look! I am a person, I have a family! It was 1998 and he was not yet at the halfway mark of his minimum quarter-century sentence. The erstwhile stream of letters to Daddy had trickled away to an erratic drip of special occasion cards because I was very busy, but Daddy still sent me, care of my mother, long letters and those handmade birthday cards emblazoned with African princesses. He wanted to see me in person.

Things were different now. I wasn't twelve years old anymore; I had plenty of money and nice clothes. I wasn't travelling as an unaccompanied minor on the plane anymore. To celebrate, I ordered a couple of glasses of wine for the one-hour flight when the cart came by. I was with Mikie, my telemarketing friend and the designated rental car driver, and fortunately he was of age in the States and liked to party as much as I did.

"We're on our way to Vine-land!" he enthused. "What the fuck kind of name is that for a city?"

"I think it's pronounced Vin-land," I said wisely.

I had heard it wasn't a city but basically butt-fuck New Jersey, the kind of place where wild turkeys still ran across the roads.

New Jersey State Prison sprawled, mega-mall-sized, across well-tended grounds whose shrubbery was shaved into neat little spherical shapes. Massive towers, horizontally bisected by a ribbon of windows (the better to see you with), overlooked the American flags that snapped proudly at each entrance. At the main gate, a bland-voiced guard called me Ma'am and told us we were late, in violation of the dress code and, because I was still a minor by their standards, Mikie would have to accompany me inside for the entire hour and a half.

I tried pleading with the guard, explaining loudly that I had been given no instructions and my letter indicated an incorrect arrival time. Besides, I reasoned, I was entitled to an extended visit because I was from Canada and had to get back on a plane soon. The guard said there was nothing he could do and we would have to come back another day. He could have been right; we might have been hungover and overslept. I might have been wearing flip-flops. I ranted at Mikie about things he didn't understand—typewriters and zippers and injustice—all the way back to our room, where we drank until I couldn't care about it anymore.

The next day, after being thoroughly frisked, wanded, sniffed by police dogs (an Albino girl who looked about fourteen begged me to pass her my vending machine tokens just to hide the smell of weed on her hands) and stamped with invisible ink as if we were about to enter an exclusive club, we were disgorged into a cavernous gymnasium where dozens of plastic chairs in primary colours had been lined up against a backdrop of murals as lurid as Mikie's blazing cheeks. As we took our seats, the mood was anticipatory. Mothers shushed their children and smoothed their hair and clothes. Abruptly, a door clicked open at the far end of the room and, in groups of three, the inmates swaggered out to find their families.

At first I didn't recognize Daddy; he seemed to have shrunk. His bushy Afro had gone more salt than pepper and was braided in cornrows down his head, and he had grown a long grey beard. I knew the beard, like his adopted religion of Islam, offered a sort of protection from the other 2,200-odd inmates (most of whom were half his age or less but at least twice as violent and insane). At least he wasn't wearing orange. At that time, the State favoured monochromatic beige for its prisoners, with street clothes allowed on visiting days. He wore a plaid shirt and tight blue jeans.

I pretended to be happily interested as he described his legal battles and reminisced about the taste of fresh produce from our garden in Toronto. With guards patrolling close by, he loudly cursed prison life, then hung his head dejectedly when I asked him to keep his voice down. He had been incarcerated for most of my life but still spoke of imminent release.

I didn't scream and I wasn't surprised when he didn't, either. I wish I could say I tried to put my consciousness into his and imagine what it would be like to see my little daughter suddenly a grown ass woman acting like she knew my life. I didn't do any of that; I was a savage by then. I held his large, oddly dry hand tightly in both of my own. I listened to his hollow promises and tried not to stare rudely into the depths of the new creases on his face.

I fidgeted on the plastic bucket seat and looked for White faces until I found Mikie who, highly medicated and probably still traumatized by the rude stares we endured at our late-night rural Denny's meal (he was White, loud and flamingly gay; I was Black, acted White and had the audacity to ask for real butter), was passing the time in the kiddie corner watching cartoons on a wall-mounted screen. He gave me an encouraging look but could not prevent his eyebrows from jumping around uncontrollably. It was the lithium.

When the penitentiary finally spit us out into the bright sunshine, Mikie, who hadn't smoked in eight years, reached into my pack and told me not to tell anyone.

"Did you see all those tongues going down all those throats?" he asked faintly. "Disgusting."

I was so grateful for Mikie at that moment. After years of friendship, he instinctively knew not to ask how I was feeling. I clutched a Polaroid that one of the trusties had taken at exorbitant expense: my father beaming as I posed for the camera looking unintentionally sultry. When we reached the parking lot, Mikie punched the air and yelled "Attica! Attica! Attica!" We collapsed in helpless laughter, draped over the hood of the rental car.

It was Mikie who coined our favourite phrase, "This is not my life. This is somebody else's life." We said it every weekend after our late-morning debrief, during which we consumed greasy hangover breakfasts in a hotel at Jarvis and Gerrard, sometimes immediately after I had seen an off-the-books customer up the street and was feeling generous enough to cover the cheque. We always filled out the customer comment card because they sent you free meal vouchers by mail. No wonder the place went out of business. It was a big chain, but incredibly, I have forgotten the name and can find no evidence that it ever existed. Our routine was to eat, drink bottomless cups of watery coffee and then stroll over to the Eaton Centre to shop with money we didn't have. I worked so hard. Wasn't I entitled to bacon, eggs and new threads every week?

I told myself my heart wasn't in what I was doing and that I was just doing research for my tell-all book. This was not my life, as Mikie always said, it was somebody else's. But when it came down to actually writing about it, I couldn't. My first novel queries, to Knopf and McLelland Stewart (go big or go home, right?) came back with personal letters suggesting I write a memoir, advice I scoffed at despite the astronomical odds against hearing back from such publishers. I figured I simply wasn't interesting enough on my own. It was the stories I heard about the pigs and perverts, the custies so addicted to porn their bosses took their internet privileges away, the girls who were there against their better judgment, that were really interesting. It had to be fiction to tell the truth.

Having lost plenty of jewelry in massage parlours, I couldn't resist addressing the issue of men removing their wedding rings before a session—as if we even cared. In one unfinished novel, whose protagonist is a schizophrenic jewelry store owner doing a banging trade in stolen gold and flashy talismans, I made myself the subject of sick, unrequited love for a change if only because it was beyond tiresome wishing for a desirable man during the day and servicing undesirable ones at night. An excerpt was published online in a New York magazine maybe a decade ago, but who can even find the URL anymore let alone my three-tone 10 karat gold hoops?

Toronto has a wealth of massage parlours, and I seemed determined to try them all like the temporary receptionist I had once been or the creative for hire I would later become. Sticking close to home to avoid prohibitive cab fares and the predatory cabbies who worked in the middle of the night, I applied to one on Yonge Street just north of College. The blinking neon signs advertised TANS and NAILS, but we girls were the only ones taking tans and doing our nails. The place was fully outfitted with expensive creams, products and manicure equipment even though no one was trained to use any of it. There was a domination room in the back from which the occasional scream issued. I became friends with a dominatrix named Holly whose claim to fame was a Molson's beer ad before she had sunk to her current level: partying all night and then trying, on no sleep, to be a good mother.

"Wonderland was brutal," she moaned. "I kind of laid on a rock all day."

After a night with her, coked up out of our minds from dusk till well after dawn, I couldn't believe she had found the strength to even leave her apartment in the sun and heat. I wasn't yet a parent.

At Lucien's, I discovered Ecstasy and let a cross-dresser thread my eyebrows while she waited to get spanked. A wall of plate glass windows overlooked Yonge Street, and Lucien was always hissing at us to "Get back, get back!" so no one at street level would see us standing around in our sexy outfits. This wasn't Amsterdam, after all, but Toronto, where selling sexual favours on an in-call basis was still against the law. We were right out in the open, a heat score.

In one of my short stories, I cast Fatemah as a pimp. She had what it took to inspire that kind of devotion: charisma, magnetism, the ability to make you feel like you were the only one in the universe no matter what you thought of yourself. A female pimp—why not? It just made sense. Although it seemed the cops who were forever raiding massage parlours wanted to prove that some of us, especially the Chinese girls, were there against their will, I never saw any Black guys with pencil mustaches and colourful suits lurking around the spa, canes at the ready to smack ladies into the waiting pimpmobile. No underage girl ever emerged tearfully from her room, make-up smeared, hair tangled and bruises visible. No one had the dead eyes of a heroin addict, no skinny teenager looked at her feet while the boss counted her money and ragefully found it short. But then, it would never have been that obvious, would it? This wasn't the movies.

The one real pimp (as opposed to exploitative boyfriend) I met in massage instantly separated herself from the rest of us. She was too pretty and too polished to belong and had no interest in trying. Girls whispered that *her* pimp—get this, a Black man who walked with a cane after being shot—sent high-roller customers in to see her for full service. It was true that she did have a lot of people asking specifically for her, but that could have been because her golden-haired Amazonian beauty practically guaranteed she would take all the business. After a while she told me she was only there to recruit other girls for her pimp boyfriend.

"But you're a girl yourself. How can you do that to another girl?" I was bold enough to ask as we sat on the cracked, oily surface of a massage bed.

Amber explained that she was performing a valuable service, that without people like her, these girls would be on the streets.

"We take care of them," she told me. "We give them a place to stay and keep them off drugs."

It sounded horrible, unfathomable. I had my own place to stay and no intention of keeping off drugs; those were the only consolations this existence offered. Hadn't I escaped a life of dependence and servitude? I would never go back to it. And, although I didn't have a formalized five-year plan, I did have the ill-defined goal of pressing on and somehow making it work for me. I would save enough for a down payment on a condo, pay off my credit cards, buy a mountain of coke and find some good people to use it with. Then I would get out of the business.

Hope is not a strategy, but this vision was convincing enough for a girl in my inner circle to insist that I get her a job. Her conservative sister, a manager at the call centre, would have killed me had she known, but Lakshmi had two small children and was sick of getting $11.25 an hour to take abuse from angry callers. So, despite my convictions, I became the worst type of pimp: the do-gooder kind who convinces herself she is only being helpful and who refuses any sort of incentive but freely shares the necessary information to drag another woman down with her.

At least I told her the unvarnished truth about what to expect. The picture I painted was dark, and I thought she would run for the hills as soon as she'd had a few unpleasant experiences because she seemed to be more aware of her intrinsic worth than I was. But instead of quitting in disgust, she worked six days a week trying to make enough quick cash to keep her car on the road and finally buy her kids the things they wanted. Her husband picked her up after every shift, and I was welcome to a ride home as long as I didn't discuss work. She didn't want him to know anything, and, as with all the married girls, I was curious as to how they controlled the ludicrous narrative that the job involved nothing untoward. Before we left each morning, she would lift her long, wavy brown hair up so I could wash her shoulders, back and the nape of her neck lest he catch any scent on her that shouldn't have been there. Beyond that, I can't imagine what she told him or why he believed it.

The more coke I did and the more I drank and the more I worked so that I could keep doing coke and drinking, the less I wrote. My observations got dimmer. Who cared if that one brushed her bleached hair so furiously it had grown as ragged as an old flag? Or that the beautiful one whose legs were bowed from rickets was obviously being forced? No one would read it anyway. No one cared that by 3:00 a.m. on a Monday we were fantasizing that the industrial-sized box of laundry soap was filled with cocaine and we were billionaires striding through the parlour half-dressed with ferocious smiles. When I did write, it was all made-up characters who were composites of the real thing. I spent a year researching Cockney slang so I could create Felicia, a hardened street girl from somewhere near London who had fled an abusive relationship and found herself in a massage parlour for the first time. This dedication to authenticity still floors me: What nineteen-year-old spends a year doing anything? *Carpe diem* became *tempus fugit*. There was no limit to how far and how fast I would try to escape my own voice which inhabited a body I hated and a mind I feared I was losing.

There's nothing like researching common Cockney expressions to waste time becoming someone else.

Every spa inevitably got busted; before the legalization of prostitution in Canada, most of them had been under police investigation for years, and my charges and tickets slowly mounted up. So much for becoming a lawyer to free my father. I pushed crumpled American bills obtained from wilted American tourists under the bank teller's wicket, converting them into money orders to keep his canteen filled instead.

There was one last house on the block. I had been warned that the place was terrible but lucrative; I had nothing to lose. It was downtown, right beside a busy Thai restaurant, and the smell was all noodles all the time. Lakshmi, my former co-worker—neither of us, by this time, could keep up the pretense of a day job—came with me. This spa didn't even have a name; it was simply distinguished by a round, red, dragon-emblazoned sign that dangled one floor above street level. To gain entry, customers pressed a buzzer and waited for James, the ever-smiling owner, or one of the half-dozen girls that were working at any given time, to buzz them in. It was the busiest place I would ever work in, and the filthiest. All the girls did eighty-dollar bodyslides, but, as ever, some were rumoured to do more than just grease themselves up with baby oil and grind naked over their client's body.

James was a wonderful boss, a kind of cross between Uncle Roger and Mr. Rogers. He would watch *Jeopardy* with us, asking me to correct his English and cheering me on when I got the right answers. He showed me a photo album with pictures of his doll-like wife dressed in red on their wedding day. He brought fresh oranges for Buddha's shrine and let me, a non-Chinese, light the incense sometimes, to offer prayers for prosperity. He was shocked that I had never been to a casino and offered to take me sometime to bring him newcomer's luck. That was James' weakness and the reason his spa had gone to shit: pai gow. He spent entire days and nights gambling, coming back haggard and uncharacteristically snappish, but his tired-puppy eyes made him eminently forgivable. As the one man I met who wasn't trying to sleep with me, I wouldn't have minded sleeping with him. But it was rumoured that he was a complete pervert in bed and only liked blondes.

I'd long since stopped drinking my way through every shift. Now I saved that till I got home. The next workday, I would nurse my hangovers with a jumbo latte and wait for the night to end so I could score some blow with one of the girls. I spent a lot of time in the laundry room because I loved doing the wash. There were certain smells, or ideas of smells, I could not get off my hands other than with harsh, grainy laundry soap; I became a veritable Lady Macbeth while my fellow cokehead thought I was crazy for enjoying chores. She flung bundles of dirty sheets at me, watching with distaste as I plunged my hands into the corrosive mix of bleach and detergent. At this spa, we knew our party plans wouldn't come to fruition until at least 4 a.m. unless James was in a good mood and let us go early.

As that first summer lingered on, we had no air conditioning and our second-floor waiting room was choked with fumes from the softening tar roof above. There was only one electric fan, under which the receptionist sat like a little prince eating walnut pastries and leafing through the Korean paper while we lay draped over the furniture like limp rags. Nights we weren't busy, I would drag a plastic chair to the one place on the roof where a slice of sky could be seen overhead between all the buildings. Sometimes that sky-sliver was completely black, sometimes midnight blue, sometimes gold or green if one of the buildings had a neon sign on. I never saw any stars. I imagined myself seated in one of the airplanes that passed by far above me, escaping, free. Then we'd get a flood of rowdy boys in from the Brass Rail and I'd go back inside to the stink of perfume, sweat, takeout, cigarettes and the ubiquitous baby oil. Sometimes I walked home, my head throbbing with the night's revenge fantasies, re-hashing what I should have said, done, charged …

My first birthday there, Lakshmi got me a gold ring, a change purse filled with little trinkets and bought Indian takeout from one of the best restaurants on Bloor. We dragged naan through rich oils and she let out a mighty belch.

"Oh, look, customers. It's about time."

I was too full and hoped I wouldn't be chosen. Our door swung open and two tall men in overalls peeked in. I stacked the food containers while everyone sat up a little straighter and smiled. The tall men didn't smile back. Instead, they announced themselves as police officers. I lied point blank and said it was my first day working. I hadn't a clue what went on behind closed doors and promised never to return. I enviously eyed Veronica, who managed to cry real tears, her cute Slavic face wrinkling like a used tissue. In exchange for this maudlin display, we all received two yellow tickets and a notice to appear before a judge in a month's time.

We stood around outside when it was over. I hadn't made a dollar, and the vindaloo churned uneasily in my stomach. One of the girls shoved her tickets in her purse without even reading them.

"I have a ton of these," she said confidently. "You just pay the fine; it's the cost of doing business."

Our second tickets where white in colour: Fail to comply. Found-in [when sworn not to be]. Inmate, common bawdy house.

One of the officers pulled on plastic gloves.

"Now, I'm gonna stick my hand in here," he said, gesturing at the couch. "Am I gonna find anything? Is there anything I should be worried about?"

I stared at him, not comprehending.

"Any sharps?"

I shook my head.

"Hypes? Needles?"

I shook my head again. There would be nothing but filth under those couch cushions.

He started feeling around, tossing cushions which had seen thousands of meals, farts, ashes, and god knows what else onto the floor, which was even worse. When they left, brows were furrowed. There was much talk of getting body rubber licenses vs. what's the point of getting the stupid license when we worked at an unlicensed spa anyway.

Time passed uneventfully after that, and to break the mundane flow of things, Jim decided to throw a party for Chinese New Year. He put me in charge of the booze, providing a laughably unreasonable fifty-dollar budget which I supplemented myself. I asked him if we would be closing up shop for the party.

"Open-closed," he replied, flipping his hand in a so-so gesture.

"What does that mean?"

"We keep door open. If client come, whoever want, take him."

"So you expect us to keep working during our own party?"

"Why not?" he grinned.

That Jim! I felt like the star of a daytime TV show. A valued member of an utterly dysfunctional but loving family, like those in the mean '90s sitcoms we watched all night long.

On party night, Jim and the receptionist came in carrying heaps of Styrofoam boxes. We cleared the table off and they set out a tremendous feast: all the dishes we'd never be served in Chinese restaurants because we didn't even know how to order them. Jim picked up a lobster tail with his chopsticks and slid it onto my plate.

"You like seafood, this is best," he said.

He would have laughed if he'd known how grateful I was to him at that moment; there was nothing I would not have done for him.

"Wait," Jim said, "before eat, Serena take picture."

I didn't know if I wanted hard evidence that I was in a rub & tug, but the smell of so much good food weakened me, so I put Jim's camera on a timer and posed with a few of the girls. Lakshmi was exuberant because it was the Year of the Rabbit, her year, and she was sure it would be lucky. It wasn't actually a bad year for me either.

The doorbell rang just as we were finishing up with dinner.

"They look Japanese," somebody remarked, squinting at the three men on the camera.

Jim looked at the receptionist, who reluctantly put down the water chestnuts he'd been scooping onto his plate and went to the front. There was a thump at the back door behind us. On the camera the three men stood back a little and leaned their heads together, looking up at us and talking.

"Ai-ya," Bonnie moaned, "more police."

Another thump on the other side of our room and someone sprang up to throw the deadbolt.

"Don't!" the girl everybody said was a crackhead shouted. "Now we're trapped in here!"

She ran out of the room. Jim was yelling in Mandarin in the hallway, telling everybody to be calm. A momentous thud came from the rooftop. If I'd been thinking, I would have scrubbed off my make-up, slipped my street clothes on over my dress and told the cops I was just there for an interview. But I was already a found-in. There was nowhere to go. I just stood in the hall as though I didn't give a shit, as the wood splintered around the deadbolt that Cindy and Bonnie were still bravely trying to hold closed. They were thrown back as two big plainclothes officers came crashing in. Bonnie fell into the coffee table hard, sending shrimp shells and dirty paper plates flying onto the floor.

We stood around as she hefted herself painfully to her feet. One of the cops punched a balloon out of his way and said, "Why would you girls do something stupid like that? Why didn't you just let us in?"

They had brought Asian cops with them this time to thwart the "We don't speak any English" act. One pulled Bonnie aside while the other interrogated Jim. Another stepped on a half-full box of fried rice, grimaced, and wiped the heel of his boot on the carpet. He plucked an orange from Buddha's shrine, looked at it thoughtfully, and tossed it up in the air, catching it with a meaty smack.

"Are you serving alcohol in here?" he asked.

"No, we were having a party," Cindy explained.

"Really? Sounds like fun! And here we are trying to save you from sexual exploitation. Let me see some ID."

They handcuffed us in the back, tight, amid the remnants of our extravagant celebratory meal and kept trying to get us to say our names. James remained silent. Cindy and Bonnie insisted that no one was in charge. We were just there for a party.

The legal process in Canada is nothing like that in the States where, according to the documentaries, innocent soccer moms get hooked on painkillers after surviving car crashes and wind up getting eight-year sentences for possession of three Oxys while their husbands divorce them and take the children. This is Canada. They are nice to people here, especially if you are troubled but functional. A kind, government-appointed free lawyer by the name of Lorne Farovitch, who I could barely drag myself in to see in his Cabbagetown office, somehow made it through the hundreds of heavily redacted pages that comprised the investigative force behind our charges and got them, if not entirely dropped, then at least resolved, consolidated, set aside. Lorne has helped a lot of people I know; he must have had big galoshes to wade through this type of soup. I will always be grateful to him for choosing to help us rather than becoming, say, a $750-an-hour family lawyer playing a whole different game.

Once in the clear legally, I decided that those airplanes I used to stare at were nothing more than dots in the sky. I would never get a passport. I stopped jotting down notes and began to write myself entirely out of the story while another part of me—the part that saw life as something to be attacked with a dull knife—frantically kept building higher and higher, right on top of the debris.

In "my" room sporting my new glasses, 1984

At home after sixth grade graduation night

Visiting my father in prison, 1990

Professional photo shoot for a modelling scam, 1994

Unknown party with unremembered people just like every night, 1995

Visiting my father in prison again, 1997

An unforgettable Chinese New Year at the massage parlour

New Year's Eve dinner with my mother, 1999

My new American family at my father's funeral in Alabama, 2003

My happily ever after wedding day, 2010

CHAPTER 17

IN AND OUT

Becoming an escort removed any constraints, moral or otherwise, that might have still applied. There was no coming out of it; the only way through, I was sure, lay on the other side of going deeper in. I couldn't keep spending time in bullpens or wasting days in court or hiding out in spas wondering if my next custy was taking his own notes. A Polish girl who lived in my building and had a fondness for pierogies and crack got me an interview at one of the very middling agencies that would hire just about anyone. It was like temping in that you had to be ready to work within five minutes of clocking in, except Altitude Human Resources had never required me to be coiffed, body sprayed and ready to fuck. I climbed into the ho-mobile for three years until my cocaine addiction, which compelled me to work and made work possible, had progressed to the point that I could not find the hotel rooms I was being sent to because I hallucinated too much to read the numbers on the doors.

I think I understand better now why I was always unable to make the story mine when writing about these events. At work, it wasn't Nicole putting on an act; Serena did that while Nicole hung back, a detached observer. I was two steps removed from everything I did, and the only things that remained authentic were the friendships I made. Of course, they were probably shallow, opportunistic situations but that was no different from the call centre. They *seemed* pure, and that was all that mattered. Climbing into the car at 5:00 p.m. pick up and sharing beers and jokes and make-up tips started the shift on a high; being paired up for group calls meant safety and companionship; having someone wish me goodnight who actually knew what my night had entailed made me feel seen. Everything in between was an adrenaline junkie's dream. Those three years probably ruined my jangling nerves forever: days of tedium, hours of small talk, half-hours of mechanical performances, minutes of anxiety, seconds of outright fear. Months that became years of pretending to be someone I was not until I mostly succeeded.

Most people got messed up escorting if they weren't already. The most sinister of all, I thought, were those who acted perfectly normal, who said they'd be a tad late because their husband had a flat tire or their daughter had taken too long in the bath. Everyone lied. There were still girls who insisted they could be in and out of a one-hour call in seven minutes with huge tips and nothing soiled but their right hand. Now there was a new species just below management: the drivers. Most of them looked down on us even though we paid them, some in trade rather than cash. They were the lowest possible form of life, but they were a necessary evil for transport and supposed protection. It was a rare driver who actually waited for me or picked me up on time, let alone would be willing to break down a door if things got dicey.

The body count piles up quickly in the outcall business. Whether it's the King Eddie or a phone booth with a blanket and a pillow, after a while the crushing sameness becomes too much to handle or you get too messed up to do it anymore if, like me, you are doing it every day. Many girls paced themselves, Hobby Hos who climbed in the car only on weekends or when bills urgently needed paying. But I was a Career Ho who didn't fear burnout—I was in my early twenties for heaven's sake! Eventually, I gave up on the agency and went to the final level: putting my own ads in the paper and working from home, a path that is not without risk. Sometimes a regular would get angry when I didn't have time for him. Sometimes a guy would explain he had shaved all his body hair because he didn't want to leave any DNA behind. Sometimes a custy would show me woodcuts of White men enslaving Black women in a handmade book and ask if I wanted to do some role-play.

And occasionally, someone came along that I thought would rescue me and love me forever—a real-life *Pretty Woman* scenario. This is what happened with Tom when I was just about done. Even I could feel that I was dying, and despite everything I didn't want to die. I wanted love. With Tom, I came as close as I was likely to ever get, so close I had to write it down to prove to myself it had actually happened.

I recall standing in front of the residence where Tom had lived a million years ago while getting his degree in chemical engineering. It was being gutted and rebuilt bigger and better. There was a rental crisis; students lived in hotels all over the city while gleaming new steel and concrete structures took shape to house them.

Tom took my hand, bringing me back to reality as we walked across the trimmed lawns. The campus was sprawling, not contained by the city but spread through it, so that greenhouses and parks opened onto the busiest streets.

The sun pressed down and I had to pull my sweaty hand from his. We were on Madison Avenue, where the fraternity and sorority houses identified themselves by way of mystical Greek symbols that probably meant little to the girls in low-slung jeans who lined the steps, smoking and drinking Coke.

"Do you want to stop for a beer? Look, we could go there. Ein Stein, it means 'one stone' in German."

I followed his pointed finger to the tiny bar, whose scattering of outside tables were crowded with boisterous students. Everyone we saw seemed to be young and carefree, probably because it was The Annex on a weekday and everyone else had jobs. There was a Starbucks on one side of Ein Stein and a deli on the other. No privacy, and way too much light.

"Doesn't beer come in a stein? Maybe that's what it means." I shaded my eyes with my hand.

"Oh," he said admiringly, as though I had said something brilliant. "I never thought of that. Oh. Well, we've got lots of beer at home."

Home was a furnished suite of rooms that Tom's company rented for him. The kitchen cupboards were so full of empty, exotic bottles and cans that there was no room for dishes. We had sampled every imported beer available at the fancy new LCBO that had opened across the street before settling on good old Bud. Tom was an American citizen now, so it seemed appropriate.

I took a shower, noting that I was running out of the good stuff to wash with and that the maids hadn't left enough clean towels. They had probably been instructed to leave towels for one, although they could not have missed my bag of toiletries, my clothes spilling out of the closet, my shoes by the door and my underwear that sometimes got trapped between the mattress and the box spring.

I picked up a towel off the floor and tied it around my waist. It wasn't the maids' fault; Tom had spent too much time in hotel rooms of one kind or another, and he went through everything like Kleenex. There was a laundry room in the building, and I could do a few loads myself in the morning. There was plenty of time. We had been so excited when Tom's company agreed to move him out of the hotel and into this palace where we could cook in the fully-appointed kitchen and enjoy the panoramic city view from our twentieth-floor terrace. We talked about rooftop barbecues and trips to the pool and sauna.

I padded over to Tom, who was pressing the buttons on the remote, angling it this way and that.

"Did we kill the batteries?"

"Yeah, but who cares?"

He pulled me onto his lap and butted my chest with his head. Over his shoulder, the picture window was showing a stunning variation of colours as the sun began its slow descent over the heads of the office towers.

"Tom?" I said later, "Let's go out tonight."

He looked at me with large, downturned eyes. "I thought you made that chicken so we could eat in."

"I know, but—"

I stopped there because everything, from the towel slung around me to the chicken in the fridge, was on Tom's dime. If Tom wanted to stay in, well, fine! My mother's old admonitions not to look a gift horse in the mouth sealed my lips at once. I was already treading on thin ice with Tom. When I displeased him by sleeping in, not getting ready enough for him, whining about my problems or getting too high and accidentally setting a fire, I went into agonies of apology until it would happen all over again. I didn't understand why I couldn't behave better when everything depended on it.

Tom and I met through a companionship service that had sent me to his hotel room three months before. The hotel, located halfway between the airport and downtown, was a long, narrow building with four floors and a tiny antique elevator. My first concern that night had been how to get past the reception desk without arousing suspicion, as surely ladies with high-heeled boots, perfect make-up and floor-length black trench coats did not often call upon the good patrons of the hotel at two in the morning. With the reception desk just to the left of the front door, there was no way to be discreet about it. I strode past the staff to the little brass elevator as though I belonged. I was drunk and high, and my new driver, a huge Black man who used to be a bouncer until he'd gotten shot and had found Jesus (and wouldn't stop talking about it), had just woken me out of a sound sleep to tell me we had arrived at our destination.

I found the right room and was greeted by an average-looking man with sandy blonde hair, full cherub lips and blue eyes enlarged by wire-rimmed glasses. He was shorter than me, round-shouldered and had a hangdog look. Here my second concern came into play: the agency's instructions were that this man needed "compassion." I had never heard such a request before.

"What's wrong with him? Is he handicapped? Bipolar? Don't tell me he's crazy. Don't tell me his wife just died and he wants me to wear her clothes."

"I don't think it's anything like that," Laila assured me from her desk back at the office, her eye-rolling visible through the phone. "He's here from the States. His job sent him over here to do some research, and he just got a divorce, and he's lonely. He doesn't know anyone …"

It sounded like a bland country/western hit, but I could do that kind of compassion, especially for only one hour.

Standing in front of the future recipient of my sympathies for the first time, I could see that he really did look sad. I had already forgotten his name; not a very good start. I told him my pseudonym and he obligingly introduced himself. I then asked the next logical question.

"Do you have anything to drink?"

Tom only had tap water. I went to the bathroom and did a line of coke to perk myself up. When I came out he was rooting through his luggage. I figured he'd say he'd never done anything like this before and then I could say something to put him at ease while laughing hysterically inside my head. But he said nothing, only dug through his clothes, laying them out on his bed as though he had just checked in. I would have to be proactive. Making sure he was watching, I put my leg up on the table and slowly unzipped one boot. The angle of my leg allowed him to see all the way up to my panties.

Tilting his head to the side, Tom said, "I'd really rather talk first."

Only the coke, still singing in my blood, prevented me from showing irritation. Resigned, I took off the other boot and crossed my legs demurely. He wouldn't let me smoke in the room. I looked at my watch without bothering to hide the gesture.

I asked him for the money, and he padded across the rust-coloured carpet in his sock feet to root around in a shoulder bag. He was like a little animal that grubbed in the dirt, a round chipmunk who had hidden its treasures and now spent all its time looking for them. He could dig to China for all I cared, as long as he had the money. The clock was ticking, and it ticked for him. I stared at the unadorned wall and let my thoughts fly until he handed me a messy mix of Canadian and US funds.

"I'm from Texas, I just got in tonight," he spread out his hands. "But I went to school here, so I'm really Canadian."

His voice was smooth and cultured, with just the hint of a Southern accent. I wanted to ask if he was part of the often-discussed "brain drain," but it wouldn't do to appear too intelligent until I knew what he wanted. If I turned him off, it wasn't too late for him to take his money back and send me away. As it happened, Tom did want intelligent. I had only a minimal knowledge of world politics but thought I faked it very well. We had a stimulating conversation fuelled by frequent trips to the bathroom where I snorted knowledge, charm and wit by the half-gram.

Finally I said, "I hate to say this, Tom, but your time's up."

He stood up from the bed in alarm. "But we didn't do anything!"

I shrugged prettily. I had an infinite universe of rebuttals to that, should he choose to engage me.

"Can't you stay for another hour? You're so beautiful, and I really want to kiss you."

His head was to one side again.

"I'm sorry, we don't kiss."

It was sometimes necessary for me to use the plural "we" when explaining personal rules of conduct. I didn't want to just tell him to fuck off. There was something actually sincere in the way he was looking at me.

"How much is another hour?" Tom asked.

I told him it was the same as the first hour, and he winced. I did not try to entice him; it was late, and my Jesus-loving driver probably wanted to get home to his prayers as much as I wanted to get home, put on my pajamas and have a couple of glasses of wine.

Tom foraged in his many bags and pockets again, and I almost felt sorry for him, but not quite. I would not be kissing him no matter how long I stayed. He handed me a wad of crumpled bills, which I counted and found a little short. I gave him the speech about tipping, courtesy and the huge agency fees, but he said, "I've just given you over $400, isn't that enough?"

We were at an impasse because I always needed more money. I was still sitting on the bed and he was standing very close to me, so that my eyes were inches from his slightly rounded stomach. His blonde hair and striped T-shirt made him look not so much like a chipmunk after all but an overgrown child who had not yet lost his baby fat.

"All right," I sighed, and he pushed me back on the bed suddenly.

All he wanted to do was kiss. After it became clear that he didn't want any form of sex, I broke down and allowed it because I was too tired to fight and I was getting let off relatively easily. I could always rinse my mouth out with the family-sized bottle of Listerine in the bathroom. Tom chewed on my mouth like a teenager and ran his hands greedily over my body. He didn't remove any of his clothes. I closed my eyes and pretended that Tom was someone I'd had a crush on for a long time and he had finally noticed me and asked me to the movies.

"Stay the night," Tom begged, as if I would even dream of staying with him for free.

Dawn would come in another hour and I had used the last of the coke, so I made a hasty exit before I could come down and reveal my Jekyll-and-Hyde personality. He insisted on walking me out.

"I'll call you again this week," Tom promised as I shut the door behind me and got a ten ready for the driver. I knew the odds of seeing Tom again were low, but the driver said if it was God's will, it would happen. I clarified that I didn't really give a shit, only I hated people who made phony promises.

Two days later Tom did call for me, and this time he had stocked his room with plenty of wine and beer. I stayed for two hours again, until my lips were chapped.

"Can I ask you a question?" he asked as I smoothed the sheets on the rumpled bed and straightened my clothes. The other bed was still covered with half-unpacked suitcases.

"Are you this affectionate with everyone?"

"Of course not," I said, and rattled off a few horror stories.

This seemed to satisfy him. He gave me his phone numbers, which of course I would never call but accepted out of politeness.

Tom was in town for as long as it took to negotiate a software contract on behalf of his company—an outfit so profitable that it didn't care how long Tom stayed, it would comp everything. That was the Texas way, Tom said. If you were strong, smart or ruthless, you could get anything you wanted. He lived in a five-thousand-square-foot home he had built for himself after separating from his big, blonde wife. The house had an in-ground pool, which was practically standard in Texas, and the garage housed a convertible and a BMW since they had agreed that his ex would take the Hummer.

I listened to him talk about these things and pictured myself sitting beside the turquoise pool on a lounge chair drinking tequila while Tom gnawed on some part of my body. I saw myself walking through the house, a grand structure with a nod to the adobe style, running my hand over modern blonde wood while Tom merged and acquired or whatever the hell he did all day.

We went on a date at a sports bar. It was raining hard, and I walked to the bar as bursts of lightning struck all around. My sandaled feet were soaked and covered with bits of leaves pelted down by the rain. This was not an agency set-up, it was real life, and I wondered what the hell I thought I was doing. I was early and decided to pretend that Tom wasn't coming so I might as well enjoy myself. I dropped an E, drank two pints of beer and accepted an NTN Playmaker from the waitress to pass the time. While frantically keying an answer into a screen I could not focus on properly, I felt a soft kiss on my cheek. I surprised myself by leaning into it as though it was very natural. Tom and I continued the game together. He was old enough to remember pop culture fads I hadn't heard of, and I was drunk enough to play boldly and recklessly. We eventually lost and cabbed it back to the hotel where I immediately threw up in the toilet. Tom laughed and put a cold cloth over my forehead. In the morning he said, "I think you threw up because you were nervous."

I spat my toothpaste into the sink. "I threw up because I was drunk and coming down off E."

"Sure," he said.

After that, we began to enjoy each other's company. Tom had a limitless expense account, knowledge of the city and time on his hands. We went to clubs, bars, dinners, plays, a harbour cruise. It was so romantic. I seemed to satisfy Tom in almost every way except for the crucial way for which I had originally been engaged. This meant that after hours of rocking the bed in drunken tantric torture where I would moan and cry out—more from the bruising than anything else—eventually he would sigh, roll off me and get ready for work. He probably thought that if anyone could rock his world, it would be a professional like me. But no matter how creative and motivated and determined I was, nothing worked. I was like a plumber who couldn't stop the leak, a tech who couldn't find the spyware, a receptionist with chronic laryngitis.

"Why are you divorcing your wife?" I asked him, though I knew he didn't want to discuss it.

We were now living together almost full-time in his furnished suite, though I still paid rent on my apartment. I had made a huge salad with avocados for dinner, in deference to the heat, which was not nearly as bad as Texas but still very intense. The laundry was done and the bathroom was clean, and I was free to relax and drink for the rest of the night.

"She's really mean," he said, looking through his thick eyelashes at the can from which he took a long, cool sip of Bud.

"Is that all?" I could not imagine leaving someone for something as subjective as meanness.

"Well, she kept threatening to leave me, so I said fine, here's your divorce. We were only married for two years," he added sadly, "and it was the biggest mistake of my life. I can't believe I was capable of such a huge failure."

I caressed his back, smooth and sleek as a child's. He was so pleasant when we weren't in bed.

I said, "You can't hold yourself responsible for failing to see that she was a bitch."

"Please don't make fun of my errors in judgment," Tom said. "You know what? Let's take a bath together."

We squeezed into the tub amid mounds of snowy bubbles. The water was deliciously hot and fragrant. It would be a nice way to let go, to sink under the clouds of bubbles and just ... drift.

"Well? Aren't you going to say anything?" Tom, behind and underneath me in the tub, squeezed my breast.

"To what?"

"Didn't you see what I wrote?"

"What are you talking about?"

Tom turned my head with his wet hands so I was staring at the wall to the side of the tub.

"I don't see anything, where?"

"Right there! I wrote it in soap, but the steam is getting to it."

I squinted at the tiles, which were dripping with condensation. It looked like someone might have written "I love you" and then a serial killer had stabbed the words until they bled into everything else.

"I don't see anything," I lied, wanting him to say it.

"For heaven's sake!" Tom said. "Forget it."

I missed more and more work, calling in sick in a desperate bid to build something lasting with Tom before he went away again. I wouldn't be the big-haired, false-breasted Texan bitch but a delightfully devoted, respectful companion. I was getting used to waking up at one in the afternoon and making a fresh pot of coffee in "our" kitchen knowing that Tom was out there somewhere thinking of me. It was nice to cross the street and shop for lingerie I felt sure would have some positive effect on Tom, then come home and leave a nice tip for the maids, who had followed instructions and left extra towels. I smoked cigarettes on the balcony, looking down at the rat race below which I no longer had to be part of because Tom would take care of me.

Needless to say, Tom found any mention of my work disturbing. Out of courtesy, I never left for work from his suite but went to a bar for my pick up because it was awkward to kiss him goodbye when he knew I was on my way to entertain other men. I began to seriously consider quitting altogether, something Tom had never asked me to do; but perhaps he was testing me, waiting to see whether I would make a sacrifice for him. For us.

I decided to surprise him with the news that I was leaving the agency just to see how he would take it. I had slept at my own apartment the night before so I could clean out the fridge and make sure the place was still standing. When I got to Tom's, not only was he not there, his shaving kit was gone and so were some of his clothes. I sat on the living room couch and tried to massage some memory into my temples: Had he told me he was going somewhere? I had a hangover and couldn't remember. He had just kissed me goodbye the night before like nothing was the matter.

I began to panic, pacing and smoking. He was seeing other girls. It was all over. He had used me and that was that. I would never take a siesta in the sun beside his pool—

The phone rang and I snatched it up. It was Tom, calling from Vancouver. Did I want him to bring me back anything?

Of course, I must have forgotten. He had to travel on business all the time. I would try harder to remember and to understand the demands of his work. In fact, I would try harder in general, all around. He was close to reaching a satisfactory contract, and when that happened he would be gone for good. There would be only memories of me to accompany him. Although I hadn't officially quit the agency yet, I went to a normal job interview to prove I could work at a normal job, but the Valium I'd taken for my nerves backfired and caused me to fall asleep during the group orientation.

As Tom grew more distant and preoccupied with contract preparations, typing reports and participating in conference calls late into the evening, I spent more time watching TV alone in the bedroom, half-longing for him to come to bed.

Tom told me I could visit him in Texas as soon as he could make the arrangements. I had known the day was coming, but it was so difficult to turn in my key, to be banished to the confines of my own small maidless apartment with its view of the asphalt roof of the building next to it. I had to go back to work again.

He called me from the airport and we made small talk because I knew if I said the wrong thing, it could shatter our connection. I thought about how different it would be when Tom finalized the arrangements and I was actually settled in, carefully furnishing his huge, empty house and hiring hardworking Mexican illegals to maintain it. I would make myself indispensable to him.

A week went by without another call from Tom, and I bitterly skipped grief and went straight to business. I had to put my own ads in the paper to make up for those months of barely working. Over the next month Tom called now and then just to see how I was doing and to tell me the divorce proceedings were dragging on longer than he had thought. He said I couldn't visit him yet, but he would send me a plane ticket soon.

I had done three exhausting calls one evening when one of my regulars called and asked to see me. He was British and liked games. He instructed me to put on stockings, a garter belt, my black trench coat and a pair of dark glasses. When I arrived at his hotel room the door would be ajar and all the lights off. I was to grope my way to the bathroom, where I would turn on the light, leaving the door open a hair, and slowly undress so he could peep at me through the crack. Then I was to chase him around the suite in nothing but my stilettos while he hid from me like James Bond.

I hung up the phone and began to cut cocaine into enough lines to keep me going, and then I realized that my fishnet stockings were in the wash and I didn't have another pair. Or did I? The phone rang and I stopped in the middle of the room, paralyzed at the centre of a triangle: the phone, the coke and the lingerie drawer. I was unable to make a decision for several more rings.

It was Tom, calling from Frankfurt. I made a point of telling him I was on my way out to work. I knew it would infuriate him that he was no longer more important than work. He told me he hoped I would enjoy myself.

"That's hardly fair," I said through a mouth that was going numb. I had a cocaine-smile plastered on my face. "Do I blame you for going to board meetings? It's my job, it's how we met."

He asked me whether I preferred cocaine to sex, and I could have been mean and said, "Well, are we talking about sex with you or sex with someone who's good at it?" But that wouldn't have changed my answer anyway.

Tom sounded shocked. "But you love sex!" he exclaimed.

I did another line. They obviously weren't big enough if I could still feel angry.

"Why all the questions? It's the same story over and over with you. You know it's just a job for me. It doesn't bother me that I don't know what you're up to every minute. Why are you so obsessed with what I do?"

"Because what *I* do doesn't involve sex with strange men."

Maybe it should. "Oh, come on, Tom," I said, pulling the phone onto the floor so I could stretch the cord farther and look for another pair of stockings. I found nude and white and even a hideous shade of taupe, but not black.

"Have you ever had sex for drugs?"

Another cheap shot. What was sex for drugs? I'd made bargains for sex involving both money and drugs. Did that count? What was the difference if I immediately spent the money I made from having sex, on drugs? Tom hadn't complained about my having sex with him even though he kept me drunk all the time. Wasn't that a form of sex for drugs? I pointed this out to him and got no answer.

Only the promise of goodwill contained in the fat white lines on the table prevented me from just hanging up the phone. Why was he being so hard on me? Weren't we friends? Weren't we more than that?

"There is a difference," he said finally. "If I found out that you were having sex for drugs, I'd never talk to you again."

"You've barely talked to me in the last few weeks. What do I care?"

I suddenly felt like I might collapse under the sheer weight of his betrayal and judgment. It was all lies and excuses; he was just trying to get rid of me. There was probably no divorce, maybe no house in the first place. I was an idiot.

"I can't care about people I can't help," Tom continued coldly.

"What? You mean if I ever became a drug addict, you'd abandon me just when I needed your help the most? You wouldn't even deign to talk to me? But I was good enough to fuck, though." I was crying and swallowing a viscous mix of snot and cocaine. "I wouldn't even treat a dog that way. I'd never, ever leave you to die an alcoholic, which you probably will, by the way. Even if you were in the gutter, Tom," I choked on a fleck of mucous, "I would do what I could to get you some help."

Tom chuckled. "You're going to learn one of these days that no one can live with that degree of compassion in this world."

I hung up the phone very carefully. I was trembling all over and there was nothing to drink in the house. I had turned my cell phone off and was now a half hour late for my appointment with the Brit. I swept a bunch of sleazy outfits indiscriminately into a big plastic bag, did a last tremendous line of coke and splashed some cold water on my face. It didn't matter what Tom thought. When you came down to it, they were all just stupid tricks.

My failure to secure Tom's love taught me that, while normal people made transactions with each other to obtain outcomes, I would never be able to do this. I was no actor. I dropped the alias and was Nicole again, collapsed, defeated, with a hard shell concealing the mush inside.

Eventually a window of opportunity presented itself from a world I had nothing to do with: the court finally concluded my sentence for an eighteen-month-old massage charge and sent me to Streetlight, a week-long program dedicated to getting prostitutes off the street. Despite my indignation—I was not on the stroll; I still had a bachelor apartment, thank you very much—I attended the classes and admitted to a counsellor that I had a problem with alcohol and drugs. He recommended a twelve-step program, and eventually, out of exhaustion more than anything else, I started going to meetings.

I fully intended to continue running ads in the back of the *NOW Weekly* and collecting johns, but it didn't quite work out that way. My nerves had frayed to the point that I couldn't stand to be touched unless I was on something much stronger than church basement coffee. My sponsor, a former stripper, didn't insist on an immediate lifestyle change but instead let nature take its course: when a client had a cardiac event in my bed and was rushed to the hospital by paramedics who looked askance at my skimpy yellow teddy, I knew I had to get out. I couldn't stay clean until I quit working.

My sponsor did tell me that any line of work which raises dishonesty to an art form was probably counterproductive to my spiritual development, but I still balked at completely leaving the sex trade. If I could even limit my using, I would be able to make back the fortune I had spent twenty, fifty, a hundred dollars at a time.

"What do I have to show for it if I just walk away? How can it have all been for nothing?" I whined.

"You get to walk out of there alive, with all your teeth in your head. Even if that's all you have to show for it, you're golden."

I took the leap of faith, pulled my ads from the paper and spent my last thirty dollars on admittance to a twelve-step convention at the Primrose, a budget hotel across the street from my apartment—the same hotel in which I'd last seen the Brit.

CHAPTER 18

A LOVE STORY

My book *A Narcissist Walks into a Bar* discusses the other relationships I had in sobriety, all of which were birthed in, and inseparable from, the twelve-step fellowship I spent almost sixteen years in. But I must at least touch on my sober life here because it led to the marriage that broke my life and gave me a new one—the impetus for this book.

So many people come into the program visibly broken, with depression and anger writ large on their faces and in their posture. Newcomers often look irritated, annoyed, sullen and closed. Some, like me, are the complete opposite: outwardly gregarious, smiley and confident. This aspect of my personality was so entrenched that it didn't feel inauthentic, though I had a troubling inability to turn off the smile even when I wanted to. Nobody was forcing me to go to meetings; they were actually far better than my alternative life of loneliness, isolation and degradation. I was genuinely thrilled to be among caring people who seemed to have found a solution to their problems and could relate to my experiences but didn't want anything from me but a voluntary spare-change contribution to the 7th Tradition Basket. Why didn't everyone feel as grateful? Naïveté closed my eyes to any facts that didn't match my new narrative of success, happiness, faith and joy. I even started wearing my hair in pigtails.

I'd never been good at seeing, much less responding appropriately to, coming storms. The SWOT analysis, I thought, was something you performed on a corporate goal, not a life. With coke, prescience should be easy: Who doesn't know that drugs are bad, m'kay? Especially when they caused devastating consequences in your immediate family? The flags were so red they were practically on fire, yet when cocaine came into my life I walked right into the flames as if they weren't there, emerging just like the pretty Targaryen: naked and burnt, with several large and hungry dragons as companions. I leaped into the fellowship with a similar disregard for reality, immersing myself completely into a new way of life that worked, until it didn't.

When I came into recovery at twenty-three, people joked that they had found more rocks crawling the carpet than I had used in my entire life, but I knew that powder wasn't child's play compared to the hard stuff. Despite my age and relative newness to the drug game, I felt I belonged, and, although I didn't achieve sobriety right away, I was willing to at least try to do what I was told. By no means did I do all the suggested work, or do it perfectly, or most importantly, do it consistently, but I did it enough to change some basic things about myself and my outlook on life. I learned to serve strangers without expectation and show up for life despite a crushing fear of everything. I got very busy, which wasn't hard, because the fellowship presented endless opportunities for responsibility, friendship and attention from the opposite sex.

As taught, I tried to abandon my thoughts to some form of higher wisdom I could trust to manage my life better than I could. The literature said I didn't have to make decisions solely with my flawed mind; I could turn to the divine for the right answers. As long as I was basically trying to be good and do the next right thing, it would all work out. This was incredibly attractive to me and, of course, supported by factual evidence in the form of legal jobs that paid my rent and bills, a phone that started ringing again and a sense of purpose I had never enjoyed before. Finally, someone had come along and given me a benign authority to submit to! The obsession to drink and use left me as I followed a basic moral code (Selling your body is bad, m'kay?) upon which anyone could build a life.

The cracks in the foundation of that life were a source of shame and distress. We were supposed to strive for progress, not perfection, but my imperfections were glaring and embarrassing. The extreme anxiety that overtook me when speaking or even reading in front of a group was self-centred fear and a lack of humility. I remained insecure and fawning, a people-pleaser in a fellowship where, despite all the voluntary service that takes place, the label is a slur. I was possessive and demanding; when friendships collapsed under the weight of my unmet expectations, I bailed, losing sleep over whether I'd had the right to be angry or, in a program whose members strive for ego death, any rights at all.

I also found myself desperate to be in a relationship. I had never been around so many men in the real world—they outnumbered women by at least four to one in my particular fellowship. I assumed they were all there to get rid of addiction, as I was, and I could definitely help them with that (wink, wink). Our shared experiences of drug use and chaos gave us an automatic bond in which all common sense was thrown out alongside the judgments we worked so hard to suppress. At meetings, you could get to know people's most intimate and traumatic details without having to do anything other than nod supportively and stack your folding chair after the hour was up. The public disclosure of private information tended to breed a sense of shared values and goals which, upon closer scrutiny, would have been revealed to be false: How could I manufacture compatibility with someone when I didn't even know who I was? Best not to look too closely, and fabricate when needed.

I was only nine months sober, not the recommended year, when I began to date a revolving-door addict who had robbed at least twelve banks in Ontario before he was caught. His grainy image had been captured by one of the security cameras and immortalized on page 1 of *The Toronto Sun* with the caption "The Polite Bank Robber." His co-workers at the treatment centre where he worked as a drug counsellor saw the paper in the breakroom and joked that the culprit looked like him; he laughed right along with them, a man incapable of showing unease. The takedown came not long after.

His kind and non-threatening notes, written in a distinctly feminine longhand, courteously acknowledged the tellers' fears but assured them they would not be hurt as long as they simply put the money in the bag. My polite boyfriend had been using the bank robbery proceeds—unlike my father, he actually got money when he robbed a bank—to buy everything from heroin to crack to ugly statement furniture. He had taken quite a lot of that cash to IKEA.

"Why furniture?" I asked him once when we were riding in the Batmobile, his new black Mazda 6.

"Well, if you're going to rob banks, you'd better have something to show for it," he replied sensibly.

I hated his monstrosity of a coffee table but understood the ideology. He had a surplus of funds and had frustrated police for a long time; he couldn't carry on letting hard-won profits go up in smoke. This being Canada, and Steve being Scottish, when he was finally apprehended—at a twelve-step recovery convention, no less, with stacks of the fellowship's printed T-shirts and other memorabilia for sale in the trunk of his car—he received two years less a day. A couple of friends packed up the contents of his apartment and put everything into storage while he did his brief Federal cakewalk. Naturally, he was assigned to bunk with the White Power people rather than the Natives or the type of ghetto mofos who were selling him the crack.

When my relationship with Bank Robber Joe imploded after four years of near-misses—near marriage, near home buying, near vacations all interrupted by his frequent relapses and my intolerance of his then-delinquent teenage daughter—I began to ask myself if what my friend Ana Maria had said about the man for me not being in Cocaine Anonymous could be true. It was a terrifying thought. I worked in a lesbian's home office and had no life outside of the fellowship. For a year I floundered in self-pity and, approaching my thirties, mounting despair: I was still pretty broke, pretty lonely and had pretty much no prospects. I wasn't willing to make the hypocritical move to a larger fellowship just to find love, nor would I pray selfishly for a mate. I threw myself even further into the program's spirituality, its service and its sponsorship, and decided to let God take care of the rest.

When I met Paul, he had just been through a break-up and seemed utterly indifferent to my existence until a mutual friend prodded him toward me. Paul had been married before, had committed fraud and theft, had smoked lots of crack. So far, so good! In the fellowship, the past was only useful for fostering mutual acceptance and providing contrast to the perfection of the present moment. He owned his own business and was independently housed. He had years of experience trying to recover and had achieved years of sobriety in the past when he lived in New York. When we started dating, he had over a year of sobriety, which maybe one in five hundred people walking through the fellowship doors attained. He did service, sponsored other men and attended meetings regularly.

Oh, I could go on, so I will! Four years older than me, he had no kids but, like me, he wanted a family. He was an intellectual, taller than me, easy on the eyes, and he didn't seem to mind my race, my sordid past or my glasses. In fact, he professed to have no such preferences at all, an incredible combination of serendipitous factors. Confirmation bias went into overdrive as I sought more evidence to confirm it was meant to be: The New York connection. The decent astrology. The love of fine dining and all things *Star Trek*. We talked on the phone every night and communicated via email several times a day. We ate out often, or he whipped up lamb-chops and roasted potatoes after we'd attended a fellowship event, tripped around the harbour on a boat cruise of the Toronto Islands or strolled the quaint, noisy shops of Kensington Market. If the synchronicities ended there, what did it matter? What else does a couple do other than eat and fuck and watch TV and go out to do interesting things?

We moved in together within a year and started building a home. I worked full-time managing a very successful real estate office at a time when it seemed the boom would never end, so we had two incomes, but I was unhappy with work; it ate into all aspects of my life far too much. How could I be the perfect housewife, the perfect girlfriend, the perfect sponsor and fellowship servant, and the perfect friend while commuting across town and slaving every day for salespeople who thought they sat at the right hand of God? I watched my bosses become very, very wealthy selling homes just like my mother's and held out hope for a profit-sharing scheme that would make it all worthwhile. Until the financial crisis of 2008. Our real estate and banking laws were very different, so the collapse merely caressed Canada, but it provided the management with an excuse to move offices and replace my assistant and I with an entirely new and far more malleable team.

I was devastated. It was Paul who encouraged me to freelance just like he did. He proposed to me the moment he returned from a tour of Europe a year later, and we were married a year after that. Within six months, I was walking a honeymoon beach in Acapulco with my son in my tummy.

Of course, we had our issues by then, none of which I put into a psychological framework because I knew nothing about it. Anyway, nobody is perfect, and if God brought you to it, He would bring you through it. Paul was depressed and I was anxious, and that was that. Friends in the fellowship marvelled at our inseparability, at the longevity of our relationship and its stability amid the surrounding chaos of musical partners, relapses, unexpected pregnancies: we had jobs, we paid our bills, we showed up, we were in love.

About nine months into our relationship, Paul abruptly stopped kissing me, which was remarkable because we used to kiss for hours, even in public. I assumed it was because all passion fades, though mine hadn't; it was troubling that he denied that anything was different. This became a pattern: nothing was wrong except in my imagination. Didn't I overreact to everything?

There had been that time we went to Niagara Falls and, in a bout of insecurity, I accused him of not being attracted to me anymore because he had gone from sex machine—angry on the rare occasions I was too tired or sick to be willing—to never initiating or wanting sex or intimacy at all. The jacuzzi room at the Hilton was intended to spark some desire, which it didn't; in fairness, I had brought a swimsuit that did my body no favours, but his rejection felt like the end of the world. I cried and somehow could not stop crying when it became apparent that no reassurance was forthcoming. I was horrified to find myself crying the entire day, which I hadn't done since childhood. Paul insisted I was just trying to get attention, a deeply unsettling thought because, like most of the things he accused me of, it could have been true if I wasn't as good of a person as I imagined myself to be.

Perhaps, after just a year or two of dating, I had already exhausted him, worn him down with my body issues and issues-issues to the point that he simply couldn't put his arms around me. The night ended with soggy ribs at the Fallsview Tony Roma's, my eyes swollen almost shut. We were both sorry.

The main ongoing conflict wasn't lack of physical intimacy; it was the fact that I didn't feel seen, heard or appreciated. That this was also the main ongoing conflict in my childhood was not apparent because, in my opinion, my mother and Paul could not have been more different. I knew I was too animated for an introverted man to bear, and his waning interest in conversation hadn't extended to outright calling me a motormouth—yet—so I learned to live with more silence. I pictured him as one of the stereotypical taciturn cigarette ad men who preferred the company of their friends to that of their women; hadn't this been the normal paradigm since at least the fifties when my mother had wanted nothing more than to serve her husband his five o'clock Scotch followed by his six o'clock dinner, no communication required? There were many such examples among my friends.

"Oh, that sounds exactly like my man," said Jenny.

"You're lucky he leaves you alone instead of pestering you for blow jobs," said Lauren.

For his part, Paul didn't like how I spoke to him. He felt pressured and harangued when I got angry at the lack of affection and conversation. He felt belittled when I pointed out, with a tongue that sharpened in proportion to his indifference, the messes I'd have to clean up, the chores that would fall to me because he hadn't done them, the little signs of neglect I couldn't help seeing everywhere.

"You're like my mother," he would say disgustedly. "I don't want a mother. I can't get turned on by my mother, and you're just like her."

I did not think I was anything like his mother, who was silent to the point of catatonia. But how could I fail to mother him when his depression and apathy and lethargy necessitated me taking charge, soothing, cheering, encouraging, performing? I tried to become more gentle, more tolerant and respectful, but on the flip side, I didn't see why I should suppress all criticism. All women nagged, didn't they? My friends often spoke of having to pick their battles with a man who, like all men, acted just like another child.

"I can never win an argument with you," he'd say, retreating to his studio.

I didn't even know we were playing.

I thought I knew all the signs of abuse and didn't really see any except, possibly, in myself. His unwillingness to change brought out the worst in me. I yelled and ranted that he didn't care even though I secretly appreciated that he didn't try to overtly control or restrict my activities; he merely, maddeningly, withdrew as if my presence were intolerable. He controlled the family finances but never my own. He made the major decisions for us (housing, cars, insurance, service providers, when to get pregnant), and I deferred to them because they usually worked out well. I was never told where not to go or what to wear; Paul was the opposite of jealous and did not inquire into my activities at all. He couldn't isolate me from my family because I had already done that. He didn't hit me, look at other women in front of me or call me names often. He didn't like my friends, but he didn't really like anyone, so I didn't take it personally.

Outwardly at least, I remained the dominant personality in the relationship, and in this we seemed to complement one another like two sides of the same coin. Shy and withdrawn in social situations, he said I made him more outgoing, though he still preferred to remain out of the spotlight when we entertained friends and guests. He tempered my fluctuating emotions with a Steady Eddie, solution-focused approach that kept me balanced. It is thanks to Paul that I learned to write everything down so I didn't double-book myself, to troubleshoot software, to stop overgiving to friends who didn't deserve it. He wasn't just talented, he was skilled in the ways of the world: in other words, he brought a lot to the table, and I would be an idiot to give that up under any circumstances.

What did I bring to the table besides a bossy and disrespectful attitude? I worked as many hours as he did, though I earned less and paid a much lower share of the expenses. I cooked, cleaned, did the laundry and the shopping, and cared for the pets, which felt very natural because I was not only strong in these areas where he was not, I actually derived a lot of satisfaction from them. I had been playing house since I was sixteen years old and was quite good at it. I understood transactions a lot better than I did emotions, so it was possible to settle into living like roommates even before the children came.

Harbour tours and Kensington Market were eventually edged out by the grind of serving in the fellowship, sponsoring people, attending meetings, seeing our own sponsors, working and social events that left us little time to consider the fact that we were often angry with each other. When simmering resentment erupted, Paul tried to convince me I had serious problems, at first with ultimatums ("You need anger management classes because I can't take it anymore"), then with insults ("You're such a cunt!") and then with personal attacks ("You don't have any friends. Your own mother wants nothing to do with you!"). I would like to think I gave as good as I got, but I'm sure my face betrayed me with shock and hurt before I pretended to be unmoved. Punishing him with silent treatment didn't work because he was better at it.

"This is all a power play," said our first therapist, incomprehensibly.

"I don't want power! I just want things to go back to how they used to be!"

"You have to wait until you are calm enough to speak to one another with respect," she continued. "This all feels very young, like it's coming from a very young place. But you're adults now."

"It's not possible. He doesn't care about me anymore."

"Well, you don't respect me! Look at how you talk to me."

The often-repeated accusation: I did not speak respectfully enough. I alternated between dismissing him as too sensitive and begging him to just tell me exactly what had bothered him so I could fix it—which he never did, preferring to reject the entirety of my tone, content and delivery. All I wanted was another chance to understand and work on it. Was I really that bad? Was I really the asshole in every conflict? I didn't know. There were no flies on my immaculate walls to report the truth. I reassured myself that it couldn't have been that bad for either of us or we would have just stopped trying, stopped smoothing it over, stopped forgetting.

Walking down the aisle was the happiest day of my life—happier, even, than when my children were born because, while they represented a vast unknown at which I was almost certain to fail, my wedding was just the opposite. It had taken a long time, but I was finally safe and secure, held by the man I loved. My rescue was complete.

CHAPTER 19

AND THEN THERE WERE FOUR

Children: First our son in 2011, then our daughter in 2012. Extravagant Christmases, catered birthdays, trips to theme parks and to the Caribbean. And, no matter how tired I was or how hard I had worked, the babies cried. No matter how sick I was, dinner had to be made. No matter how much I begged and raged, I was alone with the children while my husband shut himself in his studio. I adored the children and doted on them, but I felt the loss of my freedom like a physical wound. My life had changed dramatically, his not at all.

"What did you expect, a higher-maintenance type of cat?" my sponsor laughed.

She was a single mother and seemed to manage just fine. Naturally, babies change your life, so why did I balk at rising to the occasion?

I knew intellectually that, as the main breadwinner, my husband had to work and I had to raise the children, but the widening gulf these roles opened between us left me feeling profoundly lonely, used, even abandoned. It was a void that any parent, particularly one who craves parental love of their own deep-down, knows cannot and really should not be filled by children alone. My feelings were usually dismissed verbally ("It's just your hormones, you'll see things differently when your body goes back to normal"), but occasionally there were more concrete reminders of my place. After an argument, Paul once locked me out of the bedroom when I was very pregnant so that I had to sleep on the floor of what had once been my office but was now the nursery; there is nothing that will make you feel low like sleeping on a floor, but, of course, childhood had prepared me for this sort of thing. When he became enraged over some aspect of our perpetual argument—division of labour—and ripped up our happy family photographs, throwing them on me while I tried to sleep, I didn't even flinch.

As I did what all the other moms did—organized birthday parties, made arts and crafts, played games and served meals—people told me it would get easier, that I would settle into my new circumstances. But bitterness grew no matter how much Oprah and Deepak I listened to. Being self-employed and ineligible for mat leave, I had gone back to work part-time when the babies were just a couple of months old. I would come home from work and they were placed directly in my arms by the sitter. On my off days, I would unpack the diaper bag from some outing, and Paul would come out and remind me that he had to go back to work again after dinner. He often emailed me his schedule with the subject line: PUT THIS IN YOUR CALENDAR so there could be no doubt I had gotten the memo.

It is difficult to bargain when there is nothing you can say that won't become an argument. It did not stop me from trying.

"You're right here. Why can't you at least come downstairs to get the stroller when we come in?"

We were living in a second-floor walk-up with seventeen uninterrupted stairs (Paul counted them when our son, encased in a snowsuit, accidentally slid down from the top). I was pregnant again and had to lug the stroller and the baby separately up all the stairs.

"You wouldn't ask me for help if I worked in an office like everybody else," Paul replied. "You'd learn how to do things on your own."

His points, usually calmly delivered and grounded in logic (however cruel that logic might have been) silenced me, but only temporarily. I still thought the situation unfair and that I needed help. I wasn't the type to call my girlfriends—most of whom thought I was lucky to have any money or help at all—for practical support. I developed casual friendships with other moms who I visited for an endless cycle of play dates and adventures, but there was no emotional reliance; they had their own children, obviously, and their own problems.

More than once I thought about leaving.

"You're already a single mom," said my friend as we unstrapped the babies—mine and hers—from the back seat of her car and loaded them into my double stroller, which I pushed into the Family Court building downtown. "You can do this. It's a lot worse having another adult in the house who won't do anything than it is to know you're by yourself."

After a long wait while the children played with a very dirty abacus, a mediator informed me that married couples had to live separately for a full year before divorce proceedings could be initiated. Paul overheard me calling rental apartments and was incredulous, furious, even though he was the one who had left me alone for two days, disappeared to parts unknown, after an argument. My breast pump had broken and I had no money for a new one. He swooped in and fixed all the problems, reinforcing in my mind just how helpless I'd be trying to raise two babies born seventeen months apart, one of whom was not developing typically and needed numerous special programs and interventions.

If Paul noticed I was drowning, he did throw me the occasional life preserver: a limp rubber ring that proved insufficient to rescue me from what I saw as the impossible waves of motherhood. We made a schedule whereby he had to spend several hours with the children and me each day, which my Christian fundamentalist sponsor thought was highly unreasonable for a working man. Casual friends in the fellowship advised us to separate, admonished me to lower my expectations, recommended that we watch *The Secret* and manifest a happier relationship. A few friends from the fellowship threw an intervention: one purposely single mother (the father had offered to cohabitate but knowing from conception that he had seven other children, she refused), one happily-married woman who had built a questionable financial services empire on the principles of manifestation, and one wide-eyed newcomer who had never lived with a man, let alone kids, in her life.

"I really think you should just pray about it," said Megs, the single mother. "Yeah, it's hard at the beginning, but it's not about you anymore. It's about those kids."

Paul wasn't in the room. It was like a baby shower: all girls until the lucky guy comes in at the end to help carry out all the presents.

"Sorry, I have to take this," said Prisha, whose phone went off constantly: potential investors, newly minted salespeople and strategic allies, fellow addicts looking for a word of advice.

"I mean, you love each other, right?" asked Susan, the girl I was sponsoring. "I can help you! I can come once a week so you can have a date night and get some time to yourselves. Like after class or after work or something."

"Once a week is a lot," I said. "Don't you work till, like, eleven anyway?"

"Well, yeah, but we can work something out! I'm here for you."

"Me too," said Megs. "You should take the help where you can get it."

"Oh, for fuck's sake!" said Prisha to her cell phone. "Hello?" The rest of us sat in embarrassed silence until she wrapped up another call. "Okay, where were we? I will help too."

"No offense," I finally said. "The problem is *he* isn't helping me enough. I mean, it's amazing that you guys want to help, but that isn't really your job."

Megs looked away. I could see the gears turning in her head: I was so ungrateful. I had a man in the home who paid the bills; her baby daddy was starting businesses and losing them as fast as he could relapse. I didn't want to be beholden to her for help when she had a young child at home herself. Prisha was full of advice, but she was the busiest, most energetic person I knew. She had already said she only needed a couple of kid-free hours a week to recharge, and I didn't want to appear needy and selfish to someone who lived to serve God and her family. After babysitting a couple of times, Susan relapsed and became Bonnie to a sixty-year-old thief's Clyde, driving the getaway car while he stole luxury goods and sold them for crack. No longer a suitable childcare candidate.

I worried that the spectacle of this intervention only accomplished one thing: to make its way around our entire circle of friends as gossipy proof that there was trouble even in upper middle-class paradise. Maybe I should have had a larger gathering and served popcorn and fizzy water.

As the children got older, I dropped passive-aggressive hints that Paul should take more of an interest.

"It was all dads at the park today," I'd say.

"Well, I had them for six hours yesterday."

I would look at him in shock: How could he make such a patently false statement? If I deconstructed the timeline, showing receipts for the ball pit I'd taken them to or the sitter who had watched them while I was at work, he would talk louder and louder, not looking at me, not letting me speak, making me feel like a score-keeping shrew.

Aggressive-aggression was equally ineffective.

"I told you not to let them eat yogurt on the couch! Do you know how hard those covers are to wash?"

"If you don't like how I do something, Nicole, do it yourself. Be a mother!"

As the children grew, our arguments shrank: a few words before Paul would simply drive away and return close to dawn. He knew that the fierce love I felt for my children competed with an equally fierce guilt for finding motherhood so difficult, which meant I would never retaliate, let alone leave him for good. Not when I had been raised by a single mother and seriously doubted I had evolved much beyond her capabilities.

"I would change the locks and put his things outside if he left overnight," said the same therapist who told me he presented as "Teflon" because of his flat affect but believed he was really "trying to save the marriage." He reminded her of "a lost little boy."

"Where does he go? You should hire a private eye or track his mileage," my best friend insisted.

She didn't understand why I didn't really want to know. We never had sex anyway, so what did it matter, really, if he was doing it with someone else? I didn't trust him, but I needed him.

"He could have a whole other family across town," she said. "How would you know?"

But I didn't believe he was cheating. How could a man who had so little energy for the family that was right under his nose, and who seemed totally asexual, muster up the balls to start a whole other relationship? That left hookers, who were meaningless except for the money they'd consume, but as long as he could keep a roof over our heads it was none of my business if I had any hope of staying married. He claimed to have slept with hundreds of prostitutes as a teenager when he was making big money playing in his uncle's band, a tidbit that had seemed less like a red flag and more like charming proof of reformation by God and the fellowship.

Paul insisted that his late-night excursions were harmless efforts to blow off steam by driving around aimlessly, sleeping in his car or going to jazz bars alone—an almost deliberate poke, as I knew his snobbery around live music would never allow him to listen to the old jazz standards the Toronto hacks played. He said he was going to meetings or seeing his friends. One night I took a knife to the air mattress he kept in his studio so he'd have to come into our bedroom and confront me when he arrived home in the middle of the night. He simply got in bed like nothing had happened, waiting me out until suppressed rage and the demands of another morning drove me from the room.

"Flip the script. Leave him alone with them for a change," advised a bold girlfriend who didn't take shit.

But I wanted a happy life *with* him, not running away. Besides the obvious dereliction of duty if I just up and left, it would give weight to the instability he'd always hinted at. Anyway, he couldn't manage the kids on his own, and I knew the punishment would be swift when I did return. I couldn't even get my nails done without being told how lucky I was because other mothers did not enjoy the perks I did.

I did leave once, in the same way his mother would when he was a child. She would say she couldn't take it anymore (I never found out exactly what "it" was) and go sit in the mall all day, returning home as if nothing had happened. It got to the point where her husband and children—Paul and his brother—would roll their eyes when she threatened to leave and ask her to bring home a bucket of chicken for dinner. My own exit was far more dramatic: He had followed me from room to room through the apartment one day, telling me I was crazy. I smashed a huge vase in the corner of the bathroom he had backed me into, creating a force field of broken glass he could not cross, then fled crying into the street. I rode the subways and walked around all day, crying in the street and worrying whether the kids had eaten and played, returning that evening in bedraggled shame.

A shrug, a slammed door. I bit back so many words it's a miracle I didn't choke to death on my own bile. Occasionally, I'd scream so loud my voice would actually crack, leaving me unable to say anything at all. The effect was very similar to that of my childhood outbursts: net zero. That is the optimistic view. The real effect was that I made myself wrong even when I was right, slammed by guilt and shame (the kids could hear), terror that I was not only an asshole but insane (who screams like a maniac like that?), and feelings of defeat and stupidity (he is smirking at you. Way to prove you are a monster).

After five or six years I began to work more and take on fewer of the childcare responsibilities. I was a non-driver, perfectly content to take public transit; Paul resented being forced to do all the driving, but he worked from home, so I started making him drive the kids to birthday parties and swimming lessons instead of taking them on the train myself, as I had when they were little. They were independent, strong children who played with each other and didn't require much companionship at these events, only a driver and a witness, so it seemed fair. This gave me more time to work on my soap-making business, a side gig I had started in 2017 when a close friendship ended, suddenly freeing up time and energy to pursue dreams I didn't even know I had.

The business, a hedge against the increasing insecurity of my college job, required me to wear a lot of hats. Paul did not approve because the effort was not commensurate to the return. I was just as exhausted as I had been when the kids were toddlers, and there was, relatively speaking, little to show for it. He often said he earned more in a day than I did in a week, so logically, his time was more valuable and my efforts vain and futile at best. I refused to give up. As my work demands increased, he took over the dental and vision appointments, as well as the daily school drop-offs and pick ups. I knew it was an atypical arrangement and worried that the other parents probably thought I was sleeping in while my husband did the heavy lifting.

The world is like that—we only know what we can see. We do not always consider the possibility that the mom has woken, fed, dressed and kissed the kids, packed their lunches and is probably doing the dishes while her partner drops them off in front of the school. Despite the poor optics, I never dreamt that my absence from the public-facing aspects of their lives was laying the groundwork for my own life to be ripped from its moorings.

CHAPTER 20

THE PENDULUM

It had been nearly a decade since I'd last spoken to my mother, so I had successfully detached from her. But that was easy; she never called or otherwise attempted contact. Her silence was as complete as her authority had been. How different it is with a husband you share a home and children with!

Professor Sam Vaknin, who is referenced later in this book, lists the most often-cited reasons that people stay in toxic relationships. It is a list that makes me feel slightly less crazy because, apparently, I'm not alone.

1. Sunk cost average: time and energy already invested. Throwing good time after bad; the human tendency to stick it out rather than cutting losses
2. Money, financial security
3. The misperception, generated either by oneself or by the partner or both, that you will never survive outside of the relationship
4. Pity: the rather grandiose belief that it is your partner who is incapable of surviving without *you*
5. Shared memories: the accumulation of mutual experiences has made the other person integral to your life and identity

6. Shared children: low on the list, but still a reason to stay. Contrary to the evidence, exposing them to toxicity is seen as preferable to splitting up the family

Vaknin, an expert in psychology, also discusses the social pressures to remain married that are found in every culture, not just repressive cultures where divorced women suffer under extreme stigma. In my case, I knew that while my unhappiness should come as no surprise to my friends, my broader network was watching my highlight reel on social media, replete with grinning vacation pics, steak dinners and anniversary posts avowing "There's no one I'd rather be with than you." If they thought it odd that Paul's page was utterly bereft of posts about me, they didn't say. I feared most people would either think me phony for hiding the truth or blame me for destroying my household, a social media backlash I had seen occur when a woman finally called out abuse or something happened to her.

Obviously, I hid the bad times well. No one said, "Nicole, you have been talking about this shit for years. You don't love him. You love steak and beaches. There is a difference." I shouldn't have needed to be told, and I probably would not have listened.

Conversations of the "If you hate me so much, why are you with me?" variety always ended in stalemate. Paul had been married before, so I figured he didn't want another failure under his belt, and at forty, neither did I. So, as I researched housing prices and investments for a shared future that remained stubbornly pixelated, I simultaneously researched rents, never believing I would actually need the information. People said I could do anything I put my mind to, that I was a warrior, a supermom. They didn't know I didn't believe them.

Having slipped into toxicity for so many years, it was only a matter of time until I graduated to external poison. In January of 2017, just one month shy of my sixteen-year sobriety date, I had a glass of wine at a fancy spa.

We had completely left the fellowship about nine months earlier. Paul hadn't been enthusiastic about it for a long time, and I finally agreed. What did we have in common anymore with the newcomers who were trying to tell us how to live more spiritually while their kids had been seized by the Crown and they were sleeping with every other newcomer who walked in the door? The constant drama that used to be entertaining when we were carefree singles seemed childish now that we had to hire a babysitter just to be able to race to the meeting on time and race back home.

I maintained friendships with the people I'd known for years but resented the real work that came with the fellowship because I hadn't adhered to the program's fundamentals for a long time. It was plain that, if I ever had, I was no longer practicing the principles in all my affairs. I was known to speak bluntly, to be arrogant and unforgiving rather than kind and loving. I couldn't stand the lack of commitment from members who didn't have anything close to my responsibilities. I couldn't stand my own hypocrisy either.

We didn't leave the program so we could drink or get high again, but once I started pondering the question of whether I was even really an addict anymore, it was only a matter of time. It had been eighteen years since I had used cocaine, and I was a different person then. Who was to say that if I had a social drink I would end up in the gutter again? The answer was: everyone; so, I didn't tell anyone. The first drink I had was not social but savoured alone and guiltily, with a kind of sneaky exhilaration that nothing terrible happened. I didn't confess to Paul until the following month, when my sobriety date came and went without remark; I couldn't believe how angry he was. I tried to flip it around: If we were no longer in the fellowship, what did it matter? It was an immature rationale, and I knew it.

"I would have had a drink with my friends all these years. I never had a drinking problem! I said no for you. Now you're sneaking around drinking?"

Paul was disgusted. He hated drunkenness more than anything. So harmless pot, always obtainable and now legal, made an appearance in our home. The gloves were off: I drank, he smoked, and rarely did the two intersect. I tried smoking so we could have something to share, but like the cigarettes I'd gone back to after nine years, any substance-induced bond was temporary, especially since a few tokes rendered me comatose. I could drink him under the table without appearing buzzed, but it drove us even further apart. Instead of giving up drinking as a failed experiment, I escalated, experimenting with kratom, an herbal opiate; with synthetic amphetamines that kept me slim and sleepless, and gave me the energy of three normal people; with benzos that levelled me off. He bought shatter, resins and oils—THC in its purest form—and spent more time sleeping than ever.

I cannot claim innocence and ignorance of the effects of all this excess and attribute all the poisonous consequences to Paul; if it is true that he was secretly collecting evidence and formulating exit strategies, it is certainly no excuse for my decision to bring drugs into my home. Did I suppose the kids didn't notice anything amiss? Did I really think my loss of a small fortune on the stock market was a random event? Did I really believe he was okay with my low income when he complained of financial pressures all the time? When I chose surgery over diet and exercise to improve my body shape, should I really have interpreted his refusal to pick me up from the clinic and the weeks of silence that followed as a sign that things were going to be just fine? Blindness isn't blindness when it is willful and deliberate.

In early summer of 2018, I accidentally became pregnant during one of our mutually unsatisfying biannual thrashings on the mattress in his studio, and the gauntlet landed.

"If you keep it, I'm divorcing you. And you know I mean that."

I knew he meant that. But I was opposed to abortion now that there was absolutely no excuse for it; I was married with children already, not a lost teen. I knew it would mean quitting drinking, having to raise a baby with a partner who didn't want one, and coping with the increased risk of autism that comes when one child in the family is already diagnosed, as was the case with our son. The fact that my doctor hadn't told me my high blood pressure medication caused fetal heart defects was another nail in the miniature coffin Paul was building with some surprising help from my therapist, who had become *our* therapist when I had asked her to help us broker a separation. Paul had won her over. She was quite adamant that, given all the instability, I should abort to save the marriage.

Paul took our son to visit his brother in New York that September and still I hadn't made a decision. I was selling soap at a massive outdoor market for three days with the help of an intern, who watched my daughter while I vomited behind my tent in the broiling sun. Bank Robber Steve came into town from Windsor to take her to the Toronto Island for a day, as he was in town for an atheist AA convention—don't ask—and the visit wasn't a good one. I was grumpy and exhausted; he said I wasn't grateful enough for his help. My co-workers and friends asked me what I was going to do. I waited for someone to come along and make the decision for me so I could have someone to blame.

The clinic was, of course, packed; several visits are necessary in Toronto to complete the process, only one of which we attended together. Many couples cuddled and comforted each other, but I couldn't bear to canoodle with someone who wanted to destroy the life we had created. As a lifelong pro-choicer, my rational perspective had suddenly abandoned me. I knew that Paul and the therapist were right; given the circumstances, and my unwillingness or inability to change them, it was the right thing to do. Still I felt as though I had no choice, a fallacy that had kept me stuck my entire life. I sat stiffly in the chair beside his and waited for my turn.

I'd had an abortion before, at seventeen, but this was somehow different. The physical pain was intense but didn't come close to touching the emotional pain, the self condemnation, the what-ifs. In the recovery room, the nurse joked with half a dozen girls as they got up from their recliners one by one to check out of the clinic. There were wry smiles as she told us all not to enjoy our new boobs too much; she delivered the post-op instructions with the practiced speed of a flight attendant telling passengers what to do when the oxygen masks dropped. I couldn't seem to get out of the chair. Mentally, it would take me three years to get out of the chair.

At home, Paul went straight back to the studio, and I began to drink and eat pills like there was no tomorrow. I met up with an old acquaintance from the fellowship, who has since had her children taken by the Crown, and she gave me a beautiful crystal pendant of memorial glass that she tied with pink ribbon, as I had believed that it was a girl.

I hung it in the window, where it fractured the light into rainbows that created a moving light show for my children when it swung from side to side.

A new phase of my life had begun, whether I wanted it to or not. I was still keeping the core balls in the air, but the lure of pills was becoming seductive enough to cause a few frightening episodes in a period of a few months: a slip and fall, passing out on the couch and not being able to get up, a Saturday where I'd slept in till 2 p.m., a mental health class at work where I'd cried and then fallen asleep at my desk. Paul did not ask me to get help or issue any ultimatums. He told me I made him sick, that I was a disgusting excuse for a human being. I already knew.

A few months after acquiring the habit, I obeyed the writing on the wall for once and quit the pills cold turkey, though not the nighttime drinking, and began writing in earnest. It was going well, so much better than expected that I sent a few pages to Paul and to his assistant, Peter, a scholarly type who lived up the street and came over to drink and smoke pot with us several nights a week once I'd put the kids to bed. I was hoping to show him that I had something viable here, something that could even sell. But one night, Paul made a point of coming out of the basement to talk to me about the book. To my surprise, he didn't want it written, even anonymously, even if no one read it, because he was in it.

"I don't understand. You're in it as the even-keeled parent. I mean, I'm literally putting a parenting lesson at the end of each chapter and showing how effective your techniques are. It's not like I paint myself as some kind of hero and you're the bad guy, it's pretty much the opposite."

He remained unfazed. "Even if you make it anonymous, people will read it and figure it out. You need to think about protecting your family."

"But this is my dream," I whined. "Everyone says I'm a warrior for doing all this shit that doesn't even matter to me. I'm tired of living down in the mud and never doing anything for myself!"

"A warrior." His eyes were inscrutable behind his glasses. "Why don't you try being a mother instead?"

To his face, I refused to back down—it was my story to tell—but internally I had already folded. How could he not want me to succeed? I had tried to support his creative ambitions. I helped with what I could, like his advertising and client communication; I contributed my Air Miles to his business trips to LA; for Christmas, I had bought him a new custom website and marketing plan from a digital content director at one of the largest banks in Canada. But instead of taking these thoughts to their logical conclusion, or any conclusion, or even asking myself how I felt about them and what that might mean, I chose to simply consider myself victimized and focus on something else.

My sins were mounting up, but I never realized how deeply Paul considered himself the saint in our relationship until the pandemic struck Toronto in March of 2020. The knowledge of what was really going on took a long time to sink in, and when it did, it was only because the whole structure fell apart so quickly that one day I just found myself staring at a pile of ruins and wondering why there was dust on my hands.

Management

Redevelopment often relies on strong coordination among many stakeholders. Successful development can accelerate when these stakeholders work together to assess and clean up the property and pursue common redevelopment goals.

-The United States Environmental Protection Agency, Office of Brownfields and Land Revitalization, June 2019

CHAPTER 21

TIDY UP, THE POLICE ARE COMING

By January of 2020, Paul stopped coming upstairs at night to sleep altogether, and I no longer knew what was in his head. Instead of asking him, I walked the usual line of my fault/his fault and assumed he'd eventually come to me with his grievances if he was serious about fixing things. I had bought a new king-sized bed so we could sleep on different schedules without disturbing one another, but it wasn't really about the bed; it had been a year since anything happened in it anyway. I knew I was letting him down: dinner was on the table by seven rather than six because I had taken another part-time job working for my union at the college, laundry was done every ten days not seven, and it took me forever to sort the kids' artwork that seemed to breed on the coffee table overnight.

We were also having ongoing problems with our landlords, a young couple who lived next door. Everything had been great; our children had played together, and they once showered at our house for a month when their pipes froze. Then I'd seen their tiny, timid three-year-old daughter with a shiner that could not be explained away by their usual excuse that she was clumsy. When her father, himself a victim of childhood violence, admitted he had hit her, I had staged an awkward intervention which accomplished only one thing: the complete isolation of their daughter behind their privacy fence where both her parents could often be heard screaming and swearing at her through an eight-foot cedar hedge.

Of course, Paul had told me to mind my own business, and I feared he was right. Surely they wouldn't renew our lease after this, but they did, year after year, until we locked in a four-year contract just as Toronto's already-overheated housing market was going nuclear. When we refused to move so they could sell the house or raise the rent, they began to wage a war of vehicular vandalism, frivolous police calls, nasty ultimatums and official tribunal proceedings, but they did not succeed in breaking our lease. Taking advantage of a legal loophole, they placed security cameras all around our house, which mostly captured the weeds growing to dangerous levels. Paul placed his own cameras above theirs in the hopes of capturing their nefarious acts. The threats and skirmishes had been going on for years, and Paul's protracted silence seemed to relieve some pressure—after all, there could be no shouting or half-hearted reconciliations if there was no conversation at all—even as it added to the constant anxiety I felt.

The bright spot on the horizon was our April vacation to the Dominican Republic for our son's ninth birthday. Trips were a contentious issue between us because, while I paid for them, Paul wanted to go to very fancy places I couldn't afford, like Italy. I had once again booked us on the budget side of the island where the sand isn't white; I didn't mind eating a lot of brown food for a week, and neither did the kids. But I feared that being cooped up together in a single, small hotel room was likely to be as awful as Cuba had been the previous year; whereas I floated in a tropical paradise of blue ocean water and pale, watered-down beer, Paul sulked and suffered without pot, the purchase of which was reputed to result in a ten-year prison sentence training roaches in the Cuban sun. So I bought an extra room for one of his clients, who in the past year had become a good friend and got on well with the children. I thought this way everyone would get some extra attention and freedom, and, realistically, how bad could fights get in front of a third party?

Alba and I discussed my failing marriage while she waited endlessly for Paul to finish her work. Soon, her smothering mother began to pressure her not to go on the trip while I pressured her to just go; why not live a little for yourself instead of in your mother's paranoid, repressive shadow? Oh, and the tickets were non-refundable. By February of 2020, I found out that Alba had been having secret conversations with my husband, telling him what I had told her and what he already must have known: that I thought he was a crappy husband, an indifferent father, and I was only there for the money.

Unbeknownst to me, there were a lot of conversations of a slightly different nature going on. Paul was messaging our friends and neighbours, laying the groundwork of a smear campaign that would paint me not only as a mentally unstable, dangerous drug addict and alcoholic, but as an abusive and neglectful mother. He did not mention, in his appeals to everyone we knew, that he didn't know his children's shoe sizes or what colours they liked or what their dreams were. He also neglected to say he had added drinking to chronic daily vaping and smoking of high-octane cannabis, which made him so silent as to be almost invisible. He told other parents that he was at his wits' end; would they help?

I am amazed at the dance he must have had to do, appealing to people he held in contempt, whose company he had often said he found torturous, to lay the groundwork for—what, exactly? I remain even more amazed that people I had known for years and thought of as friends never told me about these messages until the shit hit the fan months later. Then they preferred to remain neutral even as they, presumably, gossiped about it to no end. It shook me to my core that they thought I didn't deserve to know about such serious defamation, in the name of impartiality. He was not accusing me of frigidity or laziness but of child endangerment. I later talked to a couple who said they really didn't know what to believe because they knew us both. He was so calm and quiet, they said, that it was easier to believe hard drugs had gotten the better of me than that he was lying.

Our paralegal who had fought the landlords in court, a friend of many years, was one such person. She didn't know he had tried to stop me from hiring her because he disdained her intelligence. She had sat with him in meetings, talking about the freedom of God, and been to our house, eating the dinners I made while he remained mostly silent as always.

"I know you both." She was adamant. "I refuse to take sides."

I realized that the majority of people who claimed to know my husband had never had more than very superficial contact with him, whereas I played with their children, entertained them, bought gifts and kept up with play dates. Paranoia crept in: Had all the friendships I had invested in over the years been corrupted? Did I only imagine I was fun and likeable when in fact I was an object of ridicule? Was I really so bad that these accusations were believable?

Alba, I later found out, advised Paul to buy me flowers for Valentine's Day of 2020 as an act of reconciliation. So a dozen red roses showed up on my desk one day with a card that said "Let's talk" or something like that. I didn't know what to say. Our talks lasted about twenty seconds before he would storm out. So I put the roses on a shelf and did what he had so often said was the only thing I was good for: I picked up a mop and began cleaning the upstairs bathroom.

He came upstairs and asked me if I had seen the flowers. I said I had. I continued mopping. He tried to hug me and I remained limp.

"You can't just get me flowers and expect everything to be okay. We haven't talked in a month. You haven't come to bed for weeks."

He turned and went down the stairs. It was not dramatic. There were no tearful recriminations, no backhanded "I'm sorry, but I'm only doing what you do to me all the time" apologies. The love had simply dribbled away until there was nothing left. It was the first time I had rejected his advances in almost thirteen years together.

Codependent people are said to have great difficulty saying no, and once they finally do, it's not pretty; an over-correction takes place in which all the pent-up resentment, disappointment and anger over thwarted fantasies is released in a toxic storm razing everything in its path. Over time, I have become a no ninja, easily able to decline requests and offers, though I often feel guilty about it. I have experienced an interesting phenomenon from many different people when answering in the negative, including online customers: silence.

For example, after pleasantries have been exchanged:

Them: "Can you do same-day delivery to a remote rural address/ add a free bottle of champagne to my gift/reduce the price because I can't afford it?"

Me: "I'm so sorry, I can't do that. But I would be happy to offer you X instead."

Them: "..."

When only one answer—the affirmative one—will satisfy, there is no further discussion no matter how friendly the relationship has been before. There's no "Okay, well maybe next time" or "Thanks anyway." Just crickets.

This is what happened when I didn't return Paul's bathroom-door embrace. I didn't know about the narcissist's discard at the time, but I believe the defining moment Paul decided I was unsalvageable was when I moved those softening red roses off my desk. My favourite flowers are, and always have been, carnations.

In March of 2020, our city abruptly went on lockdown to stop the spread, flatten the curve or whatever else they were saying about the COVID-19 virus. But right before this happened, the elementary school teachers in Toronto had been going on rolling strikes. Before they could ever know they would be forced by civic duty to work around the clock and adapt curriculums to online learning models, they were already agitating through their powerful union for a better deal. It meant my children would be home for almost three weeks instead of the usual week-long spring break, during which they usually went to camp anyway.

I was working part-time in my own union office at the college, in a windowless basement across from the plumbing lab, when students began trickling in asking for masks and hand sanitizer. Of course, I thought it would blow over. I am not one to worry too much about enormous macro events; it's the little things, like people blocking the subway doors, that can ruin my mood, not the looming end of the world.

The government said the city would soon close. My children were used to outdoor activities rather than staying home; it helped keep things calm among siblings who were such polar opposites. They also attended after-school and summer break care right at their school, in the YMCA. I knew they didn't love it—they would rather veg in front of the TV—but it allowed me a proper workday, and we hit the weekends hard with birthday parties, fun farms, amusement parks and other day trips, so I tried not to feel too guilty about not keeping them at home. I couldn't understand how other parents didn't get bored staying inside building train tracks or doing puzzles all day; the only time I got down on the floor was to conquer dust, spills and clutter.

What I didn't want was to spend two weeks refereeing arguments and making endless rounds of snacks while trying to churn out content for real estate agents and purveyors of wine racking, updating my website and captioning financial news reports. So, I drew up a calendar for my children with March break-type activities I hoped would tire them out every other day so they would be content at home when I really had to get stuff done. This chart included things like horseback riding because I was nothing if not optimistic that the government couldn't possibly shut *everything* down.

First, I took my six-year-old daughter and one of the neighbourhood girls she played with almost every day, Dora, to the salon to get their first grown-up manicures and pedicures. Later that week, I took both children to a cavernous indoor playground that was eerily empty despite an army of teen employees who sanitized the ball pit with frightening frequency. Next, I took my daughter overnight to a hotel where we could just be girls, ordering takeout, making funny videos and doing nail art. My son never got his next turn before the city shut down completely; I told him I'd make it up to him with an extra-fun trip to the DR which, of course, never happened. Here is the interesting part: my husband catalogued these activities we had already done and presented them to the court as evidence of unfit parenting—child endangerment in a deadly pandemic—in a custody case that I didn't know was being prepared, on the heels of a separation I didn't realize had happened.

Now we were all stuck together in the house. March in Toronto is a month where if the temperature breaks freezing, it does so only tentatively. Daily outdoor exercise in the absence of the fairs and festivals we had depended on so heavily became less than pleasant. Outdoor dining, even in a parka, must consist of fast food that is tepid at best by the time you have shoved it down your throat. To say the children were bored, and that I feared their boredom, was an understatement. My daughter had wanted a hamster for a long time, but the pet stores were closed, so to help pass the long days, I surprised her with supplies before purchasing a pair of dwarf rabbits online. We had already been to the Humane Society in search of fluffy animals to keep the family cat company, but they had suspended adoptions due to COVID-19.

The man who showed up to deliver our bunnies spoke with a Vietnamese accent. He wore a mask, of course, and came into the living room to show the children how to handle the little furballs, a fact Paul could only have known via the security cameras that he was, unbeknownst to me, constantly monitoring. He detested the bunnies and would never look at them, let alone learn their names, but the fact that I had allowed an Asian stranger into the home during a global pandemic would appear on his emergency motion to remove me from the home for risking the well-being of our children.

Dora, my daughter's playmate, had been to China a month before for Chinese New Year, and though she had quarantined in both countries, though her mother was a nurse who wore full PPE just to walk down the street, she, too, was evidence. The landlords next door screamed at her family to get indoors when they saw them on the street, mysteriously leaving all the Caucasian joggers, bikers and strollers alone. But Paul went a step further: to flesh out his court filings, he included the video footage of the night I allowed Dora to play with the bunnies on the lawn with my daughter. Dora was masked and gloved, but although they did not touch, they weren't always six feet apart, which was in defiance of COVID-19 protocol.

This is where the story becomes difficult to tell because it is so fantastical that I can hardly believe it. When an unkind inner voice tells me to be ashamed of what happened, what I allowed to happen, and how I responded to what happened, I remind it that I have come a long way since those days of willful blindness. There is so much about that period that I still don't understand, but it could have been much worse.

We had learned from our experiences with the landlords that the concept of first mover advantage is very real—whoever lays a paper trail by calling the police, however frivolously, establishes a victim precedent. Paul took this lesson to heart and began to call the police, creating supporting documents to the legal motions I did not even know he was filing. The first time he called them, it started with me telling the kids they had to help me carry groceries. He told the three of us that they did not have to do as I said ever again because their mother was a drug addict and would not be around long. He ushered the children into the basement, which they did not protest because they had never had to help with errands before and were not exactly eager to begin.

"You want to see drugs?" I said.

I followed them all downstairs and grabbed his huge glass cannister of all things cannabis—pipes, vapes, bud, papers, oils, resin—and dropped it to the concrete floor where it smashed in a million little pieces. It was the second thing I had broken on purpose in our marriage, the vase in our apartment five years before being the first. He told the police I was violent and dangerous and demanded my arrest. I was crying and in shock, and the police left without saying who, if anybody, they believed. A few days passed in a numb fog. I did not realize that all accusations of violence have to be reported to the Children's Aid Society if children are present in the home.

"You need to take your children somewhere!" I fumed one morning in the studio entrance, looking through the pass-through at his computer monitor, which was paused on a Netflix cop show. The kids were getting ready for breakfast and asking me what we were going to do that day; my soap orders seemed to have multiplied overnight. "You're the one with the car and you don't do anything around here!"

I did not understand, at first, that he was calling the police until he put them on speaker.

"Yes, my wife has become violent again and is abusing our children."

What should I have done? Laugh, cry, scream, leave? None of these options seem viable when the police are on speakerphone on the other end. I went upstairs and washed my face and tried to arrange my hair so as to look less like a madwoman; without a job to report to, I didn't usually shower till I had gotten at least four or five hours of work and chores in.

"Tidy up, the police are coming," I told the children.

I would end up saying this seven more times.

CHAPTER 22

ON THE GASLIGHT EXPRESS

"**N**etflix isn't working," I said irritably to my daughter one afternoon.

Such a small thing, but with everything else that was going on, it seemed like the pinnacle of personal failure. I didn't want to banish the kids to a solipsistic world of individual devices, at least not all the time, so we had planned to find a movie to watch together. I was trying to keep things normal for them, but I was also terrified of losing their love amid the chaos. As I scrabbled in the drawer that held the ancient DVDs of their favourite movies—*Brave*, *Tangled*, *Polar Express*—the phone rang. It was my cell phone company informing me that my account had been suspended.

No signal, however piercing—the liquidation of the store card points I had been collecting for years, the sudden removal from every shared account and subscription, the notice from my bank that a credit increase had been requested by the supplementary cardholder—was able to penetrate the fog of my denial. Instead of fighting back effectively (cataloguing my own evidence, stashing money, laying plans, or even throwing myself down the stairs to fake bruises, as some people advised), I did nothing more constructive than fall apart. Interpretations and theories raced around my skull in an endless loop that could only be quieted with more alcohol as I tried to figure out why he wanted the children when I knew he didn't; why he pretended to be terrified of COVID-19 when I knew he wasn't; why he was pretending I couldn't function when I functioned every day.

"Just leave. We don't need you anymore," he'd sneer whenever I came close enough to hear. "Loser. Whore."

Children's Aid had mandated that he stay in the basement so as to not contribute to the toxic environment which they had found to be the only threat facing our children, but he walked through the house with his phone, recording my interactions with the children, recording pre-emptively so I didn't say anything to him. He'd pop upstairs to grab lunch and casually tell the children that since I was a drug addict, a whore soon to be dead, they'd better enjoy the day with me as it might be my last. My son would scream at him, my daughter would leave, and he would retreat to the basement. The kids duct taped his door shut one day and wrote LEAVE MAMA ALONE on the chalkboard wall behind it, which resulted in another call to the police for blocking a fire exit.

When the Children's Aid worker, dressed in mask, face shield and plastic overalls, came by to make sure we were abiding by the terms of our agreement—the one I felt I had no choice but to sign and hadn't even asked what would happen if I didn't—the children told her everything was fine. I had told them to tell her only the truth, always the truth, feeling certain the truth would come out, but they told her nothing.

"I have never seen such a complex agreement before," the worker told me.

Apparently, we were unique: there were no injunctions to get drug testing or treatment or attend parenting classes or find safer housing. Instead, everything revolved around social distancing from each other within our own home. Paul agreed to stay away from us except for two hours a day providing the children with outdoor exercise, while I was to make seven lunches and five dinners a week, put them to bed every night by 9 p.m., supervise all their toileting, wash the laundry every Thursday (and only Thursday), and presumably run my business and do everything I had done before without taking the children with me due to COVID-19. The judge signed off on this plan.

"It's my house," Paul fumed to the CAS investigator. "I can go wherever I want. She's the one who should have to leave."

"Daddy, stop," said my son, always quick to defend me.

"How am I supposed to take my packages to the post office without bringing the kids?" I asked. "If he was really worried about transmission, wouldn't he just drop them off himself so I don't come into contact with anyone on the TTC?"

"Yeah, I definitely will not be doing that," he said.

Anyone who has been admonished by a store clerk to adjust a slightly lopsided mask will understand the fear and paranoia that gripped Toronto harder and longer than just about any other city in North America. COVID-19 panic was, apparently, a valid reason for all sorts of things that were formerly unthinkable; by using the age-old principle that people see what they expect to see and exploiting the unprecedented global situation, Paul's strategy was astonishingly effective.

"You need to take this seriously," insisted my matronly Christian lawyer who had been provided to me free of charge by the government in response to the surge of domestic abuse during lockdown. "People are losing their children because of this. You can take them out, I'd say, max three times a week, but just on side streets, and only for an hour."

Within two months, my athletic, cheerful son—who had spent his ninth birthday crying while his dad made churros and flung the hot frying oil over a stack of my packing boxes, grinning because I had sworn not to film anything in the house as the children found it traumatic—put on twenty pounds, started painting his nails black, opened an online video account, and began filming gender-fluid videos several hours a day. Paul ignored my pleas to at least drive the children to a remote location so they could run around in a cornfield somewhere and have a picnic. My kids were both abandoned: I was in survival mode, so afraid I would lose them forever that the possibility of fun was squeezed entirely out of our lives.

"How am I supposed to buy groceries?" I asked my lawyer. "The line-ups mean I'm gone for over an hour, and I can't carry everything I have to buy."

ON THE GASLIGHT EXPRESS

"Hail a cab."

"Cabs are slower than TTC now. They have to wipe down the cars every time. It's expensive."

"Buy a cart."

"I already have a cart. It's not big enough. This is ridiculous, he has a new seven-seat SUV that never leaves the driveway."

"Buy a bigger cart."

My lawyer was implacable. I sent her at least twenty surreptitious audio and video clips of Paul verbally abusing me, and she said she could not open them, even though the few friends I still had left could watch them on any platform or device. She said it would only hurt me to show I had been recording in violation of the agreement, never mind that Paul laughed at the agreement and did what he wanted. Nothing mattered but being an exemplary mother and behaving beyond reproach. It didn't matter what anyone else was doing because they weren't under scrutiny from the law. I was the one whose character was under assault, and mothers are held to a much higher standard.

"Do what you are told," she said above all my weak, self-doubting protestations that I was already a good mother.

Paul had provided the court with a very good reason why I had suddenly snapped and surrounded my family with dangerous Asians and their deadly viruses: alcohol and drug use. Completely omitting his own drug consumption despite the cannabis that showed up in every urine test he took—voluntarily, since I hadn't requested that or anything else—he created the narrative that drugs had affected my judgement to the point that I was now risking his and the children's lives daily by exposing them to COVID-19.

I agreed to a new agreement, this one signed by the judge who wanted to monitor our performance in a legally-binding agreement since Paul's lawyer fretted that the Children's Aid had been "utterly useless" in removing me from my home. Pee in the cup, don't leave the house unless absolutely necessary, don't let the children see anyone, don't take them on the subway, don't talk back, don't raise your voice, don't take pictures, buy your groceries online, don't drink, get a new cell phone that you can be sure has no spyware, don't tell your children how you feel or talk to anyone on the phone where they can hear you or where he can record you. Turn the other cheek and keep turning it. If all those pirouettes make you dizzy, have a chat with God.

In a city like Toronto where social pressure rather than aggression tends to be what keeps everybody in line, people were terrified and very, very compliant. When they weren't, other people shouted at them, and the media shouted at everybody. As non-essential stores shut down and supply chains were interrupted, I had to go farther and farther afield for business supplies that couldn't be ordered online; people were suddenly buying my spa gift baskets like they were going out of style because no one could go to an actual spa or even a gift basket store. This would have been a very nice problem to have under any other circumstances, especially with the college closed; I needed the money.

Instead, life became a frantic, scrambling, repetitive hell: Rise at 5 a.m. Do the soap/product-making dishes. Do the food dishes from the studio kitchen that have been left, still spilling food, on your desk by the man who you believe is trying to drive you to suicide. Try not to trip over the overflowing recycling he will not take outside; remind yourself life is not the same, the gravy train is over, he does not take the garbage out anymore. Open tin to make coffee and discover typed note buried in the grounds: "Only with God's help can I be a better mother." Save note with all the rest even though there is absolutely no proof of where it came from; if you present it in court, you'll be accused of printing it yourself. Make products for two hours. Wake children, spend some time with them. Absent yourself while your murderous husband comes up to make breakfast and floods the sink by clogging the drain with balled-up tinfoil so the tiles buckle on the spot you have to stand in making products for the rest of the day. Clean the kitchen. Avoid your children's questions about the soaked, greasy rug because you aren't supposed to drag them into your adult problems. Field calls and emails from Americans frustrated by the delays; pretend it has more to do with Canada Post than it does with the fact that you are one person who is going insane, not a thriving company of cheerful artisans. Forward Paul's continuous written accusations of mental illness to the Children's Aid, adding denials and pleas for intervention, even though they will say they cannot take sides, open videos or indeed read emails at all. Clean bunny pee and provide fresh vegetables for the kids to litter train the bunnies. Inject diabetic cat with insulin. Take some synthetic uppers purchased from an online lab. Use energy surge to make two more batches of products and heat frozen pizzas. Rope kids into helping you with packaging. Go to post office to mail finished goods. Come home and order in because you have no time or space to cook. Open a bottle of wine. Repeat, repeat, repeat.

The first day I heard the washing machine running without having started a load, I thought that the machine, always in need of repairs, had somehow started itself. Paul doing his own laundry for the first time since long before we had even moved in together was more jolting than the fraudulent police calls. The one time I had removed his clothes from the machine saying I was done being his slave, he threw them back in and threatened to kick me out if I didn't complete the wash. His designer shirts had to be carefully smoothed and air-dried, and if cuffs were wrinkled, I heard about it.

"I could replace you with a maid, you know. Do your job, Nicole."

It had stung at the time, months before, but I never would have believed that I would be relegated to my own laundry room on Thursdays only. I couldn't fathom that my children's clothes would be pulled out of the dryer a few minutes into the cycle just out of spite and strewn on the floor so that I had to go back downstairs again and again to put them back in; that every time I went downstairs to add a load I would be filmed "entering the basement" and threatened; that when I tried bringing my daughter, his favourite child, down to help, rather than showing restraint, he would call us both losers. If my mother had been a squid on the second floor surrounded by a black cloud of her own ink, he was a pale, eyeless lizard guarding the basement, with an enormous, toothy mouth that devoured everything that strayed too close.

Drowning was proving to be a slower death than I had ever imagined. I did not know that internal processes of decompensation, switching to different personalities or self-states, acting out and self-trashing were all at play; I thought he was doing everything *to* me. But where a sensible person would have marshalled their resources, sought counselling for the stress, taken their damn anti-anxiety meds, I crumbled. I had been a consistent, loving and reliable mother for nine years, but suddenly I wasn't even able to act like a decent human being. When the lockdown closed the bars for good, I'd hit the illegal after-hours gambling den that had opened a few blocks away. I'd leave at 10 p.m. and wouldn't come back until 4 in the morning, having shoved whatever I could up my nose and down my throat that would make me feel good enough to face the exact day I would have coped with a lot better had I stayed in. I was usually the only woman at this little club, and the drug dealers, once they had determined that I wasn't a cop, were solicitous. Who was I, where had I come from, and would I be staying?

"You remind me of my mother," said one who was indeed young enough to be my son. "She was a soldier, like you. You're gonna get through this."

I stared at him, bemused. Was this how soldiers fought their battles?

My handful of departures and returns was captured on camera, as was every cigarette I went around the block to smoke in order to avoid the surveillance instead of just staying in the yard. It was like being Britney Spears without the looks, money or fame. I went to hotels twice to get away and do the freelance work I couldn't concentrate enough to do at home. Curated in the context of the pandemic, these movements painted a picture of a crazy, irresponsible, unfit mother, a reputation that seemed so inevitable there was no point doing anything different. In this warped reality where nothing made sense, I did exactly what Paul expected me to do: I went crazy and dismantled the shaky structure of my self so he didn't have to. I isolated myself because who would believe or understand his bizarre actions—or mine? During the first police visit, I'd had a taste of what the public would think of my story when I told an officer that I was being gaslighted. He said if I stopped lighting the gas I could avoid the problem.

I turned down freelance gigs, quit my position on the union's executive committee, quit clearing my piles of soaps and products and supplies off the dining table where I filled orders because, without access to the basement storage, I had nowhere to put them. I stared at the clutter in despair and made my kids eat at the coffee table for six months.

"This place is such a pigsty," he'd say, grinning, which in itself was terrifying in a man who so seldom smiled. "I bet you never thought you'd end up worse than your mother, did you? Look how you're trashing my house. You're disgusting."

Where was all my bravado now? I sobbed while he followed me through the house. I wrote the sender's address on gift baskets instead of the recipient's. I stopped renewing my prescription for high blood pressure medication. Instead of implementing daily body-breaks, vocabulary-building scavenger hunts and kid-friendly recipes we could make together as I once did even before the schools closed, I drag-and-dropped the at-home learning resources I received from their teachers straight into an email folder "for later" rather than even trying to educate my kids at home. The only thing I didn't do was leave. Or try to leave. Or think about leaving. I thought maybe he was having a nervous breakdown and it would all just magically go away, or that whoever was paying for his lawyer would stop, or that the children would speak up to the authorities, or that someone would come along to save me. I assiduously avoided any contact, even eye contact, with Paul, not from a place of stoicism but from a place of complete hopelessness.

"This is a game, Nicole," he said. "And you're not winning."

I began to consider suicide. The only thing that stopped me was the knowledge that however much I yelled at the kids' messes and bickering, however much I drank and worked, I wasn't a bad mother, whereas the man who had compared so favourably to my own father was, I now believed, a psychopath. I just couldn't prove it. The police were already showing signs of fatigue and irritation, taking the stance that I must be doing *something* for my husband to keep calling them. They told me to leave if it was so bad, which under the law is an act of voluntary child abandonment and would result in Paul getting de facto custody. Taking the kids with me, on the other hand, constituted kidnapping unless I took them to a battered women's shelter, which I was too bougie and scared to do.

"You need to just ignore him and keep your cool," one of the officers advised.

I didn't like her. She had made me put down the butter knife I was using to cut up strawberries for the kids' breakfast one morning.

"I do ignore him. I don't say a word to him."

My employee assistance program at the college, newly opened to part-time workers due to the unprecedented times, had assigned me three sessions with a counsellor who advised against this strategy, recommending instead that I practice a face in the mirror that was half-smiling and non-committal. The theory was that unless I acknowledged him, he might snap completely from being ignored; but I have always lacked that type of subtlety. You could, in fact, accuse me of bringing a sledgehammer to a knife fight and you would not be wrong. Yet I did nothing when he jumped out of the shrubs to startle me when I was smoking, told me through the rear camera speaker that I was going to die, or followed me around the yard in a sadistic game of musical chairs. He became agitated and jumpy in my presence, his face uncharacteristically contorted. My phone went missing several times, turning up hours later in places I had repeatedly searched.

On Mother's Day 2020, I came home after an outdoor lunch with the children—our first in weeks—to find dirty cat and bunny litter all over the front carpets and the front door blocked by the oversized garbage and recycling bins that had, for the better part of seven years, been stored out back of the house. Sitting atop all the boxes and cans in the bin was our silk-bound, dove-bedecked wedding guest book. Inside the house, grinding the spilled animal detritus into the Persian runner, were the boxes of soap-making supplies that had been delivered, so I could not open the door an inch. I reported this, but Paul, as usual, had been proactive, telling the Children's Aid that since he had to isolate in the basement, this had been no more than a gentle hint that I should take the waste to the curb.

That same evening, he sent an email to twenty-one people: our mutual friends, family, neighbours and a few of my customers. It was almost 9:00 p.m., and I was sitting in the car with an equally psychopathic, if less sophisticated, man I'd known twenty years earlier in the fellowship who had heard of my plight through the grapevine and was driving me to the post office daily in exchange for whatever it is that love-starved, worn-down and abjectly grateful women are willing to do in exchange for a little support. The email contained an attachment: an audio file he had secretly recorded and, with the same audio software that made shitty singers sound passable, had filtered and distorted my voice so I sounded like a monster when telling my son that I was disgusted with the mess he had made.

Subject line: No child should have this mother.

He had blocked the list, but an old frenemy who wanted to be seen jumping into the fray unblocked it. My immediate response, other than tears, was gratitude for her allowing me to see who was getting the smear; how quickly I forgot that my feeling in the friendship had often been that of walking through sunny woods to find myself suddenly in a pocket of quicksand. She was the type of person who, if you dared to suggest she looked nice, would interrogate you on whether that meant she hadn't looked nice before. In response to the email, she offered to take the children for a sleepover (during a global pandemic while I was under threat of losing them both for allowing one to play outside a few feet away from another girl) so we adults "could have a date night and work things out." She had never taken my children for more than two hours before, usually with heavy financial incentives.

As usual, my response was tone deaf. I replied to the email with a rambling, defensive explanation; he replied that it wasn't really my fault that I'd had a narcissistic mother who had turned me into a vicious abuser and a narcissist myself. Frenemy said she'd talk to him directly, as they had always had a great relationship—hadn't he said he loved her? (He actually couldn't stand her.) As the emails flew, more and more people—all from the fellowship—weighed in, offering variations on the same theme:

"Think of the children!"

"I will not get involved in a he said, she said drama."

"You are both sick. I used to fight with my ex in front of the children and it didn't stop until I realized that I was only hurting them."

"You admitted to addiction, Nicole."

Paul's former sponsor, to whom he had not admitted his current drug use in years (innocuous as it may seem to many, marijuana was considered as bad as crack in our abstinence-based fellowship), was particularly vitriolic, telling me to remove him from the mailing list and that he would, in the meantime, pray for the true victims: my children. We had seen this sponsor and his family several times a year, and our kids played together. I had recently congratulated him on his new job working as a drug counsellor and on the acceptance of his children's book by a New York publisher. He told me I would be better off relapsing than putting my children though this.

Now the Children's Aid asked me if I had a plan. I didn't even understand the question. Wasn't someone from their agency going to put a stop to this and tell the judge they had found no wrongdoing?

"We haven't found any wrongdoing on either of your parts," said the investigator. "I'm not supposed to say this to you, so this is off the record, but why do you want to stay? You need to have some kind of plan to get out of there, and right now you're not doing anything. The children can't stay in this toxic environment. This is going to be decided by the court unless you do something, and I don't want to see your home and your life get swept out from under you."

She advised me to look at furnished rentals, which had come down in price and were being offered on longer lease terms due to the COVID-19 restrictions on nightly rentals. I packed while an old lawyer friend shared strategies for the next conference call court date, the bedroom door tightly shut to muffle my voice; it felt like surveillance was everywhere. In phone court, I could not listen to one more minute of Paul's lawyer's indignant claims that only Dad could provide the specialized care our autistic son required, and that he had been doing all the cooking, cleaning and chores as well as continuous childcare while I disappeared into drug dens and bars. Sounding as though she were choking back tears, she said that it was unfortunate, but I should be restricted to supervised online video chats only as soon as His Honor kindly ruled that I be removed. I started speaking out of turn, saying that this was a systematic plan to destroy me. The judge quickly shut down my rant. My lawyer said it had worked against me, bolstering the hysterical Black woman narrative that my husband had been crafting.

"You have to be perfect and instead you showed a lack of self-control. If we'd been sitting in a physical courtroom," she chided, "I would have elbowed you hard enough to leave a bruise."

Paul had done that, too, but I was cursed with dark, thick skin that didn't bruise up so easily. This time I was the one to call the police, but because he was the breadwinner, I begged them not to do anything except tell him to obey the court order and stay in the basement. It wasn't hard to do; they were tired of our inconclusive domestic bullshit. Paul laughed at me triumphantly, so sure of himself that he began to shove me out of his way on the rare occasions that our paths crossed in the house. When he pushed our son (who always came to my defense) so hard he hit the opposite kitchen wall, I woke up, if only a little. We couldn't stay. I told myself I was no saint; on some karmic level I must fully deserve this because it was happening. There was no way to fight it, but I could give him what he wanted. I could leave. Just not without my children.

I agreed to lease an apartment and leave my home of almost seven years within thirty days. The judge stipulated that both parties must co-operate to make this the best possible outcome for the children, despite refusing to seek their opinion directly (that was the Children's Aid's job, one they apparently did without considering how hard children will fight to maintain even the worst status quo). He divided custody straight down the line, 50-50, saying I had done nothing to alienate my children. Paul was to assist me in finding a suitable home and facilitate the move, including financially.

"Does your client have sufficient resources to pay a deposit on a rental unit?" the judge asked my lawyer.

"Your Honor, if I may," cut in Paul's lawyer. "That is also under dispute."

He was now claiming I had stolen $70,000 from him over the years, and he wanted his share of this mythical treasure pile back. I did have a small retirement savings for myself that I'd liquidated to pay the moving costs, a modest college fund for each child and a bundle of stocks that volatile markets had rendered virtually worthless, but he had never contributed to these. Now they were in jeopardy while his own money was untraceable.

Needless to say, Paul did not help me pack, or move, or watch the children while I went to rental offices and got money orders and produced identification. He would not give me the children's passports required by my new building, a glorified housing project on the border of Toronto's most-maligned borough, or allow me to take the furniture I had bought over the years. On this issue I agreed out of the strangest of emotions: pity. The children would need beds to sleep in and tables to eat on and couches to sit on at what would soon become his house. I did not think he could or would manage this; as long as his music studio had the latest equipment, he didn't care a bit about the rest.

Helpfully, his lawyer demanded I make a spreadsheet detailing everything I would take with me, stating that it was all, in fact, Paul's, and that I would have to prove otherwise. I have never been a keeper of receipts, so when he disputed the only two items I wanted—the Persian runner and the storage unit containing the children's toys I had bought and an old friend had assembled while we were on vacation one year—I folded, though even I could see by then that I didn't legally have to. My new apartment wasn't big enough to accommodate all that anyway. I would sleep in the living room on the couch, and my son would sleep in a donated bed, which left only one bed to buy for my daughter. I didn't know Paul would replace most of the furniture just days after my departure, commissioning a home makeover with the help of the same service he began to hire maids from. He bought a piano to fill the space where my desk had been.

The race was on. I had to pack up seven years worth of possessions while still maintaining the household, looking after the children all day and running my business. A close friend's husband came once, masked and gloved, to help me package boxes of products for shipping, and Paul called the police, accusing us of smoking crack in the living room and telling our son that his beloved "Uncle" Tony—the first visitor to the home since before the pandemic—was a degenerate drug addict. He walked around filming us the entire time with such a strong expression of contempt on his normally blank features that Tony remarked that he had never seen a case of demonic possession until that day. Of course, Tony would not be back, and nor would anyone else, not during a lockdown where such meetings were, in any case, forbidden by law.

On moving day, June 15, 2020—just three months after their first visit—the police were once again in attendance, this time called to make sure I didn't steal anything from my own home. Paul did nothing at all while my friends packed my things into a fifteen-foot van. It took three hours, and the female officer who had insisted I put down my butter knife told us to hurry up.

"We can't stay here all day."

"But I wasn't the one who called you. Why don't you tell him that?"

She looked at me with annoyance. My phone had mysteriously gone missing when I'd gone to the convenience store to get snacks for everyone. Paul insisted that one of my "criminal" friends—friends, former students, and a couple I had met through an autism program years before—who were helping me move had stolen it. The student who had tried to invent the website that told you whether or not you were an asshole used his computer skills to track the phone via GPS, and it said the address showed that the phone was at Paul's assistant's house. The police refused to look there, saying they didn't want more drama. A good Samaritan teacher found it and returned it to me a week later, after I had missed my IKEA furniture delivery because there was no way to know when they were coming. The phone was useless anyway. It had been smashed with a blunt object and discarded six blocks from our home.

The court had granted me two extra days to retrieve the family pets and my business supplies, but Paul changed the locks as soon as the moving van drove away. When I showed up, he called the police, claiming I was trying to kidnap my children because they wanted to come with me to get the pets in place. Ultimately he agreed to sit in front of us for a few hours, staring at his phone while a girlfriend, her daughter, my kids and I struggled in the summer heat with huge boxes. Nothing felt complete; I kept thinking, *I have forgotten something, and I will never be able to set foot in here again.* I stared at the bits of paper and dust bunnies that had emerged from under the radiator in the frenzy of moving, and they seemed to confuse me.

Think, Nicole, think.

But I hadn't forgotten anything tangible. And anyway, there was no time to think. It was over. Everyone needed to be fed. Everyone was hot and exhausted. To my surprise, when the last of three trips' worth of haphazardly packed items had been piled in the car, he thanked my friend, standing in the side yard that had been churned to mud by the endless trips in and out of the house.

"Nicole can really use a friend right now. You're the only one standing by her."

There are a few photos of me standing in my shiny, bright new apartment once my kind friends have helped me get everything in the door. The light is behind me. I'm smiling, showing off, my arms flung wide as if to say, "All you see before you is mine." There are bloodstains on my white shirt because the rigors of moving had torn open a cut on my stomach, one I'd given myself a few days before to remind me how stupid, useless and disgusting I was for letting all of this happen.

CHAPTER 23

THE ECHO CHAMBER

I would love to say that the realities of suddenly living alone—the non-stop work of buying, unpacking, setting up furniture and rooms, and taking care of the kids all during the confusing but colourful iterations of lockdowns (we were alternately in red, white and grey zones, but radio personalities joked about slate and puce)—awakened me to a new life of bootstrapping success.

They did not.

The intensely busy weeks with children followed by the intensely busy weeks without them only drove me deeper into hashtag mental health crisis. I no longer heard my husband's voice hissing sinister threats or came home to acts of sabotage. Instead, I heard his voice in my head as I continuously replayed everything that had happened, leavening the actual events with crazy theories, self-judgments, *Dateline*-type re-enactments and revenge fantasies. Everything seemed nightmarishly difficult; as I accomplished the needed tasks, twenty more sprung up to replace them. Of course, this is just a fact of modern life, but it seemed especially oppressive under the weight of constant rumination and crushing loneliness.

The obvious solution? I'd start dating again! Of course! Reaffirm that I was desirable and valuable rather than the untouchable pariah I imagined myself, a Black woman over forty with two kids, no money or property, no job security, almost no formal education, and no prospects. I started trying to convert the man who had helped me with the packages into a boyfriend, an idea he had the temerity to laugh at to my face. He was sixteen years my senior and went very quickly from stern father figure to emotionally-distant booty call. I wasn't about to chase an old man. Why not a mob-connected drug dealer twelve years my junior or the guy who saw my open call on social media for day labour and came to help me put my daughter's bed together? Really, why not, though?

Far from restoring my sense of self-worth or making my life easier, indiscriminate dating brought me to my knees faster than any amount of solitary rescue fantasies would have. I was abandoning myself completely, getting into situations that were humiliating, degrading and downright dangerous. I seemed to be attracting—or attracted to—one lunatic after another, all of whom made me pay a steeper price for the scraps of affection they scattered than Paul ever had. I was going from the frying pan to the fire, as my mother would have said, and I didn't seem able to stop it. I had to learn what the hell was going on lest my romantic life stretch before me in an endless parade of interchangeable jerks who took not only time and energy but money as well. In a vicious twist of fate, I wasn't the prostitute anymore; I was paying for my own abuse. All other addictions aside, if I didn't face myself soon, I knew it was going to be the men that killed me. I had slid down the social hierarchy scale and acted as such.

In order to solve a problem, says the twelve-step literature, we at first must admit there is a problem. I could do that. But then, we have to identify the precise nature of the problem. The definition of the problem in *The Big Book* of Alcoholics Anonymous—Step One—constitutes more than half of the original text because it was so important to the founders that we understand what was wrong with us, and the fatal nature of the flaw, so we would be willing to go to any lengths for a solution. For someone with an obsessive nature to begin with, this made perfect sense. It's still the model for every solution-focused therapy program in the world. The only problem was, despite what people said, the twelve-step model was not designed to identify, let alone solve, problems other than alcoholism. No therapist or doctor had ever told me, to my satisfaction, what was really wrong with me or the other players in my life. *I have to be my own doctor*, I thought, *just like when the GP said my son would eventually talk but I knew something was wrong. The internet told me exactly what it was within about an hour, and I was able to get him the right help immediately. So now I can be my own psychologist. I have to diagnose the problem, define its parameters and devise a solution.*

The silence of the apartment started getting to me. I had never used music or TV as background noise, but in these desperate times, I streamed '90s alt rock playlists at full volume. Then I discovered YouTube. To say that I discovered YouTube at forty-two, in the year 2020, is pretty embarrassing, but there had never been a need for noise before, not when I'd grown up in silence and then given most of my waking hours to the sights and sounds of commuting, work and parenting. I didn't know anything about YouTube or what might be on there; I literally thought it was just music. My Christian lawyer had sent me a link to a YouTube video entitled something like "The Demonic Games of a Narcissist" without any sort of note or comment, and I couldn't figure out whether it was intended as a resource or a dig, so I forgot about it. Now, months later, I began listening to podcasts on YouTube about narcissism.

As with the platform itself, I was exceedingly late to the narcissism/cluster B party. I had only become aware of the clinical term in 2019 when my stock market losses had prompted me to rather narcissistically Google "How to get money out of a narcissist" on the crazy idea that maybe, after ten years of exile, my mother might be willing to spot me a few grand, thus satisfying the twin goals of making Paul happy again and buffering my investment failures. Everything I read on the topic—mostly on Quora and a few articles I could tell were shallow at best, the kind that are set up in slideshow format with dramatic pictures of beautiful couples enacting irate and despairing poses to punctuate every point—convinced me not to bother because narcissists were said to be cheap, remorseless and paranoid unless they were being adored.

When we were still talking, I had sent my husband some of the articles and perhaps introduced him to the concept too. In my article captions I pointed out that while he had some of the symptoms of grandiose narcissism (was there any other kind?), I had all of them, a fact he reiterated in that infamous Mother's Day email thread. The lack of empathy, which I conflated with a lack of compassion for others, bothered me in particular. I wept at sad movies and even sad commercials, and I had to restrain myself from leaping in to help anyone who even hinted at having a problem of any kind. I sent for-nothing gifts to my friends all the time when they seemed sad or stressed. But for the significant other in my life, or indeed anyone who seemed to hold all the power to hurt me, I felt little compassion.

Gods, Men and Monsters had figured prominently in a childhood full of books, so I understood the bare bones of the ancient myth, if not the current obsession: Narcissus had so fallen in love with himself that he wasted away staring at his own reflection in a pool of water, but not before cruelly rejecting the talkative but cursed nymph Echo, who had fallen in love with him, too, but could only repeat the last few words he said. I identified much more closely with Echo, what with all the unrequited love, although I had to admit to having considerable experience gazing into toilets during my youthful drinking days. But the current narrative seemed to be that narcissism was a disease of pathological selfishness that masked deep insecurity.

I didn't know, until YouTube enlightened me, that narcissists can be broadly classified into classic or grandiose forms and covert or vulnerable ones, the former trumpeting their greatness to the world while the latter feigned humility and suffered from an inferiority complex. There are cerebral narcissists who revere their own intellectual prowess, and somatic narcissists who find their superiority between the sheets. There are collapsed narcissists who, failing to obtain sufficient narcissistic supply—adulation and services from others—retreat into solipsism, and psychopathic narcissists who, with ruthlessness and contempt, wreak the maximum amount of havoc. But I wasn't ready for any of this insight before my marriage blew up. Why get technical and risk hitting a nerve when there were so many fun articles about which astrological signs were most likely to be narcissists (sorry Taurus) and what happens when two narcissists get together (expect fireworks!).

Conflicting theories about diagnosing the narcissist abounded: A narcissist will casually admit to being a narcissist if asked. A narcissist will never, ever admit to being a narcissist because they believe they are perfect. A narcissist doesn't know they are hurting you. They are well aware they're hurting you but they don't care. They could change if they wanted to, just like they do when someone is watching. They could not change; the pattern was set in infancy. Narcissists are born of abuse. Narcissists are made via spoiling. A narcissist will never, ever go to therapy. A narcissist will totally go to therapy but only to complain about how the whole world is wronging them.

It seemed clear that the fundamental state of a narcissist was emptiness, whether they overcompensated for it with the finest things and the grandest of dreams or skulked around blaming others for failing to recognize their genius. I could relate to both of these. This was terrifying because it meant I could be a narcissist. You didn't have to possess all the traits to qualify. The reasoning goes that if you walk around wondering if you are a narcissist, you probably aren't unless you just happen to be unusually self-aware, in which case maybe you are. But we used to say in the fellowship that normal people aren't concerned that they might be alcoholics; that the internal debate as to whether or not you were a "real" alcoholic and thus potentially eligible for any loopholes, was a spurious one because regular drinkers did not fearfully sign up for rehab after having wine with dinner. Was there really something there?

The desperate mission to confirm that I was not, in fact, the asshole, began with me in my apartment, alone, doing endless repetitive, manual tasks that left my mind free to listen to everything that had ever been said about narcissism and cluster B personality disorders in the past five years. The YouTube algorithm obliged, sending me hour upon hour of content that I tried to apply to my own situation. Not for a moment do I suggest that this was a particularly good idea, but it was certainly addictive and made me feel like I was doing something to make sense of my life in general and the past year in particular. Many of the speakers pointed out what should have been obvious by the number of views their videos garnered: that as the world itself grows more narcissistic, so does the fascination with it. We are driven by the idea that our suffering has to be labelled to be legitimate. We are compelled to see our stories corroborated by fellow survivors of narcissistic abuse. We want to make sure that we really *are* the victims.

The easiest way to figure out whether or not I was a narcissist was, at least at first, to compare myself to others. Of course, I am not qualified to make any kind of clinical diagnosis on myself or anyone else; any conclusions I reached are based only on my personal opinions, written in one of the millions of books that will be released this year. Everyone, even the people writing "Six Ways to Tell If Your Gardener Is a Narcissist" articles, warns against a layperson naming someone a narcissist. The more responsible experts caution that even experienced psychologists struggle with diagnosing such a complex disorder, while still others remind us that the best way to provoke a narcissistic tantrum, sound crazy in therapy or lose your job is to walk around dropping n-bombs. There is also the problem that everyone, to some degree, has narcissistic traits, many of which are encouraged and even rewarded by society. Even the most abject doormat or selfless volunteer has some level of self-interest at play, some voice that whispers vainglory in their ear.

I could live with the idea that I was sometimes, or even often, a pompous fool or a snide cynic. I just didn't want my behaviour to be so all-pervasive that I qualified for the dreaded diagnosis of narcissistic personality disorder. If I did, it would mean that what happened with Paul was my fault. It would mean I had used him, then tortured him so maliciously and for so long that he finally turned on me. If this were true, with the horror and guilt would come a kind of relief. Since the disease was said to be incurable, I could then take the only logical step possible to make sure it would never happen again: swear off relationships forever.

So I started with a simple comparison exercise. In a repetition of the very first war I had ever fought and had never really stopped fighting, it was once again Me v. My Mother. I had spent so many years trying to make sense of her. In my childhood she was a bitch, as a teen I called her evil. In my twenties she was once again an ally, if one I had to buy with the proceeds of my dishonest labours to try and win her affection.

I had made amends to her for running away, calling her names and disobeying her so much, as the twelve-step program demanded. She replied that I had nothing to apologize for because she had never wanted to be a mother so, naturally, she had made some mistakes.

By my early thirties I had realized she would never change, never stop undermining me and others. When her husband, a diagnosed schizophrenic on permanent disability, volunteered to assist a local political candidate, she had followed him through the streets at a distance, ripping down the campaign posters as fast as he could staple them to the telephone poles. She was the president of her condo board because no one else could run the place and was trying to put through an initiative to penalize residents for going onto the sunroof. She controlled her husband's pension and doled him out funds to buy herbs, just as she had with Mamma, only the herb he was interested in was very expensive, so he was on a strict budget. She giggled when she spoke of how she thwarted him at every turn but sternly insisted I call him Daddy even though I had been eighteen when they married and he was closer to my age than hers; to keep the peace, I had let him, rather than my uncle, walk me down the aisle.

Did any of that sound abusive? Or were they just personality quirks to be humoured because, well, *honour thy parents*? Just another day in the life of a Scorpio? The only way to treat a man who needed to be led? A little controlling, but we're all adults here, right?

I didn't particularly like her husband. I told myself he was probably giving just as good as he got in his own way; they clearly hated each other, so it was none of my business. But I couldn't leave it alone. It was as though in my absence, she had found another semi-willing victim to enslave, rob and infantilize. It was maddening. Why couldn't she see it? And if she could be so blind, had the apple really fallen all that far from the tree?

My therapist was the first human being alive to tell me that what my mother had done—that amorphous collection of behaviours that left me feeling so unloved—was wrong, but she insisted that my mother did love me. Like Iyanla Vanzant, she subscribed to the theory that all mothers loved their children, they just didn't know how to show it sometimes, or not in the way that *you* needed or wanted love to be shown. They had been raised wrongly themselves, obviously, but were doing the best they could with what they had.

In the fellowship, many people came from terrible backgrounds, but this was rarely discussed and certainly not offered as a potential cause of alcoholism because that contradicted the literature. And no one was a bigger proponent of the literature than me. My sponsors were thus able to mislead me better than any clinician could, better even than I could myself, because they had been through things that could be simply and clearly described: Sexual abuse. Beatings with closed fist. Smoked crack with mom. Locked in closet while mom gets high. Burned with cigarettes. What the hell was wrong with me?

"She put a roof over your head and took care of you, Nicole. Would you rather be right or happy?"

I couldn't forgive my mother even using the most lenient definitions of the word. I mostly forgot about her, but then in my late thirties, thoughts I had assumed to be safely locked away began to return as strongly as they had when I was pregnant with my son. Instead of praying for her as *The Big Book* advised, I started wishing harm on her when she crossed my mind in the shower or as I cleaned the house. *Fuck her and her money and her fucking White privilege in her fucking millionaire condo.* I would never get revenge, but karma would get her. She was getting to be an old woman, the one thing she dreaded most—ha!

By day, I was bitter; by night, my dreams that she was trying to kill me resumed. My waking thoughts about her manifested as physical aching in all the bones of my body. I bought books like *Mothers Who Can't Love* and *Narcissistic Mothers* and studied them as though prepping for an exam until the crisis with my husband had effectively taken my mind off the distant past. Now I burned to resolve the issue once and for all: Was she that vilest of creatures, a narcissist? And had the curse been passed on to me?

It was all there: the enmeshment, the competition with me, the self-interested everything, the rage, the refusal to learn from others or admit to any flaws, the inability to respect others as independent people, the lack of empathy or access to real feelings and emotions, the mockery and verbal attacks, the inevitable discard once I stopped providing her with supply. Her utter disinterest in any form of introspection was explained: self-analysis might contradict a world of her own invention, one that she had shrunken to a pinprick consisting of only what she could control. The black-and-white thinking, the grandiose notions that she knew what was best for society, the authoritarian desire for power that justified all her actions … it was definitely all there, maybe with a touch of sadism stirred in for good measure.

The brave writers on the phenomenon of narcissistic mothers—brave because acknowledging that not all mothers are good and loving is one of society's last remaining taboos—often list the effects this mothering style produces in their daughters. Working backwards can be another way of determining whether your mother has a cluster B personality disorder like narcissism (though other household dynamics, such as the presence of strict religiosity, addiction or other mental health problems like anxiety and depression can produce similar effects). If you are a perfectionist with no self-compassion, never feel good enough, don't have concrete goals, can't make decisions, don't feel like you can trust yourself and tend toward people-pleasing as a life strategy, these are all indicators that your childhood probably wasn't all that and a bag of chips. Apparently, I was way ahead of most troubled people, who struggled to admit to childhood trauma. If the biggest trick the Devil ever played on mankind was to make the world believe he didn't exist, the biggest trick bad parents ever played on their children was to make them believe nothing happened, and if it did, it was all their fault.

All right, so my mother had been narcissistically abusive. But being raised by a narcissist cannot only make you seek out the same dynamic in romantic relationships (i.e., marry a narcissist), it can also make you *become* one. I thought it must be a classic "if you can't beat 'em, join 'em" response; I later learned that there are unconscious processes going on as early as the first year of life in the formation of narcissistic personality disorder. To discover that I could have become my worst nightmare before I even had conscious control over the process was horrifying, like discovering you had killed someone in your sleep. I knew that, like most daughters, I had become more like my mother than I could comfortably admit, but I wanted to believe there was still another person there: a kinder, more thoughtful person whose voice, though sometimes weak, could still be heard.

    I didn't want to be one of those malignantly arrogant people in the articles who went around treating people like shit and tossing them the occasional bone. I didn't want to be incapable of deep feelings or step on other people to advance myself. But I had been accused of selfishness, entitlement and superiority since childhood. I began to seek out real experts on narcissism because if I had this curse, I wanted to be sure, at least, that my husband had it too. If that isn't narcissistic, I don't know what is.

CHAPTER 24

THE GRANDADDY OF NARCISSISM

A little research led straight to the source: Sam Vaknin, a professor of psychology and the only absolutely credible online source about narcissism—quite a claim, except it happens to be true. He has devoted his life to the study of often-misunderstood cluster B personality disorders. He wrote the definitive book on narcissism, *Malignant Self-Love: Narcissism Revisited*, from a prison cell and invented the phrases commonly used today in the community: narcissistic abuse, gaslighting, love bombing and many others. He has amassed the world's largest database of people with narcissistic personality disorder and invented the first therapy that goes well beyond behaviour modification, which is mainly for the benefit of the narcissist's loved ones, to actually eradicate the core disorder.

When he's not lecturing at prestigious universities, proposing ground-breaking theories or synthesizing data from the kind of densely-worded research studies that would make me poke my eyes out, Sam is sipping coffee from his favourite mug, Minnie. Minnie is to Sam what Wilson, the soccer ball, is to Tom Hanks' character in *Cast Away*. You could say that Minnie is his only friend because Sam is not only the granddaddy of narcissism; with official diagnoses of both narcissism and psychopathy, he is also a client.

Sam's videos are difficult to listen to, not only because they're an intellectual challenge but because they are brutally, painfully truthful. Every word (and there are a lot of words and no ads to interrupt them) is a poke, a pinch, or a punch in the gut. He has hundreds of videos on narcissism and cluster B personality disorders, including borderline personality disorder and psychopathy, and to a lesser extent, histrionic personality disorder. If you are hoping for a witch hunt in which you are cast as the victim of these evil creatures, keep scrolling; even when Sam is describing the horrifying behaviours exhibited by people in the cluster B, he manages to remind you how and why they got that way: childhood trauma so severe that, once it interfered with the child's natural developmental processes, cannot be reversed.

The theory that therapy does not work on narcissists is usually presented in the context that the narcissist will not seek therapeutic help in the first place because he or she thinks nothing is amiss. After all, if you're perfect, why try to fix it? It is said that only after a narcissistic mortification—the complete collapse of the fantasy world by means of a calamitous event such as being left by their spouse, losing their job or some other terrible loss—does the narcissist voluntarily seek help. Even then, it's more so that they can rebuild, shore up the false self and become better at doing whatever is necessary to place themselves firmly in control once again.

I had heard this before, but Sam explained why. Therapy works on the premise that there is a patient who has a self. Obviously, if you are sitting in a therapist's chair, there is a *you* who is doing it. But narcissists do not have a core self in the way most people do. Instead, they have a constellation of selves, a constantly shifting hive mind. This false self is based almost entirely on what others think of them. I had thought of narcissism as basically a problem of an over-developed ego, but it turns out narcissists have no ego whatsoever, no ability to self-regulate, no core sense of self. Their minds are like a social media platform with the narcissist as an avatar. They constantly aggregate information and feedback—preferably adulation, as in narcissistic supply—from friends and partners and colleagues in order to regulate who they are, formulate memories and maintain a positive self image. Increasingly, we all do this, but the unfortunate narcissist can never close the app or go offline because there is nowhere to go back to.

This explains why people are absolutely expendable and interchangeable to the narcissist. It doesn't really matter who is providing the attention, stimulation and feedback, as long as someone is; he or she needs it like oxygen. When you stop providing it or try to negotiate change, this new reality diverges too much from the ideal in their mind and the narcissist simply empties the recycling bin and moves on to a new target. Despite what it feels like, this isn't done with malicious intent unless sadism and/or psychopathy is also present. In a life and death game of survival, there will necessarily be collateral damage.

Narcissists feel little to no remorse when their actions hurt others because they either feel entitled to those actions as a means to an end or, in the case of the covert narcissist who is constantly surprised and defensive when accused of wrongdoing, don't see how their actions could affect anyone. They cannot afford to consider foolish things like the feelings of other avatars or, as Sam calls them, snapshots: images taken of you and immediately internalized into the narcissist's fantasy so that the narcissist is never really interacting with a real person, only with a frozen image they can idealize, manipulate, abuse, devalue and discard at will. Without a partner who is willing to provide them at least two of the three S's—sex, supply and services—the narcissist must find a new source or else they will collapse. And you really don't want to see a narcissistic collapse.

This information disturbed me greatly because it seemed to suggest that severe, early abuse or neglect was necessary in the formation of a narcissist. This was a damning indicator that my ex-husband, with his prosperous and pampered childhood, could not be one. But Sam said that when it came to childhood abuse, there was more than one way to skin a cat. When I was growing up, predators came out of bushes rather than the kitchen; in the intervening years, the definition of abuse had expanded. Anything that interferes with a child's ability to separate from his primary caregiver—usually the mother—constitutes abuse. I made a list of some of the lesser-known ways to break a child's ego boundaries:

1. Parentification – turning the child into an adult by forcing them to assume adult responsibilities or emotional caretaking for other siblings and/or the parent
2. Objectification/exploitation – refusing to allow the child to become their own person by forcing the child to fulfill the parent's own unfulfilled dreams or become an extension of the parent's will
3. Emotional neglect – the phenomenon of the "dead mother" who doesn't fulfill her primary function of being a safe base from which the child can explore the world. She is too depressed, indifferent, preoccupied, etc. to notice or respond to her child's needs
4. Spoiling – the child is highly praised for a certain group of behaviours or skill sets, but only for their performative value, never for who the child actually is. When they fail to perform, love is withdrawn

Even when it came out in therapy that Paul's parents had been financially irresponsible, emotionally neglectful and argued frequently, I had seen these as garden-variety problems, a dismissive attitude that was bolstered by everyone in the room. If anyone saw us as two sides of the same coin, I was definitely the side that had lain in the mud for so long as to be almost unrecognizable. Paul had been spoiled with material goods and unreasonable freedoms, though beyond a certain point, his parents took his prodigious talent for granted. He had been allowed to do what he wanted, when he wanted, without attracting much attention. He was also morbidly obese as a child, as were his parents, who did nothing to reverse the situation. Therefore, he was tormented at school but adroitly managed to turn this around by being the richest, most gifted kid with the most permissive parents. He told me that laughing along with his bullies then inviting them to his palatial home for a swim in the grand-piano-shaped pool converted them into fast friends.

Both Paul's mother and mine had told us that the vast majority of people are stupid but we weren't. We were special and superior, and, being so smart, we both knew it but the rest of the world didn't. Paul was fat and shy, I was a stick-thin geek who looked like a boy and dressed like a refugee. The evidence showed we were exceptional in certain areas; that was just fact, not bluster. Unfortunately, this exceptionality set us apart in a world that valued conformity a lot more than genius and didn't hesitate to make us miserable for it. Throughout his life, he had enjoyed much more success than I did, admired not only for being the superior talent in his universe but for possessing the lion's share of the charm, looks and precociousness, but as an adult he still fell short of his goals of fame and money, which bothered him greatly. He realized early on that he was smarter than most and frequently complained of others' undeserved success, including that of his parents, who were, of course, from the generation where you only had to roll out of bed to be able to afford a house, a car and a family. I avoided the question of success entirely by putting my creative goals aside long before he did.

In Paul I seemed to discover my mother's shadow. Unlike other boyfriends who had viscerally reminded me of her, Paul was so silent on his true opinions and beliefs that I suspected he didn't really have any, leaving me to safely assume he was agreeable rather than secretly seething with resentment. But scratch the surface and you'd find someone even more dissatisfied with reality than me. In private, we often spoke of how other people frustrated us, in my case emotionally, in his case with their unmerited wealth and success. Our clients thought they knew better than us, the members of the fellowship were hopeless degenerates or religious nuts, our neighbours were loud and annoying, our friends unreliable and cold. He cared very much about this state of affairs but would never say so to anyone else because it would have exposed his laid back, easy-going image to be false.

Being a narcissist is a full-time job. It reminds me of when Paul described the endless, hopeless cycle of waking up each day and planning how to steal enough to pay for his drug habit: you can't do it for one more day, but you also can't stop. Pretending, often with great success, to be a well-adjusted person when you are not is nothing if not exhausting, which is why narcissistic people are often diagnosed with depression. The narcissist is happy when they are winning, but it's a fragile, short-lived happiness constantly threatened by both the inside and the outside world.

When I was not busy losing my mind, I drew up a little chart to help me compare my own narcissistic symptoms to those of the man who, I believed, had given me the best life I'd ever enjoyed and then mercilessly destabilized it. Were we both narcissists? If so, was I the grandiose, classic narcissist or the equally grandiose but secretive, subdued covert narc?

Narcissistic Personality Disorder Symptom	Me	Him
Low tolerance for boredom	X	
Demonstrates remorse for hurting others	X	
Surprised that actions can negatively affect others	X	X
Usually feels actions are justified to achieve goals	X	X
Builds fantasies and tries to maintain them against all evidence of reality	X	X
Focused and dedicated to goals		X
Dislikes weakness or flaws in others	X	X
Feels like a victim	X	X
Defiance for authority figures and rules	X	X
Avoids mundane or routine tasks; considers adulting beneath them		X
More concerned with optics than morality		X
Seeks fame by association with more talented/successful others		X
Has trouble with equal relationships; sees others as better or worse, not equal	X	X
Triangulates, pitting significants against each other for personal gain		X

THE GRANDADDY OF NARCISSISM

Manipulates helpers or "flying monkeys" to carry out their own goals		X
Refuses to accept responsibility for wrongdoing or acknowledge mistakes		X
Has difficulty respecting others' boundaries	X	X
Never stops trying to mould their partner	X	X
Uses sex only to obtain results from intimate partner		X
Gaslights their partner, pretending events never occurred or that the partner is insane		X
Prone to substance abuse	X	X
Becomes angry and defensive when confronted	X	X
Easily wounded by criticism, even when it is constructive	X	X
Punishing response when others don't meet expectations	X	X
Rushes intimacy and idealizes partner in early stages of relationship	X	
Was the golden child in the family who could do no wrong		X

To receive a diagnosis of narcissistic personality or indeed any other psychological disorder, you must exhibit a certain number of symptoms across all situations. For example, you must equally be exploitative of your friends, your partner, the postman, the government, your children and everyone in between. This is important to note because narcissists are said to infect their partners with their own symptoms; the more time you spend with a narcissist, the more narcissistic you will become because you are seeing everything through the same Machiavellian lens. But when you move on from that abusive relationship, you're supposed to eventually be restored to your former self, the self that has always interacted in a healthy way with the rest of the world. Narcissists are no more than one out of every hundred people. But unfortunately, I had always been a little different.

In many of his videos, Sam also explores the phenomenon of psychopaths. Like most people, I had previously thought psychopaths were serial killers, crazy-town personifications of evil. For the first time I learned this is not true. While one must certainly be a psychopath in order to be a serial killer, psychopathic traits will also make you an excellent CEO. Primary psychopaths do not have emotions, empathy or remorse as we understand them; they are predatory and parasitic in pursuit of goals, reckless novelty-seekers with little regard for societal norms.

Unlike the narcissist, who presents a false self even to themselves, the psychopath has no such false self. They are always themselves, they just pretend to be you in order to reel you in. The psychopath makes up concepts like right and wrong according to their own whims and aims. Deceitful, callous and often charming with the uncanny ability to tell victims exactly what they want to hear, psychopaths impulsively seek stimulation at all costs even when it tears down their own lives.

Sam says that when narcissists of any stripe experience devastating pain or loss—in other words, narcissistic mortification—they become primary psychopaths. A psychopathic part or state steps forward to protect the narcissist from whatever harm has befallen them, acting in antisocial, aggressive and seemingly irrational ways that the regular narcissist never would. Thus the quiet, brooding person who has suffered in silence for years suddenly becomes vicious, even violent. It explained why a man who could not muster the energy to do the dishes without first having a two-hour nap suddenly roused himself to plan and execute an incomprehensible campaign to erase me from his life as opposed to, for instance, getting a divorce.

As dangerous as a narcissist is in a psychopathic state, some experts on narcissism, including Sam, believe that covert narcissism is the most frightening form of the disorder because it is so well-masked. Both grandiose and covert narcissists take on the role of children in a committed relationship. They are looking for a mother so they become childlike as a form of test: Will their partners love them no matter what, under any provocation or circumstance, as a mother should? This is initially as irresistible to a woman with strong maternal tendencies as the narcissist's other iteration, the stern father, is to women with daddy issues. Neither state is conducive to anything like a healthy relationship because of the switching that takes place: the paternal figure suddenly becomes a helpless child and the partner feels confused and betrayed even while still loving this cuddly toddler who only throws a fit when demands are made on him.

But in a covert narcissist, who has such a negative self-image, this child is a sad, self-effacing one, which makes victims even more empathetic and fervent in their attempts to build them up. As pitiable objects, covert narcissists get away with a lot more because they have a sad story that happens to be true: they keep failing at everything. This is the narcissist who, unlike my mother, will apologize—even if the apologies are of the frustrating, "I'm sorry if you feel I did something wrong, but ..." variety. There is always the illusion that progress is being made when underneath the superficial placating is a seething mass of rage waiting for an outlet.

Then there is the inverted narcissist, with whom I shared the habit of seeking out grandiose types to bask in their reflected glory. Subtypes of, and synonyms for, different sorts of narcissists proliferated like clowns jumping out of a tiny car: somatic, cerebral, collapsed, malignant, vulnerable, malignant covert anti-narcissist. My head was spinning. I thought I might wake up one morning to find the walls covered with tightly bunched red writing, but instead of "redrum" it would be a terrifying word salad of narcissistic terminology that I'd written in my sleep.

I ended up feeling sorry for narcissists—they couldn't help being such dicks because their boundaries had been so transgressed in childhood that they had simply worked out the best way to avoid being hurt again and it didn't even work. People acted like they were innocent victims of these demonic people, which might have been true for them; maybe they had run afoul of psychopaths or such complete, utter assholes that even my friend's faulty website would sprout flashing red pop-ups from six miles away.

I knew in my heart that whether I blamed astrology, alcohol, birth order or personality testing, I had high narcissistic traits myself. I was not an innocent victim, but nor could I believe I was a terrible person. Despite all the reading and listening and note-taking, the question of whether Paul was a narcissist or not, or what type, remained unanswerable, but the presence of so many telltale signs in both of us provided a possible explanation for how our relationship had gone wrong.

Still, I now knew I had empathy and access to emotions in a way that a narcissist didn't—perhaps too much, if the tears I shed for Sam were any indication. His own background was one of abuse so severe that it is a miracle he survived it. His genius IQ both protected him, allowing him to escape into realms limited only by his own brilliance, and condemned him to live as a brain a jar, detached from and repelled by the very people he depended on to keep himself alive. He knows everything there is to know about narcissism and shares it freely to help others, but he can't save himself. As I felt the pain and injustice of this Promethean punishment, I wondered if there could be another scientific explanation for being just plain fucked.

CHAPTER 25

MEMOS FROM THE BORDER

As my marriage was imploding, I had texted Alba about my fears that I was a narcissist.

"Weren't you diagnosed with BPD?" she responded almost immediately.

I was taken aback. Had I been? Well, the psychiatrist who had done my intake when I heard about a program for people with sexual flashbacks had offhandedly said something about borderline personality disorder within an hour of meeting me. I had been randomly assigned to the same psychiatrist who treated my mother's husband for schizophrenia and who, according to my mother, had failed to ever mention that she might not be helping his situation.

"He's the sick one, Nicky," she had told me with a loud sigh.

This psychiatrist had whipped open the *DSM-IV* and told me that of the nine symptoms of borderline personality disorder, I appeared to have at least six. But I was in recovery from addiction and no longer self-harming or indulging in substances. I hadn't been looking for a psychiatric diagnosis, especially one that I thought was totally unrelated to the program I was trying to get into (which turned out to be for sex offenders, so I was not admitted). I was horrified at the label, even without knowing anything about BPD; it sounded like multiple personalities!

Years later, an old friend from the fellowship came over to buy soap and recommended I read a book about BPD called *I Hate You, Don't Leave Me*. I finally opened the book months later and read most of it during a short vacation to Niagara Falls alone with Paul. He was warm and supportive that weekend, so I shared a lot of the book with him. I was relieved that the book said such individuals had been warped by childhood abuse, so at least there was a reason for all that self-destruction, promiscuity and instability. If icons like Marilyn Monroe, whose picture graced my living room wall, could have developed BPD through no fault of their own, I was certainly in good company. I didn't know then that *all* cluster B personality disorders, including narcissistic personality disorder, result from disruption to the normal processes of healthy attachment, separation and individuation. Whoops.

One helpful thing I had learned was that BPD exists on a spectrum. I could understand that; it was what made my son a talkative genius who could discuss the smallest details of his passions for hours while some children on the autism spectrum do not talk at all. In psychology, severity is measured by its impact on the subject's life (i.e., is what they are doing working for them or harming them?). Yes, I had mood swings, but that didn't mean I was doomed to go back and offer the elderly psychiatrist a quickie on the exam table, trash his office when he rejected my advances and threaten to kill myself unless he un-diagnosed me, only to show up the next week sporting a radical haircut and demanding a second opinion. I wasn't that person anymore, if I had ever been, so I kind of forgot all about it.

The subsequent version of the *Diagnostic and Statistical Manual of Mental Disorders*, the *DSM-V*, has a much clearer map of the borderline. When I heard it read online by Sam Vaknin, I felt that every hair on my head might be turning white at the same time, so well did it depict my inner world. I remember not wanting to do anything for the rest of the day. I had thought myself safe because I was decent at not acting out in a distinctly borderline-y way; it certainly helped that there was a lack of targets. I worked, very hard, for myself and was no longer hanging out with many people, let alone other addicts, because of the lockdown. But I felt the potential lurking there, waiting to spring once the masks came off.

According to Richard Grannon, a life coach and content creator with a psychology degree who had pursued his own healing and then developed courses over the previous decade, NPD and BPD are closely linked (look, they only have one letter different!). In collaboration with Sam Vaknin on numerous video series, he describes how their origins are very similar. Grannon first expands upon how a narcissist is made, saying it requires three elements:

1. Having your sense of self torn down in childhood. Receiving the explicit or implicit message from one or both parents that you have no intrinsic value as a human being. Unconditional love is replaced by the constant communication that you are only as valuable as what you can produce or how well you behave. This message can be conveyed directly, such as by telling a child they are a piece of garbage, or through actions such as ignoring, punishing or neglecting the child—anything that smashes their boundaries and leaves them with a deep sense of unworthiness.
2. Being highly praised and adored—not loved—for a certain skill or ability. For this ability and this ability alone, you are elevated above others and receive the message that your performance entitles you to special treatment. This breeds the arrogance and sense of privilege narcissists are known for but also causes the impostor syndrome, anxiety and deep feelings of inadequacy.
3. Being made to stay within limits of personal development invented by one or both parents. These children are made to believe they can never surpass their parents; they are allowed to excel only at certain specific things, within certain limits, but the parent always maintains superiority and takes credit for the child's accomplishments. Thus even being the "golden child" in a family is sufficient to create the entitlement, grandiosity and lack of empathy that characterizes a narcissist.

In contrast to Vaknin, who goes into fascinating detail about the formation of these personality disorders in infancy with a deep dive into concepts like inconstant object relations and splitting (and which I explore in my parenting book, *Don't Fry the Children*), Grannon has said that the only difference between the development of NPD and BPD is that borderline patients are conditioned with those same three messages from *the same* person. Unlike the narcissist, who is usually being mistreated by one authority figure (father, school, mother, institution) and spoiled in compensation by another, the borderline is receiving conflicting messages of "I hate you, you're awesome, you disgust me, you're the best" from one central person.

I began to watch Grannon, Vaknin, and Grannon-Vaknin videos as I made bath salts and skin creams, my hands moving mechanically while my brain raced to absorb information. At this point, I was obsessed with diagnosing myself: Was I a covert narcissist or a borderline? Sam's work on the subject was, as always, well referenced, and his videos are infused with quotes and study findings from authoritative texts by authors with crazy sounding names. One theory that stood out was that borderlines are, in fact, failed narcissists. The reason a borderline has empathy and emotions—indeed, a surfeit of them—is because they failed to erect a narcissistic defense and therefore walks the border like some skinless ghost who is prone to abuse over and over by all the people who will obligingly step in to mess them up if they aren't already doing it to themself.

My counsellor, assigned by a non-profit I once supported with my chequebook, told me not to listen to Vaknin because his opinion is so negative when it comes to borderline personality disorder. Evidence included his need to repeat, in every single video on the topic, that a full 10% of borderlines commit suicide rather than live with their condition. They try so hard to be good, but they never can. The tears I had cried for him became tears for myself; if there had been an option to simply not be, at many points in my life I would have gladly taken it.

Grannon seemed to speak of BPD with something like revulsion, often referring to exploitative and malignant elements I didn't think I possessed—but isn't that always the way? The schizophrenic, after all, thinks the voices they hear are real. BPD became the diagnostic bogeyman I now hoped to avoid. His most compassionate video on the borderline's shifting sense of identity, which he described with the horrific image of a crumbling statue toppled from its shelf and falling endlessly through the air, contrasts to most of his much harsher commentary on the borderline. I was not sure whether the literal and figurative shuddering resulted from his being hurt by borderline women in the past or if I was merely being hypervigilant, seeing attack where there is none (a classic borderline's trait). The fact that I sometimes cheered the harshest criticism of the narcissist but felt mortally wounded by descriptions of the borderline's antics probably speaks volumes.

Other experts online—Vaknin would call them "self-styled experts"—said that if the narcissist's one goal was to win and the psychopath's was to have fun, the borderline's was to be loved. Some said that genetic factors played a role, which seemed to render the situation even more hopeless, although all the experts unanimously agreed that BPD was the most treatable of the cluster B group of disorders, perhaps because the borderline is more likely to seek treatment. If this was the case, then why had my former therapist insisted that labels are unhelpful? Why did I read that many therapists will not take on a borderline patient at all?

Ironically, while seeming to repel even the professionals, borderlines are supposed to be terrified of abandonment, which gave me hope because I wasn't; that hope was dashed when I realized the only reason I didn't fear abandonment was because I accepted it and often initiated it pre-emptively. Were being in pain and wanting love such bad things? The *South Park* social worker had the answer: Wanting anything so badly that you will manipulate people to get it is bad, m'kay?

Sam acknowledged that the remorse and self-loathing borderlines feel after each compulsive outburst is not solely demonstrated to ensure their victim will pity them and stay. By all accounts, the horror at having made a mistake that will hurt someone else is real because borderlines do have empathy. I felt guilt and remorse every time I snapped at my children, the more so because I felt that it wasn't really me doing it. The person who got so angry at messes and back-talk seemed to get a little more carried away than I would ever dream of doing. We always talked it out (this is my problem, not yours), but unless I could rein in my temper, I knew the day would come when talking wouldn't fix it.

It caused me great distress to feel that online giants in the field like Vaknin and Grannon, who seemed like funny, intelligent, reasonable, compassionate lovers of humanity (yes, even Sam), would, if they met me on the street, recognize that telltale borderline neon glow and treat me with a mixture of fear and contempt. It was so unfair. It was time for another chart.

Borderline Personality Disorder Symptom	Me
Emotionally dysregulated; disproportionately strong reactions to emotions	X
Difficulty establishing own boundaries and respecting those of other people	X
Strong fear of rejection	X
Anxious and hypervigilant	X
Tendency to enmesh with significant others while simultaneously fearing engulfment	X
Poor whole object relations; tends to see others as all good or all bad	X
Anticipates and initiates abandonment	X
Prone to substance abuse	X
Feels guilty and responsible when things go wrong	X
Feels fundamentally flawed and unlovable	X
Tries to secure or "buy" love with money, acts of service, perfectionism	X
Tries to provoke massive emotional reactions in others to keep them off balance	
Uses "word salad," gaslighting and other manipulative mind tricks	
Goes through cycles of idealization, devaluing and discard in relationships	X
Looks to significant other for identity	X
Judges behaviour through a moral lens and punishes others for moral infractions	X

Frequent dissociation and adoption of different self-states or "personalities"	X
Acts out (risk-taking, self-harming, addictive behaviours) under stress or rejection	X
Pervasive feeling of inner emptiness and lack of purpose	X
Craves intimacy but decompensates in the face of it	X
Switches to a secondary psychopath (psychopath with access to emotions) in extreme adversity	X

In one of the college psych classes I audited in my job captioning for deaf students, the teacher once said that BPD was the modern world's answer to the hysteria diagnosis because it was diagnosed almost exclusively among women, much as men are pronounced narcissists and psychopaths far more often than women. She asked the students to think critically: If a disorder shares so much symptom overlap with other disorders that you can really throw anything in the borderline basket, and the condition is acknowledged to be a response to childhood mistreatment, and treatment aims to reduce excess emotion, was its ever-expanding deployment in the mental health community just the establishment's way of controlling women by pathologizing them? Isn't BPD—or hysteria, for that matter—a pretty natural response to the kind of provocation dished out not only by abusive parents but by a repressive system and society itself?

Sam Vaknin and others said that borderlines were the natural partner of the narcissist because they thought they wanted perfect love but unconsciously felt most comfortable when re-experiencing the original abuse that had made them borderlines in the first place. I didn't want to keep doing that, but having encountered many women in recovery who seemed to have pronounced traits of the disorder, I wasn't fully convinced I was a borderline. Either that or the disorder was, in addition to being unfairly stigmatizing, beyond my full comprehension. Sure, I could be pretty extra, but was there any other possible explanation for my emotional dysregulation, temper tantrums and the uncontainable pain that seeped out to poison the foundation upon which I built my life?

CHAPTER 26

BACK TO THE FUTURE

My brother, Jay, came to visit me from Alabama twice, once as a new father and then, ten or fifteen years later, when my own children were young. Imagine: thanks to my dad's infidelity, the desperately lonely only child had not one but three brothers. The twins were too young to bridge the age and culture gap, but the eldest, a mere four years younger than me, had grown up feeling like an outsider too. He was driven to self-improvement and introspection and was relentless in his self-discipline, perhaps a holdover from his army career. He is now a successful professional bodybuilder, competing across America, and owns a fitness training business where he works with people across the fitness spectrum whether their goal is to get healthy or to attain 3 percent body fat.

The first time I met him, he did not have such a sculpted physique but merely looked like a young man of the type you didn't really see north of the border. For one thing, he stood six or seven inches taller than me, which is not something you see every day. I felt an instant bond where I never expected to feel any at all for Daddy's secret family. But with Jay I felt I was in the presence of someone almost holy; kindness and innocence radiated from him like a soothing balm. When he was able to come to Toronto in 2017, I was beside myself with excitement, but there was something off about the plan from the very beginning.

There wasn't enough notice; I couldn't get enough time off work, Paul wouldn't take any time off at all, and I was scrambling to figure out where my brother would stay in a small house where two little children lived. Then his arrival was delayed. Apparently he had been pulled over by the police, who had found a gun in the glove compartment.

"Why did you bring your gun?" I ranted. "What were you thinking? We don't roll like that. This is Canada. What would you need a gun for?"

All misgivings were erased when he put his arms around me. He was simultaneously baby brother, dad and link to the past I could have had if I'd been raised by my Black family. We toured around town a bit, driven by a friend. We had a tense dinner, with Paul and I fighting over his having smashed the chandelier accidentally just as the table was being set. We made some plans and talked. And then my brother went out and didn't come back till 3:00 a.m. I waited up anxiously and confronted him in the morning but got only vague answers. He didn't drink or do drugs, and he had a serious girlfriend at home, so where the hell had he gone? The next day, he missed our restaurant dinner because he said he had to do something with his lawyer over a charge.

At the time, I was bewildered, annoyed and hurt. Of course not everyone lived a life as rigid and structured as ours, with kids' nap times and routines dictating every move. Of course there was tension in our home, but it was only a few days—couldn't he just show up for my sake? Irritation at his irresponsible behaviour turned me cold, and I couldn't control it. He was just like Daddy. I had put so much emotion into this short visit and felt like a failure already for not having the time or money to really show him a great time. When we parted, it was with the unsettling and sad feeling that, although I loved him with an inexplicable ferocity, maybe I didn't know his true character.

As most stories do, the details came out over time. The three tours he'd done in Iraq had made him start to act a bit funny. He had always been a little different—not difficult to accomplish when growing up as a free thinker in a large blended family amid rigid societal expectations for Black men in America—but now he was acting, well, strange. He told me he had post-traumatic stress disorder, just like his fellow army friend who had beaten an Arab man to death in a Denny's during a flashback and gotten away with it because he was a vet.

At first I met this news with skepticism. PTSD? I knew absolutely nothing about it. I remembered once sending Jay a care package of poetry, jokes, articles and art that my friends and I had put together for him, wondering if he would even receive it on his base in Iraq. He did and told me a bit about his daily life there, how tired he was of wearing forty pounds of uniform and equipment in 130 °F heat. He worked on computers, and if he had seen or at least heard about nearby IEDs, shootings, suffering of the type I saw in the patriotic American movies, he didn't mention it in his descriptions of that alien world. I understood PTSD had to do with flashbacks but couldn't imagine what it would be like to literally think you were somewhere else, like a war zone, when you were actually staring at a plate of bacon and eggs.

The next time I heard about PTSD was from a doctor who was analyzing the results of a sleep study. Paul had informed me I snored unbearably. He did, too, but because I always woke up feeling tired rather than energized and had several risk factors, I thought I might have sleep apnea. I could fall asleep easily but never stay asleep for longer than a couple of hours at a time, a condition made worse by having babies; I was sensitive to their smallest noises. It would be just like my body to be secretly waking me up all night long while I thought I was asleep or to starve my brain of oxygen—it just figured! After spending an uncomfortable night strapped to a box of wires connected to the electrodes on my scalp, sheepishly bothering the attending technician to go to the bathroom multiple times as I always did, I fully expected to be fitted with a CPAP mask to help me breathe at night. I'd heard that people made fun of the mask, saying it would guarantee you'd never get laid again. Well, I already wasn't getting laid so what difference did it make? But the doctor told me to have a seat and asked me if I had ever heard of PTSD.

"Do you go to therapy? It can help," he said.

There didn't seem to be a lot of information forthcoming. I already went to therapy but that didn't stop me from startling awake with such force that my feet would hit the ground, commando-style, as if responding to a bomb threat rather than the cat coming up the stairs. I was still afraid—terrified, actually—of the dark, a fear that didn't leave me until after I turned forty. If you suffer from a similar phobia, there is hope: prayer helped, although drinking myself to sleep, while I don't recommend it, was another strategy that kept the closet monsters at bay.

A couple of years later, the frenemy who would later unblock the recipient list on Paul's Mother's Day email suddenly told me she didn't have an anxiety disorder after all. She had berated me for selfishly not wanting to take anti-anxiety medication when I obviously had anxiety just like her, but now, whoops! She did not have anxiety but at least now she knew what was wrong with her. All the last-minute cancellations, the self-sabotage, the extreme emotions, the lashing out (she did not acknowledge this part) was due to C-PTSD: *complex* post-traumatic stress disorder. Here I was, after reading *I Hate You, Don't Leave Me*, privately thinking that if I was a borderline, she was a lot further along on the spectrum than me. Despite her therapist's diagnosis of C-PTSD, I thought she was grasping at straws to avoid the more serious borderline diagnosis. Now with my life still in shambles, obsessively and sometimes despairingly looking for answers, I was doing the exact same thing.

Richard Grannon popped into my feed saying that the signs and symptoms of borderline personality disorder are often conflated with C-PTSD because repeated trauma causes emotional flashbacks which lead to dysregulated emotions, high reactivity and codependence on their abusers (though not the shifting sense of identity of the borderline). Vaknin says the two diagnoses are virtually indistinguishable. Unlike my brother, who felt like he was back in a literal war zone, people with complex post-traumatic stress disorder have been traumatized repeatedly over a long period of time, so their flashbacks are not visual and auditory but emotional. In the grip of a sudden flashback, the personality switches to another state altogether in response to even a minor trigger. When someone tells a certain joke or the washer breaks down or someone cuts them off in traffic, they experience the same intensity of feeling—rejection, frustration, anger—that they used to feel when their mother said they were a piece of shit, and they react accordingly.

This could explain my bewildering outbursts when my kids ate the last cookie or refused to lend a hand with the pets. It explained my internal fight and flee responses when a friend said she couldn't have us over after I had hosted the last three times, or a boss told me to mute myself on a Zoom meeting when it was my turn to speak because my kids happened to walk by in the background. I often didn't lash out, but my mental reaction was swift and disproportionate; I never wanted to speak to them again. Then I would be tortured by guilt and the worry they could read these irrational thoughts, that I had hurt their feelings. I felt I would never escape these behaviours or their consequences, that I was doomed to be that statue, falling, falling, falling, smashing, trying to glue myself back together, and not understanding why any of it was happening.

The possibility that I had C-PTSD gave me hope. It is not, of course, an excuse for bad behaviour, but if it wasn't a full personality disorder it could be healed because it was not purely psychological but also neurological—the brain's pathways are literally changed by trauma, and they can be changed again. I listened to the C-PTSD discourse online, turning to specialists like Anna Runkle and Marisa Peer, who both said brain injuries of this type could be overcome.

Grannon, with his Spartan Life Coach program, teaches clients to reduce emotional flashbacks and break the hold of a toxic superego—what he calls the inner critic or the internalized voice of the bad parent, which is trying to destroy us with vicious commands that constantly signal that we, and the world, are screwing up badly. He proposes emotional literacy work on the theory that people with C-PTSD often have a lot of trouble identifying any but the most basic emotions; they don't know what they are feeling at any given time, let alone why.

I began writing my feelings down every day and trying to drill into the deeper feelings behind them, as he instructed. I wish I could say that my love of language served me here, but although in literature I had never met an adjective I didn't like, I could only identify my most superficial, monosyllabic emotions: Sad. Mad. Lonely. I had always received the message that feelings didn't matter, and that message had served me well, allowing me to power through and keep going no matter what the insides looked like. It had also led me to betray myself over and over in the dogged pursuit of things I didn't even want. I didn't want to feel, but as with anything else in life, consistent effort produces results: the exercises began to help. By witnessing my own feelings without judgment, I gradually began to accept them, which lessened their ferocity.

The borderline/C-PTSD jury was still out. In one of his videos that is, as usual, peppered with references to the scholarly literature, Sam Vaknin cites that the International Classification of Diseases (ICD), the international equivalent of the *DSM*, does not draw significant distinctions between C-PTSD and borderline except that there has to be trauma present for a C-PTSD diagnosis. As he points out, however, what borderline hasn't experienced prolonged trauma?

In the twelve-step fellowship I had heard speakers say there was a part of their minds which, for some reason, wanted to kill them. I had always parroted this because I believed it to be true without realizing that this destructive part didn't really belong to me but to my mother, whose commanding internalized voice had taken on immense proportions in my psyche. The childhood truce had solidified into a kind of inner merger in which she still called the shots with enough force to edge out my own thoughts and feelings. To try and escape, I continually formed new bonds with one mother substitute after another in an endless attempt to prove my worth and goodness … to her … who had become a part of me … who believed I was bad and wrong. It all sounded so codependent.

CHAPTER 27

IT'S NOT YOUR FAULT, DEAR ONES

Another prolific speaker I discovered in those first months of the separation, working frantically to meet the demands of the discerning mid-pandemic online shopper, trying to figure out my life and escaping frequently into fantasy to take the pressure off, was Lisa A. Romano, the reigning queen of codependency. Because she had dozens if not hundreds of videos on recovering from narcissistic abuse, I began to listen to her a lot, but in smaller doses. Unlike Vaknin and Grannon, who discussed complex concepts in granular, clinical terms, and a host of others who attempted to explain high-level psychological phenomena, Lisa spoke plainly, conversationally and in a spiritual context of self-empowerment that I found a little woo.

Listening to Lisa's distinctive New York accent, which reminded me of my primary school teachers so long ago, I realized I had heard of codependency in a personal context. Just as I had introduced narcissism to my ex-husband, he had introduced the concept of codependency to me. Now I wondered if we hadn't, as part of some cosmic healing intention, each exposed the other to their true nature. Or maybe Lisa's woo was rubbing off on me.

IT'S NOT YOUR FAULT, DEAR ONES

Paul attended Co-Dependents Anonymous (CoDA) meetings regularly at one point in our marriage. When he had announced his intention to try CoDA, I was already too weary to argue; he would do whatever he wanted, regardless. It meant one more night of the week alone with the kids, which I remember resenting even though it didn't change much of anything. I didn't know where he got the idea that he was codependent but since most members of the fellowship attended more than one type of meeting, whether it was for sugar or sex or gambling or debt, I figured he heard it there.

I didn't know much about codependency but assumed that a codependent person was one who desperately needed other people to like them. I have never met anyone who seemed to need people less, but Paul said he wanted to understand why he was always trying to make me happy even when I didn't reciprocate. *This is you trying to make me happy?* I thought with an inner smirk. He seemed to resent needing me, and I knew I wasn't meeting the need, so I said I was happy he wanted to be more independent.

"You're my only friend," he would say, reproachfully. "I have no one else to talk to."

"That's too much of a burden," I'd retort defensively to conceal my remorse. "You can't make one person responsible for all your happiness. I don't do that with you!"

"You're my wife, though. If you're not here for me, who is?"

Following me around the kitchen with a pleading look that was normally nowhere in evidence, he had a way of guiding me straight back into a state of inadequacy. I thought I was there for him, I tried to be, but it wasn't good enough. All my misgivings about the relationship would evaporate in the face of his vulnerability, and to assuage my guilt for not loving him properly, I'd remind him he had friends of thirty years that he was still in touch with. Sure, they weren't perfect, but they were around! I told him what I did to nurture my friendships and connect with people online, but he shook his head: too much effort, and that is not what he wanted. He wanted his wife and to stop feeling like he had to try so hard for her love.

He attended a couple of CoDA meetings and didn't like them until he found one that his former sponsor, a very, *very* woo lady, had started in the basement of her friend's house. He went every week, and though we didn't discuss too much of what happened there, he had an astute observation: every recovering codependent in the room was single or, as they called it, abstinent. He didn't approve, and I agreed. How are you supposed to learn how to have healthy relationships if your philosophy of healing revolves around avoiding them? I teased him that the meetings were just a bitchfest about the uncaring partner, except these people actually knew to whom he was referring. He said it wasn't all about me.

At one point I suspected he wasn't going to codependency meetings at all—after all, how would I know?—but then I realized he had to be because they were writing their own book over there and his sponsor asked me to edit the first draft. It was essentially a rewriting of *The Big Book* of Alcoholics Anonymous with the word "codependent" inserted in key places. The authors were traditionalists known as bookers and muckers, people who highlighted *The Big Book*'s text in different colours, circled key words and wrote comments in the margins as one would when studying for an exam. The difference was these were not a student's independent notes but text copied verbatim from one book to the next at the sponsor's direction. The actual CoDA text was said to be far too watered down, and therefore a return to basics was required. The editing did not go well. I said it was too derivative and not even that useful because some things just didn't translate; human relationships are not a zero-sum game. I recommended they write originally from their own experience. They said I was too negative to be the right person for the project. The house was sold, the meeting eventually dissolved, and Paul did not find another group. The subject was never mentioned again.

Lisa A. Romano was the daughter of two adult children of alcoholics and describes her childhood at length both in her videos and in her first book, *The Road Back to Me*. Her mother was codependent and her father exploitative, and both acted in ways that were cruel, mocking, malicious and condescending—in short, the opposite of loving and responsive. Lisa and her siblings developed a poor sense of self, a natural consequence of receiving the constant message that it wasn't okay to have needs, wants or desires. When you are told it's selfish to want anything, even the basics, and that you are downright crazy for having emotions, you naturally find unhealthy ways to cope: self-denial, fantasy, shame. Under such circumstances, the only safety Lisa could find was in a man, someone who would give her a purpose and shore up her sense of self-worth. But, of course, he was also a narcissist, so he only reinforced her childhood conditioning. Fortunately, things got bad enough that Lisa woke up. She successfully disengaged from her toxic family, learned to assert boundaries, is happily remarried and has a healthy relationship with her three adult children. She then became a life coach to help others break this cycle as well.

I had to take notice because here was a woman who had done all the right things: initiated the divorce, worked three jobs to rebuild her life, took healing seriously, wrote books, started helping other people. She didn't sit around waiting for the discard or, once liberated, proceed to fuck everything up.

Lisa said that all narcissists are codependent, a novel idea because I thought a codependent was someone who acted like a doormat. Although Paul said I treated him like one, that everything always had to revolve around me and my needs at his expense, I couldn't see this no matter how controlling of my household fiefdom I had become. Rather it made sense that a narcissist, who depends on narcissistic supply from those around them to maintain their identity, absolutely needs people— well, maybe just one—for their very survival. How hard it must have been to rely on me totally for his sense of self when my own wasn't even intact! If you had held a gun to my head and demanded what I felt, wanted or needed at any given time, I would have had great trouble telling you. Did that make me, along with those pitiable and acceptably feminine traits like poor self-esteem, caretaking and people-pleasing, a codependent? Lisa said that in a relationship with someone with high narcissistic traits there are two people who only care about one person in the room. If the narcissistic partner is unhappy, the codependent will blame themselves and assume responsibility for solving the problem, pouring tremendous amounts of energy into maintaining a caretaking dynamic that the narcissist is happy to exploit.

But my marriage hadn't been so black and white. In addition to trying to meet everyone else's needs, I was also irritable and annoyed when things didn't go my way. I was always busy but impossible to please; I craved more time alone until I got it and felt useless, guilty and empty. I often moped around, depressed and anxious about my own affairs. I could be manipulative and bullying.

"When you felt anxious and depressed, dear one, what did you do?" I can imagine Lisa asking me in her no-nonsense Italian-New-Yorker way.

"Well, I went down into the basement and asked him if it was going to be okay," I would respond.

Like a child, though I knew that the state of not being okay was not something he had necessarily caused and certainly couldn't fix, I would plead with him to hug me and make it all right. Experts said that being raised in a narcissistic family system can create codependents who feel responsible for the emotions of others and focus their attention on others more than on themselves to regulate their own sense of self. Thus the codependent, according to Lisa, is the perfect companion for the narcissist, having been already trained in childhood to attend to another person's needs to prevent pain. I took Lisa's codependency quiz and scored a perfect 18 out of 18. How could I have forgotten all the friends whose houses I cleaned, who I bankrolled and fed and lavishly gifted while living in perpetual disappointment that they failed to reciprocate all that dirty, guilty giving? Or the doctor who had diagnosed me with burnout, put me on medical leave and provided me with a two-page list of activities that might bring some joy into my life because I had lost touch with everything but duty?

Like all my YouTube heroes, Lisa advocated the journey back to the true self as the only way to heal from toxic relationships and avoid getting into new ones. She admits that, after a lifetime of self-denial, she "wasn't always Suzy Sunshine" until she recognized what had happened to her in childhood and began to heal from it. She complained, whined, became physically ill and generally gave up playing the dutiful, adoring wife, but even if she was just reacting to the perpetual dissatisfaction of the relationship rather than causing it, she knew nothing would change unless she did.

Lisa cautioned, as did Grannon, against demonizing the narcissist and thinking that you were some kind of superior being because you won the personality disorder lottery and wound up merely codependent. Codependency is an ugly thing. No one can pour all their selfhood into someone else without becoming resentful when little comes back. The whole raison d'être of the codependent is to secure love by becoming the perfect partner, which of course is impossible on both counts. Set with this Sisyphean task, anyone would fail, and failure produces misery on both sides. The codependent is unhappy because they don't feel seen, heard or appreciated. They may hold it in and continue to try to please their partner, but they don't forget the injustice of having to make these compromises. The narcissistic person is unhappy because their source of supply has gone from a gushing well to vapour in the pipe; it's the difference between your partner serving your favourite meal by candlelight to soft music and making sure leftovers are always on the table by six.

Unmet needs can lead to a vicious cycle of sulking and nagging and begging and reconciliation and deliberate forgetting and, essentially, enslavement. The codependent will apologize to keep the peace, but there's more to it; we know that through poor communication of our own needs, we have contributed to the fouling of the emotional air. We know and we are sorry. But the underlying dynamic, the issues in the relationship, never get addressed. Everything stays on the surface, right where both "predator" and "prey" want it to. Though I still could not be sure whether I was a garden-variety codependent or something more sinister and entrenched, Lisa's videos comforted me because I needed to believe that change and healing were possible.

Of course, Richard Grannon threw a monkey wrench into the works in his video about counter-dependence. In stark opposition to the codependent, a counter-dependent does not like to depend on anyone, so they practice approach avoidance, trying desperately to connect with others and then pushing them away. They tend to be workaholics, blunt and harsh in their speech, grandiose and self-centred, judgmental and lacking in compassion. This diagnosis also fit me like a glove. Perhaps Sam Vaknin was right and, with my ever-shifting sense of self, I cycled through personality styles the way other people cycled through their newsfeed.

Whether I was a narcissistic and therefore codependent, a true codependent or counter-dependent, none of it was serving me. All the cooking, cleaning, mood boosting, emotional support and sex I had poured into my relationships had only made me self-righteous, exhausted and embittered. I still didn't know what was wrong with me, and although I was thinking about it a lot, I suspected that true change would require nothing less than an act of God.

CHAPTER 28

GETTING OUT OF THE MUD

Finding myself single for the first time in well over a decade, I was desperate to fill the void of loneliness and fear. Of course the sensible thing would have been to work on myself, like Lisa had when a therapist diagnosed her as codependent, to find out why my life had blown up (again), to work on my business, to focus on the mental health implications of the pandemic on my children. Instead, I hoped all these things would go so much easier with a romantic partner—even though that had hindered, not helped, me to focus on myself in the past.

Codependents are said to seek out a project specifically to avoid doing their own work. But the whole world, I thought, or at least people of my generation, seemed to want to attach to a romantic partner. I was sure it would focus me and provide release from the tedium of working twelve-hour days with only my assistant for company, panicking about bank accounts I had accidentally locked myself out of while trying to outwit my husband's surveillance, often brutally hungover and perpetually exhausted. The strategy of moving on quickly certainly seemed to work for Paul, who I later discovered had been dating on Plenty of Fish before I was even gone and within a month of my departure had settled down with a wonderful woman who immediately picked up the childcare duties during his weeks with them.

Of course, it doesn't always work out the same way for single mothers because of the double standard. There are hilarious memes of women chastising single mothers for not trying harder to keep their families together while lining up around the block to fellate a single dad for having learned to braid his daughter's hair (something Paul refused to learn, resulting in my daughter's fine, wavy hair matting so badly it often had to be cut). If I added a boyfriend to the mix, I'd be doing more cooking and dishes and laundry, not less. I'd have less time to myself, not more. But as I sought dominion over my little girl's knots with spray bottle and brush, I craved distraction and adult company as though they were powerful drugs. Intimate relationships do, in fact, provide them: dopamine, which cocaine will give you faster, and oxytocin and serotonin, which are naturally released by the hugs that I simply lacked 50 percent of the time.

The problem with pre-vaccine dating in the midst of a global pandemic is that the only people who may be willing to date in person are degenerates just like you, people with a bit of a death wish. I'm sure the men I dated—if you can call it that—in those first months saw my screaming loneliness as carte blanche to be their worst selves because why not? I thought I knew them already, but suddenly the gloves were off. Coffee dates consisted of me listening to tales of sexual conquests in excruciating detail, jokes at the expense of my height, glasses and even skin colour, or waiting at home alone, coffee in hand, being ghosted. No fewer than three out of the four talked about Black gangbangers as being the true scourge of society (I am a Black woman in Toronto where you'd be hard-pressed to find real gangbangers in our population of three million).

Despite the unsuitability of these men, who didn't want to call, text, hear about my children or my job or even pay for a burger, I couldn't seem to be alone for days on end without the discombobulating feeling that the ground under my feet was so unstable I might lose my footing and plunge off the side of the balcony. As always, the people I wanted to be around were usually those who didn't feel the same, a C-PTSD trait that Anna Runkle, a.k.a. The Crappy Childhood Fairy, called "eroticized abandonment." In this potent brew of self-loathing, toxic hope and self-betrayal, and while still frantically trying to diagnose myself, I stumbled across that pastor's video about narcissism that my lawyer had sent me long ago. Her Christ-like strategy of turning the other cheek had at least prevented me from losing my children altogether, so maybe there was something to it.

Pastor R.C. Blakes looked kind and benevolent. He didn't shout like a Black Baptist preacher, or at least not too much, and his New Orleans accent reminded me a bit of my father's Alabamian one, what little I could remember of it. He spoke of the narcissist the way almost everyone online did: as evil, probably demonically-influenced individuals who should be avoided at all costs. In a biblical context, Satan had been the first narcissist before other characters like Jezebel took up the cause, but the pastor spent a lot of time in his line of work counselling modern-day victims of what they believed to be narcissistic abuse. The bulk of his message had to do with prevention rather than clinical diagnosis, which he didn't get into whatsoever; he didn't pretend to be a counsellor or a psychologist or even a life coach, humbly describing himself as a pastor and a man.

I was interested in his theory that the father wound—the epidemic of missing or absent fathers everywhere, but especially in Black America—had a lot to do with the insecurities women faced that compelled them to settle down with men who had not learned to love or commit from their own fathers. He said people no longer knew how to be happy as individuals, finding purpose and meaning in God and in life; we had instead been indoctrinated by toxic culture to derive identity from physical appearance and relationship status, frantically casting about for external validation. Even when the resulting relationships led nowhere or were characterized by cheating, lack of commitment or abuse, we put up with it so as not to be alone.

To counter this broken consciousness, he developed a philosophy of female empowerment called Queenology, founded on the basic assumption that all women, from the professional in corporate America to the one on the street corner, were queens according to the

Bible—they just didn't know their own worth. Some of its tenets sounded paternalistic—certainly there was the black-and-white simplification of problems and solutions that one might expect from a man who had dedicated his life to applying two-thousand-year-old principles to the letter. But to a person who had "reaped the wages of sin" all her life, the message of accepting personal responsibility, developing relationship standards and boundaries, and building the self for its own sake was a welcome one. It saddened me that I still had to be told that I had intrinsic value as a person, but I needed to hear it from outside before I could believe it myself.

Over a period of a few months, Pastor Blakes became the wise father I'd never had, supplying me with guidance on everything from moral and spiritual principles to communication, attitude and healthy financial management as I washed dishes and folded laundry. He didn't mince words when it came to bad habits, but I didn't mind; whether or not I believed it was really a sin to fall into bed with someone and then try to work backwards to achieve compatibility, it certainly hadn't been working. My life was filled with "soul ties" to inappropriate people, substances and beliefs that hadn't served me for a long time, if ever.

"You all shouldn't be dating for six months and then you find out they're an axe murderer!" he exhorted. "God has more in store for you."

I tried to set aside what I saw as the rigid, outdated and contradictory religious principles that would always prevent me from accepting evangelical Christianity and focus on those interpretations that made good sense: Become the person you want to attract. Avoid the lust of the flesh. Take the time to get to know a person, ask questions and observe behaviours to find out if you are equally "yoked." Be intentional and clear about your expectations. Get your self-esteem right so you feel okay and authentic when setting clear boundaries. Respect gender differences and don't shy away from gender roles; they exist for a reason. Value intellect, work ethic and character above looks and bank accounts.

The revelation that if people don't protect themselves with boundaries, the world was full of those who would string them along with crumbs may not have been a common one for a Baptist minister to address, but it made my naïveté all the more shocking: everyone knew about this stuff, even and especially your daddy, but nobody talked about it. I had been giving every part of myself to people who probably didn't even deserve a conversation with me—not because I was too good, but because I sought out equally unhealthy people who would gladly race me to the bottom. The pastor prayed for my deliverance in the name of a deity whose existence, to me, remained in doubt, but his advice was practical and I began to follow it, along with that of another preacher's son.

Life coach Tony Gaskins showed up like holiday magic in my feed at my lowest point since the separation, just before Christmas of 2020. We didn't have a tree yet because I usually waited till mid-December to get one for optimal freshness, but trees had sold out early, like seemingly every other commodity. It didn't feel like Christmas. It felt like I was on a hellish hamster wheel of working around the clock, trying to fill orders, drinking myself to sleep every night and obsessing every day about how to organize fun winter activities with my forcibly home-schooled children. I lied to them about how Santa worked in cases of divorce, and it backfired. I was trying to keep our ancient, diabetic cat alive for one more holiday, and I wasn't sure I was worthy of the same effort.

As a published author, speaker and social media influencer, Tony Gaskins has acquired quite a following of mostly Black women who presumably want to be told what to do as badly as I do by someone whose authenticity and humility keeps dogma at bay. Like Pastor Blakes, he said I could be happy as long as I found purpose and lived along spiritual lines. In a direct response to a question I posed, Tony said I should focus on providing my children what they didn't have and on my health and appearance; he said I still had a lot of years left. I clung to these words like a life raft when, reacting to loneliness or emotional pain, my fingers twitched to text a former fling or drug buddy just to see what was going on. I knew I had to leave old habits behind me and become independent and content with my circumstances but given how much I'd been pathologizing myself and everyone else, I no longer knew whether this was even possible or whether my life would stay broken indefinitely.

Yet words like narcissism would not cross Tony's lips. He maintained, correctly, that NPD is a rare disorder and one that must have a significant impact on someone's life across all situations for the diagnosis to ever be made. Most people online were hung up on the theory that there were many more undiagnosed NPDs than we knew about, but even if this were true, Tony, who had worked in a residential care centre for people with disabilities in a past life, refused to use the label. That is not to say he didn't talk about narcissistic abuse. In fact, he discussed a whole kaleidoscope of behaviours that would have been familiar to anyone in the narcissistic abuse community. He just maintained, rather frighteningly, that *every man* would do the narcissistic, psychopathic things—cheating, beating, abandoning, abusing in every conceivable form—his beleaguered listeners talked about in the comments. For the first time in my career as a content consumer, bad behaviour had been uncoupled from personality disorders and brought into the realm of everyday living where it could be dealt with more easily.

According to Tony, a successful entrepreneur, life coach and happily married man of God, unless and until a person becomes willing to live according to spiritual principles, abusive behaviour is the inevitable result because of the inherent selfishness of human nature and society. He reframed the psychological vocabulary I had gotten so used to hearing and applying to my own life.

> *Love bombing* = having your representative show up for the first three months on his best and most manipulative behaviour primarily to get you into bed but also to obtain other services.
>
> *Devaluing* = what happened once you slept with him right away and/or put up with unacceptable behaviour.
>
> *Discarding* = when he doesn't really want you.
>
> *Hoovering* = pretending to have changed so as to keep his options open, only to abuse you even worse the second time around.

Breadcrumbing = he has a whole other relationship (or several) on the go at the same time, so there is only so much time and attention to go around.

Histrionic = all the boo-hoo crying that women do instead of setting boundaries in the hopes of producing different results.

Codependency = staying through verbal, emotional, financial, sexual abuse because you think you don't have options.

Tony said that what we now called narcissism was really just grown-boy behaviour that is exhibited by nine out of ten men because they hadn't been properly raised, they just grew, resulting in a grown boy inhabiting a man's body. The grown boy was usually produced by a combination of spoiling by a single mother, overcompensating for the absence of the no-good daddy and the social pressures of everything from Instagram riches to institutionalized racism, resulting in an immature, predatory creature masquerading as a man. Unless held to account by a woman's boundaries and standards, he would never evolve because he didn't have to when so many women were willing to accept cheating, beating and other forms of abuse while cooking, cleaning and washing his musty drawers.

Tony lives in Florida, and refreshing glimpses into his normal family life (taking his kids to their soccer games, world travel, dining out) while we were so restricted gave me hope that somewhere, life was going on. His no-nonsense talks and affordable online courses on life, love and business were the tipping point, finally empowering me to start writing again; his was a voice that had risen from a less than desirable past to "get it out the mud." His conversion to a moral life had led to enviable material wealth and personal contentment, but it was his relationship advice that really helped me. Having broken every possible dating and relationship rule, it was time to reclaim my dignity at last.

"Stay off your back," he said, the word "back" sounding like "bike" in his slow drawl. These and other rules, like breaking the hold of addictions, using your gifts and eliminating dishonesty, were so simple but so elemental. How did I expect to change and grow without renewing my mind with new knowledge and then applying it? Acting contrary to a moral philosophy for most of my life, even against my own self-interest, had made me forget how I wanted to live.

Tony doesn't get too deep into the specifics of healing other than recommending the help of the Lord and qualified professionals; he answers specific relationship questions to a fine point, then says something I find maddeningly vague like "Heal before you deal" or "Do the work," a phrase I knew all too well from the twelve-step program (which at least provided the twelve exact steps to take). So I focused on his concrete advice around the Three B's: Brain, Brand and Body, which I translated to information, integrity and health.

I realized that every speaker I was drawn to had a singular message of personal responsibility. They didn't say I hadn't been victimized, like the twelve-step program did by omission; they said victimhood was not a life strategy. I had been a passive bystander in my own life for so long that I didn't even know my own actions had real power. Now here were all these people—philosophers, psychologists, coaches, independent thinkers—telling me I had agency and the responsibility to use it, not just to defend and protect but to change and improve no matter what barriers, imagined or real, existed in my path. It was time to stop analyzing, ruminating, blaming and shaming. It was time to stop over-thinking, drinking too much and shrinking away from myself, other people and the truth. More chilling than the darkest descriptions of psychopaths, sociopaths and other vile creatures, the thought came that it was time to grow up.

From what my online mentors said, I would have to embark on a program of personal growth to get over what had happened and to change my own shitty behaviours so it wouldn't happen again. The little problem of what the hell was wrong with me began to seem less important as the realization came that labels, while massively insightful, were only the beginning, not the solution. My emergence from this psychological miasma didn't happen instantly, however. I still listened to videos and read articles, but more to reinforce my learning and doing

GETTING OUT OF THE MUD

than with the feverish intent to solve problems just by naming them. I still indulged in a little fantasy in which the experts argued over what was really wrong with me, knowing that even if a psychiatrist right here in Toronto told me, I probably wouldn't believe them.

> Vaknin: "She had become dissolute and then she became a schizoid. Look—she doesn't talk to anyone except these introjects! She is obviously a borderline. She said it herself."
>
> Grannon: "Hang on a second, mate. These are just models. But when you've been through forty years of trauma, you're practically living in an emotional flashback. That's why she's like a different person every day."
>
> Vaknin: "Well, the narcissist is a different person every millisecond! They're the most traumatized. I mean, it's not possible to be more traumatized than to not have a self."
>
> Romano: "Doesn't anyone notice that she has very high codependent traits? I mean, hello! It's not her, it's her programming."
>
> Gaskins: "She was loose booty 901, hot 'n ready like Lil Caesar's. She's living for the Lord now."
>
> Blakes: "Amen, amen, amen! She used to be one of the silly women in Second Timothy, now she's behaving like the woman at the well. Glory to God."
>
> Vaknin: "At least you didn't mention mindfulness, which is possibly the only way to make your statement more absurd."
>
> Grannon: "She's finally realized no one is coming. That's where the healing begins."

"Do you want to do therapy?" my CAS-appointed counsellor asked as our sessions drew to a close. "We can explore some sliding-scale resources that have a waiting list of under a year."

I was about to retort that if I couldn't figure out my own symptoms, which seemed like a tossed salad of trauma responses with a congealed anxiety and depression dressing, then I could easily spend years and a fortune I no longer had on therapists who would be as confused by my shifting traits and identities as I was. Then I remembered that arrogance had prevented me from accepting help and trusting that things could get better more than once.

Pete Walker, who wrote the ground-breaking book on complex post-traumatic stress called *C-PTSD: From Surviving to Thriving*, had been to therapy three times a week for years, an indulgence I could not possibly imagine, before ultimately identifying and resolving his own problems. I signed up for online programs and, with the global reopening rendering my online business less overwhelming and my freelance gigs irregular at best, took advantage of the extra time to pursue my recovery, beginning with a dialectical behavioural therapy, or DBT, group. I had heard about DBT long before from a couple of acquaintances who had said the therapy helped them a great deal. One was on more or less permanent disability from the navy and still struggled with depression, though he was at least functional. The other told me about DBT as we shared an eight-ball of cocaine. Both had only one thing to say about the therapy:

"There are no 'buts' in DBT. It's, 'I'm doing the best I can, *and* …'"

It seemed a reductionist takeaway at the very least, but I was willing to try anything. Sam Vaknin said that borderlines had the best prognosis of any cluster B personality and that DBT had been proven effective, although that wasn't saying much among a group that is notoriously hard to treat.

Dialectical Behavioural Therapy was invented by a woman named Marsha Linehan, who recognized that some reactions to life are, let us say, unhelpful. The underlying principle was that everything we did was for a reason but that it was not always helpful or effective (Outbursts are bad, m'kay?) and that, more importantly, we could improve on these behaviours through a process of radical acceptance of ourselves and the world, non-judgmental awareness of our thoughts, feelings and actions, mindfulness and problem-solving skills.

My group would take place online because of the pandemic. It was two hours a week, leaving plenty of time to go through the enormous binder of skills we'd been given to practice at home and the other, more basic life skills program I'd enrolled in just to lend some kind of structure to my life. Two of the other women initially in my group had children with autism and abusive ex-partners. One sometimes showed up high, staring fixedly at the screen and sharing unfiltered thoughts that all too often mirrored what I was only thinking. Another lady needed medication to function in daily life. The lone man who stuck with it had received excessive medical interventions such that he felt nothing at all and, unlike we women, was there to gain access to his emotions as opposed to dampen their intensity. My vicious inner and outer critics sometimes frolicked, but fortunately, one of the DBT skills is becoming aware of your own judgments without judging them. I enjoyed connecting with my fellow group members almost in spite of myself. Spring of 2021 saw me literally hugging trees, practicing willing postures and writing letters from Paul's point of view.

"These are skills that everyone should develop!" said the enthusiastic group facilitators.

I wondered if it was really true that ordinary people had to put ice water on their temples in moments of stress or examine facts in writing to determine whether their thoughts were even connected with reality, but I certainly needed to. Cognitive behavioural therapy hadn't done a damn thing for me, most meditations felt like torture, and endless twelve-step inventories over the years only rehashed the same fears and resentments while providing a solution—asking a God I didn't wholly believe in to remove flaws I didn't think were all mine—that often left me frustrated. I instinctively trusted DBT, sensing that any system of regulating my emotions and helping me see the world and my place in it more accurately as well as relying on my own resources rather than berating myself or indulging in magical thinking would make life a lot better.

My DBT binder contained a dozen pages of descriptions of emotions because it is designed for people who are confused about what they are feeling at any given time. As Grannon and Romano both said so often, when emotions are dismissed or punished in childhood they tend to become hazier even as they grow out of control. This meant that, within minutes or even seconds, I could experience a profound rush of anger, fear or sadness without knowing what had triggered it, lash out and make the problem worse, thus setting the old familiar cycles in motion again. Grannon emphasized the importance of becoming emotionally literate *before* problems struck, so I spent time each day writing down what I was feeling and exploring the feelings with as much specificity as possible without trying to change them or push them away.

It was like trying to cut a new path through densely-wooded forest instead of taking the highway; the amount of resistance thrown up by my mushy brain was shocking. I had never understood why I, a go-getter in other areas, was so averse to spiritual exercises, but it had never been this bad, probably because I had had some external world to impress. Now there was only me, or me and my children, who wanted me to be less sad but who also wanted a whole lot of other things I could no longer give them. As well, this was different work that was centred solely on the emotions I had spent a lifetime trying to get rid of. After a year of isolation amid the ruins of my former life, I could already hear the siren song of isolation tempting me to stay safe by shutting down completely, a path from which I feared there might be no return.

Fortunately, my recovery background had taught me that sometimes the only way to get things done is, ironically, to ignore your feelings of laziness, apathy, fear and avoidance and proceed anyway. I remembered that every time I had quit anything, I hadn't exactly wanted to but that didn't stop me. I had been terrified of a life without cigarettes, alcohol, drugs, but realizing that there might never be a "good" time, a wholehearted desire for change, I took the actions anyway and hoped for the best.

With whatever shreds of willpower I could gather, I set a low bar and decided if I could take even one healing action per day, no matter how brief, it could grow from there. And it did. Grannon's daily emotional literacy exercise, which took less than ten minutes because I resisted the use of coloured pens to have fun with it, was joined by his daily goal-setting exercise. He was right; I couldn't just wake up and fling myself at the day, as I had been doing, and expect satisfaction, no matter how many items on the to-do list got crossed off. I needed a very regimented morning routine that involved first setting an intention for each day, such as "calm" or "focused," and then writing a bit about what had to get done and how I wanted to feel while doing it.

He always said to assume positive intent, and this instruction had an unexpected side benefit: I found myself attributing it to others as well. For the first time, I began to consider my mother's methods as secondary to her intent to keep me safe from what she considered to be a hostile world. This wasn't an exercise in willfully ignoring or reframing the truth to make things more bearable, nor was it a lie or excuse for what had happened; it wasn't even done deliberately. The thought just came to me one day. I made a list of all the positive things she had tried to teach me, and when combined with the content that was actually getting through, the one overriding message was this: fight. There are worse messages to give a child. And I realized that the less energy I spent on a mental battle with my internalized mother, the more energy I had to fight for myself.

I began to do a longer exercise two or three days a week and, harkening back to Julia Cameron's teachings in *The Artist's Way*, I had to find a way to make them fun. These were my excuses to get out of the house during lockdown and, later, when I felt too bored and depressed to bother. I would take the DBT binder to a golf course, sit there and do whatever it said—examine blades of grass, walk and breathe, notice everything around me—for an hour. Hop on a bus with an internet list of values in hand à la Grannon and narrow it down to five core values I couldn't live without. Sit on the beach and do a twelve-step list of everyone I have harmed and then put it away when the anxiety gets to be too much; I could look at amends another day. Do something for someone else, even if it's impersonal, like donating blood, or personal, like helping someone make a website.

During this time my blood pressure had become dangerously high, so I had to monitor it daily, and on my doctor's orders went on more medication. I had never paid attention to my body except to criticize it, but now it seemed to make sense to get more exercise, eat better, take supplements, try to develop a healthier relationship with sleep.

"It sounds like you're doing a lot of good stuff," said my counsellor. "How are you doing with self-compassion?"

She had me practicing this concept which had been totally absent from my life. I had thought that without whipping myself with guilt, harsh commands and mocking self-talk, I would never get anything done, but the opposite was true. When I was gentle with myself, I could accomplish most of what I had to and sometimes more.

Of course, she also asked the once-dreaded question: "How are you feeling?" It was a question I could finally answer with more accuracy and without verbal pyrotechnics. Everyone said that the back story was less important than how I felt about it, and while writing this book (because the story still demanded to be told) I paid attention to my feelings as it unfolded. Anger. Sadness. Disgust. Shame. Regret. Sympathy. Compassion. Hope.

That is not to say that the details don't matter. Experts and laypeople will say you should stop telling your story over and over because it is actually re-traumatizing, and I understand the logic; the problem was that I had never really told my story or felt that I even could. It came out in whatever size of piece I thought the listener could handle, and then I tried to make sense of it by their reaction. Having once been silenced, I then continued the censorship myself. Now it was all coming out on the page, not as a series of furtive disclosures fit for a particular person's consumption but as a narrative that was as whole and complete as I could make it. If my role as a storyteller was, as James Baldwin said, "to make you realize the doom and glory of knowing who you are and what you are," that was fair enough, but telling truth for myself, finally, has become the goal.

So, am I the asshole? Like anyone else, I hope not. But from where I am, I can see it and accept it and work to do better. After so much study, I have chosen to lay the blame for my mistakes at no one's feet: not my parents, not my marriage, not even my own malfunctioning self. This is not precisely the same as forgiveness, which I have learned cannot be forced. It is more like the radical acceptance of knowing I need to look for the actual facts, feelings and solutions in each individual situation rather than chalking everything up to incurable personality traits or an unjust world.

It is tiring sometimes, and I often wish that "Dear Abby" website had worked. But the more I am willing to know and accept myself instead of fleeing from the parts I don't like or ruminating on circumstances, the more a sort of internal intelligence is activated, showing me how to move on and learn from my mistakes. I am open to input but not enslaved to following advice. There is no one to impress anymore, no love and acceptance to desperately yearn for but my own.

My anxiety and panic have not vanished, but rather than seeing them as enemies to be subdued or evaded, I stay with them—with myself—speaking to myself compassionately, as I would a child. Hunger for expression makes emotions grow, so I don't try to starve them now, not even the ones I still think of as ugly, like jealousy or irritation or judgement. I can feel anger or upset without drowning in them, letting them pass through me rather than accumulating and calcifying, which made and kept me so sick.

Why me? has become *Why not me?* From this foundation, I can at least manage to not stay furious at myself and others, which is progress indeed. When I slip into an emotional flashback and act out of character, it is easily identifiable, allowing me to bounce back and repair any damage quickly. While panic attacks have lessened their grip, I still fall into periods of depression where the weight of life feels like it's pulling me down. I get through these times not by checking out of life but by letting myself grieve for every agonizing moment of existence if need be. I can let the tears fall, secure in the knowledge that I don't always need to be *up*, that maybe *down* has its answers for me too.

By no means is this the final word. I have only been practicing these skills less than a year at the time of writing this, and I'm still putting the pieces together as to why and how I got here, and what it might take to step into the life I really want. In the meantime, life goes on. I grind, but take the time to feel, to stay conscious of what supports me and what doesn't. It's helping me to be more present as a parent; my children are the great joy of my life, the two people on earth I still struggle to say no to even as I have learned to listen to myself and honour my own limits. My ex-husband and I typically maintain perfunctory, very sporadic communication; we have perfected the art of contactless pick up every week. His past motivations and future plans for our children are a mystery that I'm no longer interested in solving because, whatever happens, I trust myself not to get lost in a toxic fog of passivity ever again. But sometimes, a switch is suddenly flipped, and we are plunged into a dank, familiar darkness.

"You're so irrelevant," he messaged this fall, in response to my email asking him to buy winter parkas for the children; after all, I sarcastically wrote, I hadn't received a penny of child support or alimony for eighteen months, so perhaps he could afford to go designer? "Nobody cares about you, Nicole. If they really need coats, why don't you turn some tricks in your welfare apartment? Twenty guys at $10 apiece should do it."

By the time I read the whole, vicious diatribe, my heart was pounding and my hands were shaking. I knew how the story would end: a game of tit for tat could last all day and leave me emotionally annihilated. Collecting pages of four-letter words for use in court felt like wandering a tangled forest, adding bitter morsels to a basket that I would later present to a slavering wolf, but I breathed deeply as I logged them. The contents of my inbox could only trigger rumination and haunt my sleep if I let them fester.

"Please buy the children a parka, thank you." I breathed and typed. And after hitting Send, I got up and walked away, a physical representation of what I've finally learned to do more generally: take life at the walking pace I've set for myself, rather than escaping reality in a series of panicked flights. It's a discipline that, if nothing else, sets a good example for my children. They are already mature beyond their years, a fact that makes me both proud of their strength and sad because I know what it is to have knowledge of adult problems and feel, at best, that you have to fix them and at worst, that you caused them. We talk about things openly; we are in this together. Our family agreement is respect and forgiveness, both of which are necessary on a daily basis, since all three of us are pretty strong-willed.

Masks haven't yet come off in Toronto, and it seems unlikely that they will in the foreseeable future. But the pandemic and the tectonic shifts that accompanied it did expose the emptiness of the life I had been living for so long. The internal and external pressure finally stripped away the false, forcing me to confront history and finally take an active role in creating my future. Now that the ground has been prepared, my goal is not just construction, but integration. If I don't continue to heal, every good and useful structure I could ever manage to build will, divided, fall. So what I am erecting now is not a monument to suffering and shame but a big, beautiful skyscraper like the ones I used to stare up at in New York. It's an edifice that can easily accommodate every part of me. It casts a long shadow.

ACKNOWLEDGEMENTS

When it comes to writing a book, no one is a rugged individualist. Inspiration, encouragement and assistance has always come from many sources, but there are a few special people without whom this project would not have seen the light of day.

My editor, Darin Steinkey, who saw potential, and applied wisdom, skill and discernment to help me tell my story, and the professionals at Tellwell, who gave me the confidence that this could become a book that someone might actually want to read.

Sydnia Yu, mom, journalist, photographer and long-time friend. This book's first editor, she is one of the least judgmental people I know; she loved me at my worst and was able to read the first draft without running screaming into the night. Her positivity has always shone a bright light that shows me a way out of whatever momentary darkness I happen to be languishing in.

Pam Mardula, whose wisdom and expertise were second only to her kindness at one of the most difficult times in my life.

Susan Fraser and Sonia Taylor-Miglioni, who never silenced my ugly-crying but gently and compassionately and wisely helped me limp back into the world.

My children, who put up with me, and without whom I would not try quite so hard to be a better person.

Manufactured by Amazon.ca
Bolton, ON